THE CHILD'S VOICE IN FAMILY THERAPY

· ·

A Norton Professional Book

THE CHILD'S VOICE
IN FAMILY THERAPY

A Systemic Perspective

• •

CAROLE GAMMER

W. W. Norton & Company
New York • London

First published in French as
LA VOIX DE L'ENFANT DANS LA THERAPIE FAMILIALE
First published in German as
DIE STIMME DES KINDES IN DER FAMILIENTHERAPIE

For information about special discounts for bulk purchases, please contact
W. W. Norton Special Sales at specialsales@wwnorton.com or 800-233-4830

Manufacturing by Courier Westford
Book design by Carole Desnoes
Production manager: Devon Zahn

Library of Congress Cataloging-in-Publication Data

Gammer, Carole.
[Voix de l'enfant dans la thérapie familiale. English]
The child's voice in family therapy : a systemic perspective /
Carole Gammer.
p. ; cm.
Includes bibliographical references and index.
ISBN 978-0-393-70541-6 (hardcover)
1. Family psychotherapy. 2. Child psychotherapy. I. Title.
[DNLM: 1. Family Therapy. 2. Child Behavior—
psychology. 3. Family Relations.   WM 430.5.F2 G193v 2008a]
RC488.5.G36 2008
616.89'156—dc22
2008021244

W. W. Norton & Company, Inc.
500 Fifth Avenue, New York, N.Y. 10110
www.wwnorton.com

W. W. Norton & Company Ltd., Castle House
75/76 Wells Street, London W1T 3QT

1 2 3 4 5 6 7 8 9 0

To Ben and Jennifer Downing

Contents

• •

Acknowledgments

● ●

There are so many people I am grateful to for making this book possible, including colleagues, patients, family, and friends. I especially thank Dr. Jean-Claude Benoit, Professor Herbert Pielmaier, David Trachsler, and Annette Kreuz for their direct help with the manuscript. I am much indebted to George Downing for continuous support, generosity, encouragement, and years of fruitful exchange of ideas. Lana Dumas has been tirelessly helpful and supportive. I thank my editors at Norton, Kristen Holt-Browning, Vani Kannan, and Deborah Malmud, for their patience and guidance, and to Casey Ruble, copy editor, for her trenchant advice.

Introduction

● ●

There is a growing awareness in the family therapy field that we need to give the children in families more of a place in our work. But how? One dilemma we face is that family therapy, like most therapies, is conducted mainly with language. We speak; the family members speak. But children are limited in their language abilities, and the younger the child, the less sophisticated her verbal resources. So how do we get around this barrier?

The problem is no doubt accentuated due to historical developments. Since the 1980s, family therapy paradigms have tended to put a special emphasis upon language. This was a valuable, productive step. How family members "construct," or represent, their world—and how these capacities can be explored—was moved more strongly to the foreground. However, as helpful as the linguistic turn proved in many areas, it did not make the puzzle of what to do with children in family therapy any easier.

The perspective I describe in this book takes both representational and behavioral process into account. What I try to add is an expanded access to the children's representational universe. On a concrete level this means putting into play a variety of techniques, some linguistic and some not. The challenge then becomes to keep the work systemic. In other words, this is a book about family therapy, not child therapy, with all due respect to the latter.

The various techniques involved are described in detail. Illustrative case examples are frequently given; all the case examples are composites of families in which I have altered identifying information, such as names, gender, and age and that I have treated or supervised. I also discuss how to organize family therapy: what can be most profitably taken up first, and what next, and so on. Much as I value theoretical questions, they have been mostly left aside, apart from a few comments in the next chapter. The focus throughout the book is upon the practical.

The journey leading to these ideas has been a long one. When I started out, in the early days of family therapy, I had good fortune. My first teacher was Carl Whitaker, at the University of Wisconsin, where I had been studying behavior therapy with children. He was an inspiring supervisor and mentor.

Although I appreciated what I learned, I was disappointed in one respect. I felt hungry for a more comprehensive approach. The lure of family therapy, novel at the time, was very strong. I felt it would give me just what had seemed lacking.

But things turned out differently. I revered Whitaker, but soon discovered that work with young children was an area that engaged him rather little. He had a fine, playful rapport with children, yet his therapeutic interventions were directed almost exclusively to the adults. This seemed to me a major—and unnecessary—lacuna.

As I became better acquainted with the field, I discovered that the problem, or what I saw as a problem, was hardly unique to Whitaker. It appeared widespread. I watched family therapy being done by the Mental Research Institute group (Watzlawick, Bavelas, & Jackson, 1967; Watzlawick, Weakland,

& Fisch, 1974; Fisch, Weakland, & Segal, 1982), Boszormenyi-Nagy, Haley, and others. Minuchin and Satir, who had clever ways to engage children, seemed exceptions. Otherwise, the story remained the same: Each school seemed to have its wisdom, but work with children was underdeveloped across the board.[1]

I was convinced something else might be possible. But I realized I had to learn a lot more about child psychotherapy in general. To this end, in another piece of good luck, I accepted a position as a clinical psychologist at Children's Hospital in Boston, a teaching hospital of Harvard University Medical School. The Harvard Child Psychiatry Department was then a center of psychoanalytic child therapy, and I had the opportunity to learn many psychoanalytic techniques and much more besides. My indulgent, if skeptical, supervisors even allowed me to test some of my budding notions about a different kind of family therapy.

I can't say these endeavors proved satisfactory. Often I ended up operating in the Wisconsin mode, with the child or children on the sidelines. Or, in a family session, I would try some play techniques with a child with a parent or both parents watching. Something would come of it occasionally, but I didn't sense that I was getting far. In the language I would use today, these attempts were not throughly systemic enough. The gains are limited if you simply transpose classic child techniques into a family therapy setting, like repotting a plant (a point I thoroughly discuss in coming chapters).

Despite setbacks, as the years passed I went on with my experiments. Bit by bit I seemed to find a path. Meanwhile, family therapy itself was going through a series of fascinating convulsions: constructivist concepts, narrative therapy, solution-oriented brief therapy, and plenty more. I absorbed a lot from this ferment, as I imagine will be apparent in these pages. Nevertheless, the field appeared to continue to live with a blind spot. Apart from the innovations of Gil and a few others, little emerged that was truly different with regard to explicit work with children.

I have tried to develop an alternative perspective. Two decades ago I moved to Paris, which led to the development of my extensive family therapy practice, as well as teaching in France and other European countries. My interactions with many seasoned professionals have been important as well.

This book gives an overview of the discoveries which seem to me the most useful for other therapists. What I have tried to do here is to emphasize the practical. I go over a number of techniques that are effective in bringing children into the foreground of family therapy, and present detailed explanations and numerous case study examples.

So as to emphasize the practical aspects of working with children in family therapy, chapters 3 through 9 outline the techniques themselves. I give detailed explanations along with plenty of case examples.

Chapters 10 through 12 delve into the overall therapy process itself. I discuss case conceptualization and how to formulate a plan for the therapy. I address how to help a family set goals, as well as what to do with different kinds of system composition: single parent families, step families, and so on. I discuss how the various techniques described in Part I of the book can be selected and woven together in a coherent manner. Chapters 13 and 14 look at family therapy with children with hyperactive behavior and systemic work with sibling relationships, respectively.

I have not tried to cover everything. While I would have liked to have covered work with infants, mentally disturbed patients, adult siblings, and victims of sexual abuse, it seemed to me more important to illustrate a basic model, and show the reader how the model works in practice.

I hope this book can serve as an aid and source of reference for family therapy colleagues of all kinds, regardless of persuasion and background. I hope too that it will stimulate others to develop similar reflections and perspectives.

NOTES

1. Significant exceptions have been recent cognitive-behavioral family therapy (Cavell, 2000; Reinecke, Dattilio, & Freeman, 1996; Kendall & Brasswell, 1985), narrative family therapy (Freeman, Epston, & Lobovits, 1997; White & Epston, 1990), and the approach of Wachtel (1994).

THE CHILD'S VOICE IN FAMILY THERAPY

• •

CHAPTER ONE

Thinking About the Family

• •

The focus of this book is upon practice. It will be helpful, however, if I mention several theoretical background assumptions before turning to techniques.

As mentioned in the introduction, when we try to give children more room in systemic therapy, a difficulty confronts us: They don't speak as well as adults. The younger the child, the more limited his verbal capacities. So what do we do about that? Fortunately there are plenty of technical answers to the problem. In order to have a feeling for how such techniques function, however, it is helpful to have an awareness of certain ideas about development.

Consider what Bowlby (1969, 1980) called the child's "working model" of a relationship. This is how the child represents the relationship. It comprises his representations of the other person, of himself, and of the tie between the two. Attachment research has demonstrated that infants already have a working model of their relationships. They even have one working model of their link with the mother and another of their link with the father. Presumably they have still other working models of a relationship with a sibling, with a grandparent, and so on. So what are these representations like? And how are they similar or different for a preschool child, a grammar-school child, or an adolescent?

The best way to get a handle on these questions is to know a little about how researchers have gone about answering them. Infant and child research is a universe unto itself, but one key type of finding can be easily and quickly summarized. Even in their earliest months, children develop extremely specific expectations about interactional regularities and patterns. They lack words, but they don't lack sophisticated representations of how things usually go between the child and an adult caregiver. These are sometimes called *procedural* representations.

For example, in Tronick's (2007) still-face paradigm, a 3-month infant sits facing his mother. Mother and son interact in their habitual way, sending an array of vocal and movement signals back and forth. Suddenly, as prearranged by the experimenter, the mother makes her whole face and body become immobile for 2 minutes. How does the infant react?

With evident upset—and with a variety of responses. He will usually try a series of devices (movements, facial expressions, sounds) to reengage the mother. He will probably "self-comfort" as well, touching his face or torso with a hand. What is very clear is that he possesses definite expectations about what normally ought to happen between him and the mother, and now these expectations have been violated. The reality occurring now does not match his procedural representations of what should be occurring.

Tronick (2007), Beebe (Beebe & Jaffe, 2008; Beebe, Knoblauch, Rustin, & Sorter, 2005), Fogal (2008), Rochat (2001), Stern (2004) and others have shown how detailed these representations are. The infant expects intricate reciprocal exchanges, with certain patterns of rhythm, certain styles of affect expression, and the like. Attachment researchers have made similar discoveries.

In the Ainsworth Strange Situation (Ainsworth, Blehar, Waters, & Wall, 1978), for example, a 12-month infant plays with his mother. She then briefly leaves the room and returns two times. What is carefully examined is how the infant, now in emotional distress, copes with the situation the second time the parent returns. Does the infant go straight to her, openly signaling his need to be consoled? Does he allow himself to be quieted, returning in a short time to a state of calm? Some do; some don't. More to the point, the infant's behavior during this "reunion" reveals a lot about his procedural representations of such interactions. In some cases he will even show how his expectations are mixed and contradictory, resulting in mixed and contradictory behaviors on his part: For instance, he might run toward the mother and then suddenly veer away (an example of a so-called disorganized attachment).

From these and many similar findings we can distill several important clues. First, an infant's or child's behavior in certain circumstances is revelatory of her underlying representations. Second, these representations are intricate. The fact that no or little (in the case of toddlers and preschool children) language yet accompanies them does not mean that they lack organization and structure. The representations are there, and they are causally operative. And they are fine-grained enough to be of therapeutic interest.

So we can now redefine our problem. True, young children are limited in what they can directly verbalize in a family therapy setting. So how can they still communicate to us, and to other family members, some of their experiences of family relationships? The answer is that we have to depend upon other representational formats. But they still can communicate some of their experience of the family relationships. We have to allow them to "speak" in other modes.

One mode is behavior itself. In the next chapter I describe how the therapist can help the family recreate selected vignettes of interactional behavior. This will elicit from most children not only communication by demonstration (i.e., acts we can observe), but also plenty of spoken commentary. The language of a 3-year-old may be restricted, but when his comments are elaborations of events in the room, they can be perceptive and eloquent.

Other types of attachment research are equally helpful. For example, with preschool and young children, forms of play have been used to reveal the child's working models of relationship, as have "story stem" methods (wherein the experimenter begins a story and the child completes it; Bretherton & Oppenheim, 2003, Steele & Steele, 2005a; Woolgar, 1999). These and other approaches can be transferred, with some modifications, to a family therapy setting. They can elucidate working model representations, as well as other beliefs and cognitions, wishes, intentions, yearnings, and so on.

So far I have been talking about children's mental maps of their world, and about how we can gain access to them. Another preliminary point that bears mentioning has to do with how family members affect one another. If you want to give attention to children in family therapy, that attention has to be in part systemic. You need to see, and think about, the child not only as a small, contained human unit, but also as she exists in a web of interpersonal relations.

The earlier family therapists, from Bateson onwards, talked about "circular causality" (Bateson, 1972; Bateson, Jackson, Haley, & Weakland, 1956). A favorite metaphor was that of a thermostat: You set it higher, the room heats, the warmth expands a metal strip, the strip turns the heat off, and so on. In later years, however, as constructivist family therapy models became predominant, talk about circular causality trickled away. The notion still could be found in the literature, and still can today, but it was relegated to the margins. However, it was an excellent idea, if flawed. Family members do affect one another, constantly and in many ways, and usually without realizing how they are affecting others or how they are being affected themselves. Videomicroanalytic (Beebe, Fogal, Rochat, Stern, Tronick, etc.) and some attachment research (e.g., Abrams & Hesse, 2006; Hesse & Main, 2006; Lyons-Ruth, Melnick, Bronfman, Sherry, & Llanas, 2004) leave no doubt here. A close analysis of even a minute of interaction shows that human exchanges have a moment-by-moment denseness—a richness far beyond what we ordinarily imagine. And obviously once we add language, the reciprocal effects are even greater.

Beebe (Beebe & Jaffe, 2008; Beebe et al., 2005) called this "bidirectional influence," referring to dyads. By implication, parents influence children moment by moment, but children influence parents as well, and parents influence each other and children influence one another. Nor is what goes on simply the sum of crisscrossing dyads. For example, Fivaz-Depeursinge and Corboz-Warnery (1999) have demonstrated that a "triadic" level of mutual influence exists between mother, father, and child above and beyond the dyadic effects.

In short, we need to consider systemic processes. Ironically, they turn out to be far more pervasive and more complex than Bateson realized. On the other hand, Beebe (Beebe & Jaffe, 2008) and Tronick (2007) have shown that more is taking place than just mutual impact. As seen in one of their videos, many of the micro-acts done by person *A* have a visible effect on person *B*, but many also do not. Only *some* of person *A*'s behavior exerts systemic influence. Beebe and Tronick argued that we ought to distinguish between "interpersonal regulation" (the acts affecting the other) and "self-regulation" (the acts affecting oneself alone). Circular causality, or something like it, is more complicated than Bateson dreamed of. It is also merely one piece of what overall is taking place.

Personal agency also needs to be acknowledged. Whenever we explain a type of behavior we must recognize the "gap"

(Searle, 2001) between determining influences, on the one hand, and the act of willing, on the other.

Systemically speaking, we should distinguish two aspects of agency. One is the concept of representations of agency. Like adults, children hold sometimes helpful, and sometimes unhelpful, beliefs and self-attributions concerning their power of effective action. Family members also often attribute either exaggerated or impoverished powers of agency to other family members. The other relevant aspect is the concept of enabling conditions of agency. This has to do with external (i.e., family and systemic) factors that enhance or decrease a child's power of effective action. In this book you will find plenty of examples of both, and you will see how these notions of agency can contribute to clinical interventions.

One more point, concerning case conceptualization. It can be very helpful to distinguish between *structuring causes* and what the philosopher Dretske (1981, 1988, 1995) called *triggering causes*. Simply put, a *triggering* cause is an event in the moment that brings about an effect in the moment. A *structuring* cause is a standing condition, an ongoing state of affairs. Systemic causation in families can take either form—or both forms together.

For example, in working with one family with an anorexic daughter, I found that the girl had first initiated restricted eating soon after the death of a beloved grandmother. The death was a triggering cause. But further exploration made it clear that the girl's incapacity to mourn the death mirrored the family's more global, long-lasting denial of loss and suffering. The family's denial was a structuring cause, a systemic standing condition. In addition, the girl and her parents were fighting intensely over food, reinforcing her anorexic behavior. The power struggles were further triggering causes, systemic as well.

More generally speaking, my model assumes *multicausality*, the notion that human actions flow from many causes: systemic and nonsystemic, conscious and unconscious, behavioral and representational, triggering and structuring. The payoffs of this perspective will be evident throughout the remainder of the book.

In sum, to work more closely with children in family therapy, we need to not only watch, listen to, talk to, and intervene with them. We must also take seriously the idea that they have a rich representational mental life, even if words mirror it poorly.

PART I

Techniques

CHAPTER TWO

Dramatization Techniques

● ●

Families arrive in our offices with complaints. "Our sons fight all day." "My father is too strict." "My wife and daughter team up against me." So expressed, the complaints are abstract. What does the family member really mean?

The usual move the therapist makes is to ask the family member to move to a lower level of abstraction. "Give me an example." "What does this mean in detail?" "When was the last time this happened?" This is, of course, absolutely necessary. However, for the most part, the representational vacuum still remains.

First, even when an example is described, what the family member actually has in mind often remains hazy for the therapist. "He came in the room and started shouting like a maniac," says the family member. This description helps, but it is still not very fine-grained. How loud is "shouting like a maniac?" What kind of gestures, facial expressions, and rhythms were being expressed? What, precisely, was the shouter saying in terms of semantic content?

Second, critical information about the participants' inner states is usually left out of these descriptions or given only in a perfunctory manner. Even if the person describing is asked explicitly to go into this, she will not be able to tell very much. What she experienced in the interaction affectively, moment by moment, will be largely forgotten, to the extent it was even noticed. What the other person experienced she can only guess.

Third, and most important, such described events often have more of a systemic context than what gets captured in the description. What was really happening on a couple level, or family level, just prior to the event? During the event? Right after the event? What circular triggering causes were really at play at different points? Typically, much of this dimension is missing in the family member's conscious representations.

So what do we as family therapists do? One route is just to plunge ahead and not worry about the lack of fine-grained information. Another route is to ask a lot of detailed questions. Many times I do one or the other of these options. But there is a third possibility that I turn to frequently and find to be an enormous help. I call it "dramatization." I have the family "play" the event. They stage it on the spot. This is *representation by demonstration*—by showing instead of telling. It guarantees a representational vehicle rich in analogic detail. It also is a lively technique and easy to use. Furthermore, it is extremely effective for mobilizing the participation of any children in the family.

The technique comes from the psychodrama tradition. In psychodrama group therapy, a patient will act out a scene from his life, using other group members to stand in for whatever persons were there in reality. Naturally when one transposes this idea to family therapy there is a large difference. In a family therapy dramatization each person must play her own role. The real actors themselves are present. And they all know one another intimately and were all originally participants in the event being investigated. This implies, for the most part, procedures and other therapeutic ends different from those belonging to psychodrama.[1] In many ways it is closer to what Minuchin and Fishman (1981) called "enactment," although, as I explain later, it is different from that as well.

I use three versions of the dramatization technique.

- A *replay dramatization* (or "replay" for short) is a reproduction of a problem event. The event may have happened yesterday or 2 years ago. It may have been a one-time event or a repetitive, daily occurrence.
- A *positive future dramatization* tries out new, more advantageous behavior. It might or might not be an altered version of the same problem event.
- A *negative future dramatization* is a more specialized, less common version. The family stages a vision of what will probably result if the problem is not altered. For example, the family may dramatize what their life will eventually become if one parent does not change his or her drinking.

REPLAY DRAMATIZATION

The first step in replay dramatization is choosing an event. Finding a pregnant, illustrative event to stage is normally not hard. Whenever possible, it should be a recent occurrence, as people can remember recent events better than those from months or years ago. Repetitive events also tend to be more productive than one-time occurrences. Families often have recurring cycles of interaction that may be closely intertwined with the presenting problem. For example, you might choose a pattern of interaction that typically occurs over dinner, or when a child is told to clean up her room, or when the family is in the car, or when mother or father arrives home from work. The family is then asked to show how the repetitive event typically happens. Another option is to ask when the problem is at its worst.

Although recurring events work best with replay dramatization, it is also possible to dramatize a critical one-time event.

This might be a trauma or something bordering on trauma. Or it might be a pivotal moment from a (past or present) more enduring crisis period. In these cases, dramatization not only helps to elicit more information but also helps family members better resolve lingering difficult emotions or cognitive perplexities.

In some cases, events that happened years ago may still profoundly affect family members' behavior in the present. This was the case with the Bryant boys.

> Mrs. Bryant insisted that her children's fighting was normal. "After all, they are boys," she said. Christian, 14 years old, disagreed. He said his brother Matthew, 13, regularly insulted him, kicked him, and threw furniture at him as well. I asked Christian to describe the worst incident the two of them had. He recalled an event when their mother was out shopping. He and Matthew were playing with knives. They argued, and then Matthew began to run after him with a bread knife, threatening to stab him. Matthew wound up accidentally cutting his own finger instead. The blood spurted all over a wall, and a neighbor had to call an ambulance.
>
> Christian told the story as if it had happened yesterday. When I asked him when it had taken place, he said that it had happened 2 years ago. But he remembered it frequently and was often afraid of having Matthew go out of control in the same way.

With the Bryant family I used a dramatization of the boys' fights. Through the forming of a rich, dense representation-by-showing, we could deal with these difficult events in a more helpful, thorough way.

There are some types of trauma, however, that are not appropriate for replay. These include sexual abuse, a directly witnessed death, and extreme violence. Such traumas carry too much intensity and need to be dealt with by other means; a replay would risk retraumatization.

Choosing an event for replay is often relatively easy, but sometimes it is not. In these cases, it is helpful to explore the contexts in which the problems are at their worst and at what time of day they occur. This is what I did with the Fish family.

Mrs. Fish, a single mother working full time, consulted me because she was worried about Joanne, her 11-year-old daughter. Joanne was fearful and timid and had frequent stomach aches. Joanne's parents had separated 3 years ago. She rarely saw her father. Her 7-year-old brother, Eric, was described as outgoing and free of problems. All three family members came to our first session.

Joanne hung her head as her mother spoke. She appeared upset. Whenever she sniffled, her mother immediately handed her a tissue. When I attempted to speak with her, Joanne responded with silence or said, "I don't know." She refused to look at me.

Eric seemed very busy getting his mother's attention. He constantly interrupted and at one point started to climb onto her lap. Mrs. Fish said no several times, but Eric kept trying anyway and eventually succeeded. This prompted Joanne to finally speak up. She commented, with obvious irritation, that Eric always got his way, just like now.

Observing all this, I was already collecting information on a systemic level. I decided to propose a dramatization. However, it was not yet obvious to me whether there was a family scene that might be beneficial to replicate. Staying with Mrs. Fish's primary complaint, I asked when and where in the day Joanne's anxieties and stomach aches typically were at their worst. "In the evening," Mrs. Fish responded. "When in the evening?" I asked. "At the children's bedtime," she answered. I proposed that it would be useful for me to see more concretely what went on among the three of them at that time, and I ask if they would be willing to show me through a replay dramatization.

Once the event to be replayed has been chosen, the therapist requests each person involved to verbally recount his or her version of what happened. The real detective work starts now. The therapist inquires about the details concerning who did what and in what sequence.

Typically I start with each of the parents' versions (if they were both participants). Next I ask the children to tell their versions. Then I summarize what I think I have heard. I emphasize whose versions are similar and how they are similar, as well as whose versions differ and how they differ. If certain family members were not present at the event, I ask them to describe what they have heard about it and from whom.

In some cases, significant differences emerge between the recounted versions. When this happens, I often have the various family members write on a flip chart the ways in which the versions differ. Other times, I have the family do the replay more than one time, staging it from different perspectives. What I *don't* do is allow the family members to get into a lengthy argument about who has the correct version. It is not that I think no underlying reality or truth about the past exists. It is simply that endlessly pursuing this would waste our time, as there are no practical means of settling the matter. I try instead to convey the message that differences in perception are normal.

Another interesting issue that often comes up is exactly where in time to start the replay. It is often useful to start a little earlier than what the family members have described as the "beginning." This illuminates the wider systemic context and reveals additional triggering elements. Sometimes you may immediately have a hunch that starting the replay earlier will be valuable. Other times you may realize this during the replay itself, in which case you can begin the replay anew. With the

Fish family, beginning the replay earlier was very helpful in eliciting more systemic information.

> Mrs. Fish, Joanne, and Eric were in the middle of their replay of the interactions taking place at bedtime. Joanne complained to her mother that she had not had any time to be alone with Mrs. Fish. I sensed that we needed more information here, so I stopped the action and asked for more details about exactly what happened starting when Mrs. Fish arrived home from work. It came out that the moment Mrs. Fish came in the door, Eric aggressively and successfully demanded her attention. He then dominated what little free time she had. I had them move to a replay of this moment.

Sometimes what occurred shortly after what the family members describe as the "finish" is equally relevant. There may be later systemic repercussions that they have failed to connect with the original event.

Next comes the replay itself. The therapist has everyone stand up and begins to set the scene with them. At the same time, the therapist continues her detective work. Often new details surface at this point. The therapist must ask questions about spatial arrangements, physical context, and the like. For example:

- Exactly where is each person located during the event?
- Who is in the kitchen, living room, bedroom, bathroom?
- Who sits where in the car? Who sits next to whom?
- Who can hear whom?
- Which doors are shut and which are open?

Everyone should be asked to help with the puzzle of organizing the therapist's office so that it corresponds at least a bit to the physical setting of the event itself. Chairs can be rearranged. A table can be moved. Toys or other items can serve as props (I even keep paper plates on hand for dramatizations of meals). Young children tend to join in enthusiastically with this task, and of course the therapist should encourage them to so do. There is no need for overly exact correspondence to the original setting, however. It is only a representation of the event that is about to be given shape and form, not the event itself.

To start out, each family member plays his own role. Depending on the family, members may feel comfortable or awkward engaging in replay. It is common, for example, for adolescents to refuse to directly participate in a replay. During the preparatory discussion they may have comments and opinions to express, but once the time comes for action, this cooperation may evaporate. In most instances, this is not a problem. I give the adolescent permission not to participate actively. I ask him to sit or stand where he can observe what is going on. If he personally had an important part in the event, I may ask him to choose another family member to play his role. Then I give the adolescent the job of correcting the replay while the others are enacting it if he experiences it as inaccurate. That said, once a replay is underway, adolescents may find it difficult to resist participating. Often, after the adolescent adds a second or third correction, I ask him to show me what is supposed to happen. At this point he just may agree to participate.

During the replay the therapist aids each person, step by step, from the sidelines. Typically a family with children will do fine for the first 2 to 5 minutes and then will need some help. This is especially likely if there are small children. When families are unsure how to go farther, the therapist helps them clarify what to do next. Typical comments from the therapist might be:

- And what happens now?
- So what happens at this point?

- So what happens next?
- So after David says that, what do you, Susan, do?

Don't worry if there is a lot of stopping and starting—that is just part of the process.

Some laughter about what is being represented is common. A replay will often bring out humorous aspects for the family. As long as they are laughing at themselves in a nonmalicious manner, this is positive. It is a sign that their understanding of the event is widening. It also heightens motivation for change.

Dramatization allows the family to represent to themselves how they mutually behave. But it also lets them discover a great deal about their accompanying thoughts and emotions. Because the replay proceeds bit by bit, there are plenty of opportunities for each person to notice more of what is going on within herself, along with what happens externally.

The therapist can also intervene on this level. One means is simply to stop the action for a moment and then ask one or more family members what they are experiencing. For example:

- Stop a second. Joanne, when Eric says this, how do you react inside?
- Christian, what do you really feel like saying to your brother right now?
- Hold on a minute. Mrs. Fish, I notice everyone else is eating but you are not. What is going on? What are you thinking? What are you feeling emotionally?

The other way is let the family get to the end and then ask them to go back and replay a certain part of the scenario.

- That was very interesting and informative. Before we talk about anything else, could we go back to . . . ? Would you please do this part again? Yes, that's right. Now, let's stop here. Christian, what is happening inside of you right at this point?

Family members often interrupt the flow as well, adding commentary, an explanation, or some additional information. In many instances these remarks are important and should be welcomed by the therapist.[2] Usually one can listen briefly, make a short reply, and then encourage the family to continue the dramatization.

An additional benefit of dramatization is that each family member learns something about everyone else's emotions and thoughts in addition to her own. Everyone forms more complex representations of the others' inner lives. They deepen their sense of "intersubjectivity."[3]

Doubling

"Doubling," a classic psychodrama technique, is another effective way to bring out more explicitly what a family member is experiencing during the replay. Doubling can be done when the therapist suspects that a family member has important unspoken feelings or thoughts.[4] The therapist moves to a place just beside this person and, asking permission first, offers succinctly, in one or two sentences, what he thinks the person is feeling or thinking. This is said using "I": for example, "I'm afraid to show you how disappointed I am right now."

Next, the statement must immediately be checked for accuracy. If the family member agrees it is indeed accurate, the therapist can request that the person rephrase it "in your own words." If the family member disagrees with what the therapist said, the therapist asks the family member to correct the statement.

Doubling can be particularly effective with young children, who, depending on their developmental stage may have only minimal representations of their mental states. If the therapist asks what a child is thinking or feeling, the reply may be only a shrug. This was the case with 7-year-old Robert and his 9-year-old sister, Samantha, who were having difficulty dealing with the arguments between their divorced parents. When I asked Robert what he felt during his parents' fights, he said he didn't know. But he looked miserable during the replay. I doubled for him, saying, "I am sad that you always fight with Dad." Robert began to cry and described how terrible he felt during these arguments. I asked Samantha if she felt like her brother. She did not answer. I then asked her, "Can I speak for you?" She nodded, so I said, "Mom, I am angry that you spoil our weekend by fighting with Dad." Samantha nodded that this was right. The children then suggested a change in the replay. They wanted to show what happened when their parents fought.

With young children, you do not need to ask that they rephrase your doubling statement. I often simply ask, "Is that right? Just shake your head yes or no."

Role Reversal

Another useful technique originating from the psychodrama tradition is "role reversal," in which two people switch their roles in the replay. The therapist stops the action and asks the two people, if they are willing, to physically move into the other's original location and repeat a segment of the replay in the position of the other person.

The primary value of role reversal is to gain insight into how life feels from the other side, but it can have additional purposes as well. Perhaps family member *A* wants family member *B* better to grasp how he, *A*, is experiencing *B*'s manner and behavior. Or one person may have "forgotten" what he said or did, so now someone else can show him. Or someone thinks someone else is not really acting like she does at home. This technique can also be effective when there is generally little empathy among the family members.

However, the therapist must also be careful with role reversal. Sometimes there is a fine line between a portrayal that conveys information and a degrading caricature. If you think anyone is going too far in this respect, you should intervene and ask the person to tone down the portrayal.

Pretend Play Dramatization

One major problem with dramatization, especially with children under 5, is difficulty maintaining a role. Young children usually enjoy the action and liveliness of dramatization, but it can be hard for them to focus on the step-by-step process that is required. Another major problem is that some events may be too painful, poignant, or intense for a family to easily replay. Here again, the younger the child, the harder it can be.

Fortunately there is a good solution to both problems: *pretend play dramatization.* Each family member selects a toy to represent himself. Usually this is a doll, a stuffed animal, or a puppet.[5] The dramatization takes place with each person manipulating and making his toy "speak." This variation on replay dramatization worked well with the Gregory family.

Mr. and Mrs. Gregory and their children—Chloe, 8, and Seth, 6—had been sent to family therapy because of Seth's eating problems. Seth had cystic fibrosis, a disease that would probably result in an early death during his twenties. What he ate had to be carefully chosen and prepared in order to limit his digestion problems. He was very small and thin for his age.

Meals in the Gregory household had recently become a drama. Seth was eating insufficient amounts and was taking 2 to 3 hours to finish a meal. The parents were beside themselves. The institutional team in charge of Seth's case had urged the parents to come to therapy. They said it was a family problem and not a direct result of his illness. They also saw the problem as life-threatening.

I proposed a replay of a typical meal. The family chose the evening meal, when they all were present. Because of the gravity of the problem, along with the strength of everyone's emotions concerning it, I decided that a pretend play dramatization would be most useful. It also fit better with Seth's age.

When I brought out the animal puppets, Chloe chose a bat, Seth chose a snake that was actually longer than he was tall, Mr. Gregory chose an elephant, and Mrs. Gregory selected a red fox. They pulled my small table to the center of the room, arranged their chairs around it, and started in. During some minutes of replay, the fox and elephant both looked only at the snake and talked only to him. They talked a lot, insisting that he eat more and eat faster. They asked him how he was feeling. Both anxiety and anger dominated their vocal tones.

It quickly became apparent that Mr. and Mrs. Gregory totally ignored Chloe, the bat. They didn't look at her. When she spoke, they didn't hear her. Finally the bat flew away, announcing that she was going to her room to play. They didn't respond to this, either. Both parents continued leaning slightly towards Seth, concentrating only upon him.

After the replay was finished, I sent the children out of the room so the parents could speak as freely as possible. I asked them what they discovered during the replay. Mr. Gregory said right away that he realized how completely they forget their daughter. Mrs. Gregory began to cry; she said she felt that she was missing having a relationship with her daughter, as their son occupied all her time.

After a moment I added some observations, noting that the parents had not said a word to each other during the meal, either. I went on to point out how it appeared that mealtime had ceased to be a social ritual in their family. It was no longer an occasion for contact and exchange—instead, it had turned into a high-pressure situation in which it seemed hard for anyone to take pleasure in being together, let alone in the food. They agreed emphatically, opening up a good moment to begin talking about possible change.

Dramatization functions best when the family's anxiety level is not too high. Some anxiety will always be there—partly because they are performing in front of the therapist, partly because they are moving toward new ground, and partly because the portrayed event in itself probably has emotional charge. This is all okay, as long as such nervousness and uncertainty remain within a certain zone. Too much would be counterproductive.

That said, the therapist should do her best to diminish anxiety. The pretend play mode can help a lot. It lets the family be in the scene and build a dense, complex representation, yet it also gives them space from the scene, as the affair takes place between toys or puppets, not between the parents and children themselves.

In this sense, pretend play dramatization is in the same spirit as many of the new anxiety-reducing techniques used today in the psychotherapy of trauma. The family members can literally "look on" at what the puppets are doing, even while the represented action is gripping and full of implications.

POSITIVE FUTURE DRAMATIZATION

Perhaps the best advantage of dramatization is that it can so easily move from a process of portrayal to a process of change. With *positive future dramatization*, the family can represent not only "how it happens" but also "how it could be different." In representing the latter, the family begins to realize—to *perform*—the "it could be different." In other words, they take steps toward behavioral change right in the session.

Often in one session I start with a replay and then end with a positive future dramatization. This lets the family profit from the focus and emotional momentum they have built up during the session. Other times I use positive future dramatization alone in a session, with no prior replay dramatization.

A decision to make, naturally, is *whose* vision of the future to portray. Often we discuss this beforehand. For example, I might ask each person to imagine how the event could happen differently in the future. Then we might together work out a kind of collated notion, putting together several family members' ideas. In other cases, everyone might like one person's picture and agree to try that. Or we might stage, successively, more than one version. Occasionally I even suggest that the family just start in and try something new without any prior planning.

After their pretend play dramatization, the Gregory family was highly motivated to work toward change. While the children were still out of the room, Mr. and Mrs. Gregory and I discussed ways of transforming meals into something more pleasurable.

They came up with a plan to alter three things. First, the parents would talk to each other and to Chloe more. Plus, they would talk about more pleasant topics, sometimes with some humor. The third idea was that for the first part of the meal, while everyone was present, they would not concern themselves with how Seth was eating. Once Mrs. Gregory had left the table, Mr. Gregory would then take over supervising Seth to ensure that he ate a minimum amount. Mrs. Gregory and Chloe would go somewhere else in the home and spend a little time playing together.

I then had the parents get the children from the waiting room. They described the changes that would happen during the positive future dramatization. Both children decided at once that they each wanted to tell a joke at the beginning of the meal. They began the dramatization with this, and everyone laughed. As they continued, they maintained this atmosphere.

When the family came the following week, they reported that they had managed to implement their ideas at home rather well. Two weeks later, Seth was eating a little better, and a month later his eating problem was much more under control.

Not all family events suitable for a replay are also suitable for a positive future dramatization. With a trauma, for example, the idea of a changed future does not always fit. However, once in a while with a trauma I do ask the family members to imagine what, if it had been done differently, would have been more helpful for each of them. Sometimes this concerns practical action and communication in a moment of emergency. Sometimes it concerns the aftermath—for example, how a child is consoled, forgiven, or helped to think in ways more useful for her inner digestion of the trauma. Sometimes simply discussing these things is enough. But I might also see if they want to try a staged representation. The idea is to develop new collaborative skills to use in this type of situation.

NEGATIVE FUTURE DRAMATIZATION

Negative future dramatization is not a technique I turn to often, but for certain issues it can have enormous power. I usually use it when there is some kind of seriously destructive behavior in the family, and especially when one or more family members denies or minimizes the consequences of this behavior. The dramatization helps the family to see how things are likely to evolve if the destructive behavior does not change.

Jesse Dumont, age 15, had been stealing money to buy drugs. His mother downplayed the implications of Jesse's behavior, returning money to the people he had stolen from and generally making excuses for him to protect him from any consequences. Jesse's sister, Grace, age 14, complained that "Jesse just does anything he wants to and then gets away with it."

I suggested that Grace organize a negative future dramatization. I asked her to imagine and portray the family 10 years from now. Everyone agreed to participate. In Grace's dramatization, Jesse was in prison. She put him in a corner, facing the wall, to represent this. Their mother was portrayed at home alone and very depressed. She now spent all her time and money on lawyers and trying to get Jesse out of jail, Grace said. Grace placed herself far away from both Jesse and their mother. She said she had left and had her own life now. In the dramatization, the mother was telephoning Grace, complaining about how unhappy she was.

Occasionally I use negative future dramatization for slightly different purposes. In the following example, I used it to help the family better prepare for a future situation they were dreading.

Mr. and Mrs. Brook arrived for family therapy very upset. They came with their 6-year-old son, Lucas. Mrs. Brook was also 7 months pregnant. It seemed that Lucas, who was an aggressive and at times violent boy, had told them he intended to kill the baby. Lucas already had a lot of trouble at school with his aggressive impulses. He recently had seriously injured another child, hitting him on the head with a large, heavy stick. The school refused to take him back unless he was followed by a psychiatrist. The parents took him to a child psychiatrist, who saw him several times individually before referring them to family therapy. Mrs. Brook said she was terrified by the idea that Lucas might harm the baby.

During a long first session, in addition to other techniques, I used future dramatization. But I decided to have them experiment with two types of representation—a negative and a positive. Both versions represented what the family interaction would be after the baby was born.

I proposed a minimal beginning scenario. The time was after school, and the baby was crying loudly. Mr. Brook had yet to come home from work. The first dramatization was of what could happen when Lucas felt very angry at the baby and his mother felt extremely afraid. The second dramatization was of what could happen when everyone had more positive feelings. I decided also to put both of these in the mode of pretend play dramatization, given both Lucas's age as well as the severity of his prior behavior.

I asked that each person pick an animal for him- or herself, and then together select an animal to represent the baby. Unexpectedly, Lucas insisted on choosing a puppet for the baby and put it on his right hand, while he put the puppet for himself on his left hand. For the baby he selected a small dinosaur that could curl inside its attached eggshell, and for himself he took a horse. Mrs. Brook picked a cat. I asked Mr. Brook to play the baby, but Lucas said he wanted to play the baby. This surprised me as well as the parents. I told Lucas that his father would play the baby now, and he could perhaps play the baby later.

They played the first version. The dinosaur baby wailed. The cat-mother acted helpless and confused, while on her own face Mrs. Brook looked genuinely frightened. Lucas just watched passively. I tried to get him to talk, asking what was going on in his mind. Finally he commented that he did not know what he felt. As I encouraged him further, he said that he couldn't stand the baby's crying and wanted the baby to go away. He insisted, however, that he did not want to hurt the baby.

Mrs. Brook, dropping out of her cat role, protested about Lucas saying he was angry. She said she thought he should not react that way. I confronted her about this, proposing that, on the contrary, Lucas was verbalizing his anger in an appropriate way. Not only was he openly telling how he felt, but he also was saying clearly that although he experienced this kind of reaction, he still wanted not to act toward the baby in an angry way. I checked with him that I had understood him correctly.

He confirmed this, adding that what made him the most angry was that his mother was just taking care of the baby and not playing at all with him.

We then turned to the second dramatization. I explained that they could now show how they would like the situation to be. But I suggested we discuss one point first. Referring back to the comment Lucas had just made about his fear that the presence of the baby would mean that his mother would not play with him, I asked Mrs. Brook and Lucas to talk about this and see if they could make a plan that would solve this problem. Mrs. Brook proposed that when Lucas first come home from school, she would take care of the baby, but that once Mr. Brook returned from work, she would then play a while with Lucas, letting Mr. Brook take care of the baby. Lucas liked the proposal, and Mr. Brook commented from the side that this plan was fine with him.

With this understanding in place, I asked them to play a new version of when Lucas come home from school. Another unexpected development now emerged. Lucas had the baby puppet cry. Mrs. Brook had her puppet start to take care of it. Lucas then had the Lucas puppet announce that he would help. Noticing Mrs. Brook seemed at a loss about what to do with this, I intervened, suggesting that she and Lucas find ways to calm the baby down together. They did so, with Lucas having his puppet act quite lovingly toward the baby. After the dramatization, I discussed with Mr. and Mrs. Brook how this side of Lucas could be given more recognition and more developmental support in the family.

Readers familiar with Minuchin's work may notice that dramatization has some affinities with what he calls "enactment" (e.g., Minuchin & Fishman, 1981). Indeed, Minuchin's provocative enactment technique is one from which I have drawn inspiration for many years. Like dramatization, Minuchin's enactment gets the family doing something rather than just talking. Additionally Minuchin often has a family try the same exchange again, experimenting the second time with new behavior.

That said, dramatization is in most respects different. Enactment normally is based upon interactions the therapist has noticed happening right in the session, whereas dramatization attempts representationally to reproduce a previous event. Also, when doing a positive future dramatization, the therapist for the most part explores the family members' ideas about change rather than instructing them on what to do differently. Both for positive future dramatizations and negative future dramatizations, there are no equivalents with regard to enactment.

A good dramatization changes how everyone in the family thinks, almost inevitably. They don't just act out the dramatized event; they *see* it, and see it with new eyes. The representational shift is often extensive. Each person emerges with a more detailed grasp of his own actions. More importantly, each gains a better sense of how the reciprocal actions fit together. A systemic point of view—a notion of "how we do it" (and perhaps even of "how we might do it otherwise")—begins to come into place. It is an awareness that the jigsaw puzzle comprises more than just the individual pieces, and that the secret is to grasp how the pieces belong to the whole.

NOTES

1. For a more traditional use of psychodrama in family therapy see Blatner (1994).

2. This is another way in which dramatization in family therapy is unlike classic psychodrama.

3. See, for example, Fonagy, Gergely, Jurist, and Target (2002) and Stolorow, Atwood, and Orange (2002). For an excellent overview of the concept of intersubjectivity, see Beebe et al. (2005).

4. As Leveton (1991) pointed out, doubling can also be used by itself as a freestanding technique in a family session.

5. Puppets manufactured by the Folkmanis company serve particularly well. The puppets are figures, such as witches, with moveable mouths and bodies.

CHAPTER THREE

Metaphor Techniques

. . . .

We rarely speak—indeed, rarely even *think*—without relying upon metaphor. It is a representational device so permeating our daily lives that we hardly notice it (Lycan, 1996, 1999; Stern, 2000). Look how quickly we turn to metaphor when referring to time, for example. We want to "save" time, or say that it is "slipping away" or that we have "not enough" or perhaps "too much" of it.

Although most metaphors are banal, some have great expressive power. This has long been incorporated into family therapy lore. Borrowing from the hypnosis tradition, family therapists have learned how, at special moments, to embed a carefully chosen metaphor in what they say. This lets us communicate with a family on a different level, often bypassing potential argument and objection. The right creative metaphor can also wonderfully condense a complex message into a seemingly simple vehicle.

Such interventions employ what I call *therapist-generated metaphors*.[1] For example, during divorce mediation, the therapist could suggest to the parents that "a custody battle is like a football game between rival teams." The implied suggestion, of course, is that they had better make sure that their child doesn't become the football (Mio & Katz, 1996). Lankton and Lankton (1983), helping a family explore how to create more balance and control, proposed that a family is "like a small boat."

Of course, strictly speaking, therapists err when they call these metaphors. They are similes. That need not worry us, however. As far as their utilization in therapy goes, it makes sense theoretically to treat metaphor, simile, and even some related types of figurative language as equivalent.[2] For example, sometimes the therapist tells a story or recounts an anecdote, intending with this longer construction to convey a deeper message by indirect means. Milton Erickson (1980) was considered a master of such indirect communication. Thanks to Haley (1963, 1973, 1985), Lankton and Lankton (1983), Zeig (1982), and others, his methods have been widely disseminated in the family therapy world.

I appreciate such means and use them myself at times. But I find there exists a much richer source of therapeutic effectiveness: *patient-generated metaphors*.[3] These are metaphors (or similes, etc.) that family members themselves produce. Surprisingly, this possibility has been little mentioned in the literature. A valuable article on couple therapy by Peggy Papp (1982) is one of the few exceptions I know.[4]

A patient-generated metaphor might be spontaneous or might be formulated in response to a question from the therapist (for example, "How would you describe that using a metaphor?"). Exploration of such metaphors can give a unique access to features of a family member's representational world. This is because often the metaphoric word or phrase has close ties to an interconnected constellation of beliefs, values, wishes, fears, hopes, and the like. By means of her metaphor, the family member makes discoveries. She can contact previously unarticulated aspects of what, at a deeper level, she believes and feels.

Perhaps even more valuable for family therapy, however, are the systemic possibilities. A family can "play" with a significant metaphor once it has been brought into focus. The metaphor can become a shared representational vehicle undergoing development and variation, like a musical motif.

Crucially, children of all ages are easily included in such work. They like to "play" with a metaphor, much as they enjoy pretend play with toys and objects. The metaphor being used for this purpose in the session must be fairly simple and straightforward, naturally.

An exchange starting out with a focus on a metaphor turns out to be one of the best ways to draw family members into a systemic dialogue. The following vignette clearly demonstrates this.

> Mrs. Morgan, concerned about her 9-year-old daughter, Elisabeth, brought her to family therapy after meeting with Elisabeth's teacher. The teacher portrayed Elisabeth as a lonely, frightened child who avoided playing with others her age. Mrs. Morgan tended to agree, although hearing this from the teacher had been a shock. Elisabeth rarely invited friends to play with her, and was rarely invited by others.
>
> As Mrs. Morgan spoke, she remarked that Elisabeth had built a "thick, stone wall around herself." This was a metaphoric representation worth developing collaboratively. Why? Not because of its poetic originality; from that point of view the metaphor was banal, a stereotype. But from a human perspective, as an ascription of a mother concerning her daughter, it was pithy and obviously extremely important. It was almost certain to reflect not one, but a whole interwoven series of beliefs about her child.
>
> I decided to use a technique I call *implication exploration*. (I explain this technique later, but first we can see it here in action.) I asked Mrs. Morgan to tell us how she imagined

34

this wall. She described it as "solid stone, 5 feet thick and 10 feet high."

Next, using what I call *systemic extension* I asked Elisabeth if she agreed with her mother's picture and description of the wall. The idea was to invite Elisabeth to engage with the metaphor.

Elisabeth's response immediately deepened the session. She told her mother that the wall was actually "transparent, made of thick plastic, not stone." Noticing that Mrs. Morgan was listening intently, I encouraged her to go on. She said she "could see the others through the wall." She also said there was "no door in the wall" and that it "protected her" and that she felt safe. However, she added that when she saw children "playing on the other side of the wall," she yearned to be with them. She was also very afraid that they would make fun of her or reject her.

At this point I posed another question. I asked Elisabeth to imagine that in the future the wall could change in any way she wished, such that she could be protected but also join the other children, or have them join her. What would this be like? This is a technique I call *future portrayal*. One builds upon the original metaphor, but explicitly with respect to possible solutions or more positive outcomes.

Elisabeth responded, hesitant at first and then with conviction, that "the wall would be changed into a fence." This fence would be "made of wood" and "painted white with flowers on one side." It would be "low enough that she or anyone else could jump over it." The fence would also have "a gate that could be locked." There would be "spaces between the fence boards so you could see through them to what is on the other side."

Mrs. Morgan was quite enthusiastic about Elisabeth's fence. They then both deliberated at my suggestion, over what the first steps to transform the wall into a fence could be. Elisabeth's idea was that to start she would wear shoes like what the other girls wear and would change her eyeglasses so that the other children would make less fun of her. Next, she would invite Melanie, a schoolmate, to a movie. Mrs. Morgan approved, and they promised each other they would continue with new ideas after the session.

This is a good example of how a mix of representations already formed and representations newly formed emerges in the discourse. The initial metaphor stimulated a series of new metaphors. Mrs. Morgan's and Elisabeth's imaginations began to function collectively.

What makes such a productive exchange possible? The answer to this question has to do with the nature of metaphor itself. In the example Mrs. Morgan said that Elisabeth kept herself behind a *wall*. *Wall* is a simple word, but it belongs to a large semantic field: We easily connect *wall* to words such as *gate*, *fence*, *keeping in*, *keeping out*, and so on. These words reflect a metaphoric grouping of concepts, an interrelated network.[5] By metaphorically using the one word, *wall*, Mrs. Morgan implicitly invoked the larger grouping.

Once a family member has employed a metaphor, and once the therapist has highlighted it as well, it is usually easy for other family members to continue along the same lines. They develop the metaphor further, adding their own nuances, as Elisabeth did. What they add normally draws upon the same underlying metaphoric grouping.

Additionally, a good metaphor, once worked on productively, often becomes a kind of representational shorthand for the family afterwards. It is enough for someone to simply refer to "the fence"—everyone immediately knows what is meant. This is often a source of humor for the family, but it is more than that, too. It is a light and easy way for them to evoke important commitments they have made to one another in the therapy session.

Sometimes the metaphor even gets translated into family life in more graphic ways. This was the case with the Avery brothers.

> Russ, age 13, Roger, age 11, Steven, age 7, and Jordan, age 4, were angry with one another because of difficulties in respecting one another's privacy and personal belongings. Conflicts often broke out because one brother would take something from the room of another without asking or would walk off with the object even after being told he couldn't have it.
>
> They also often hurt one another's feelings. Steven described an example of wanting to play with Russ and Russ yelling, "Leave me alone!" It turned out, however, that Steven had barged into Russ's room without knocking, which had angered Russ.
>
> As we discussed this incident, Russ explained that it was not true that he disliked Steven—it was just that Steven "misread his signals." This spontaneous metaphor of "signal misreading" was picked up quickly by the others. Everyone agreed that Jordan, the youngest, always "went through red lights." Steven also complained that he never knew if he had "a red or green light" from Russ or Roger when he wanted to hang out with them. Russ replied, "If my door is shut or half open it is a red light."
>
> We talked about how the boys could send clearer signals. They decided to make a sign for each of their doors with a red light on one side and a green light on the other. This system helped to reduce the conflict among the brothers.

The second fact is that even small children can do this. And they like to do it. This is somewhat surprising, as they are hardly facile with language in general. But something about metaphor can "click" with them. They become interested, even excited, and with some support form the therapist they can usually make their own contribution to the family exchange.

SPONTANEOUS METAPHORS VERSUS REQUESTED METAPHORS

Both *spontaneous metaphors* and *requested metaphors* can be helpful in therapy. Spontaneous metaphors are like that of Elisabeth's mother. They occur in the flow of a family member's speech without prompting. If the therapist guesses the metaphor might be rich enough for joint exploration, he simply expresses interest in the word or phrases used and asks if the family member would be willing to explore what might be implied. For example:

> *Brother:* My sister is a spy.
> *Therapist:* What kind of spy?
> *Brother:* A spy that is very clever and really thorough.
> *Therapist:* For whom does she do her spying?
> *Brother:* My mother. My mother even pays her to be a spy.

A requested metaphor is normally easy enough to obtain. For example:

> *Grandmother:* My son and my grandson just don't communicate.
> *Therapist:* Could you find a metaphor to represent their not communicating?
> *Grandmother:* My son speaks Greek and my grandson answers in Chinese. I don't speak Greek or Chinese.

What is interesting about both types of metaphor is the almost inevitable response of the other family members. The moment a specific metaphor is on the table, so to speak, everyone goes into high alert. There is something about metaphors examined close up that can be instantly catalytic.

USING METAPHORS WITH YOUNG CHILDREN

Starting at 2 years of age, children do something analogous to linguistic metaphor use: They engage in pretend play. They pick up a banana, for example, and pretend it is a gun. But the capacity for linguistic metaphor seems to come on-line only later.[6]

This is an area which has not received a lot of attention from researchers. Worth mentioning, however, are David Foulkes' (1999) wonderful studies of children's dreaming. It is only around four to five years—the same age when family therapy metaphor work becomes possible—that children start to have dreams with story-like narrative content.[7] (Interestingly, one of their statistically most frequent types of dream image is animals.)

The fact that pretend play begins so early has a beneficial practical consequence. With metaphor work with small children, the hardest part is the very beginning—soliciting a metaphor for exploration in the first place. After that is accomplished, however, their already highly developed pretend play capacities kick in. This is one of the reasons that metaphor work is so useful with young children.

Because young children have little linguistic sophistication, their range of what they can come up with in terms of metaphors is limited. Usually they will think of animals, which is fine. An animal metaphor is an easy one to use for further steps on a systemic level.

When a young child has difficulty thinking of a metaphor— or difficulty even grasping what is wanted—there are ways the therapist can help. One way is to provide a "menu" of possible choices. For example, the therapist might say: "Can you think of something that is like this? Some person or thing? Maybe someone from a TV program? Or something from nature? Or something or someone from a book?" Another option is to use stuffed animals, toys, or dolls. The therapist can propose that the child pick one out to stand for whatever is supposed to be metaphorically described.

Once a young child has found a metaphor and it has been discussed a little, how do you go further? Metaphor enactment, discussed later in this chapter, is often the most obvious means. Small children adore acting out their stuffed animal metaphors, and the rest of the family—siblings especially—can quickly join them on this level.

An alternative is to turn to systemic art techniques (see Chapter 4). A chosen metaphor can be drawn on paper by the child. After that, there are several ways to proceed. Other family members might be asked to comment on the drawing. Or they can be asked to draw their own versions of what they think the child's metaphor means. After drawing what they think the child's metaphor means, they can then think of their *own* metaphors, and draw them, too.

Metaphor work can be done with children as young as 4 or 5, as long as the child has support from the therapist. Once children are 7 or 8 years old, they begin to have much more facility with metaphor. The therapist can proceed with them more or less the same as they do with adults.

IMPLICATION EXPLORATION AND ASSOCIATION EXPLORATION

We can help clients to explore a metaphor in two different ways: through *implication exploration* or *association exploration*.

My exploration of Mrs. Morgan's metaphor was an example of implication exploration. In this instance, the therapist poses questions that utilize language from the relevant metaphoric concept field. If a daughter says her mother "is a volcano," the therapist can make a series of volcano-related interventions. Depending upon the context, examples might be:

- How often does the volcano *explode*?
- Volcanoes often *give signs* just before they explode. Does your mother give signs? What are they?
- When there is an *explosion,* who gets hurt most by the *lava*?

With *association* exploration, the therapist simply asks the family member to name her own associations to the metaphor she has produced.

As you can see, although implication exploration is akin to work with associations, it is not quite the same. The therapist's questions—and for the most part the client's answers—remain guided by the underlying metaphoric grouping.

Both procedures are of value. I turn more often to implication exploration, however, because I find that it teases out responses that, at least in part, are different from what would have emerged if the family member had simply been asked to associate.

The feel of using the two procedures is also quite different. One advantage of implication exploration is that it almost always becomes lively—usually very quickly and for the whole family. This is probably because metaphors used by family members often have a provocative edge. They can be slightly characterful, cartoonlike. This quality of exaggeration easily stimulates everybody's responses. It may also be due to the fact that implication exploration tends to stay near to the semantic concept field. This helps the other family members to follow, empathize, and find their own related ideas. Everyone is guided by an underlying shared frame of reference.

Association exploration has a looser feel than implication exploration; it is more idiosyncratic and more likely to evoke a piece of a family member's personal history. A wider net is cast. The following example illustrates this.

In a session with both his parents, John, age 15, complained that his home was a "prison." He said he felt "trapped" in this jail. His parents were the "prison guards" who watched everything he did and "locked him up" each evening and weekend.

I asked John what came into his mind when he thought of prison and being a prisoner. He let a flow of thoughts come slowly and gradually. I continued to encourage him by asking, "What else?"

Eventually John said that prison reminded him of a time 6 years ago when he was hospitalized for leukemia and had to undergo several months of chemotherapy. His mother moved into his hospital room, staying with him for most of this period.

This remark prompted John's mother to begin crying. She recalled aloud how horrible it was for her when he was ill, saying that she still lived in perpetual fear that John would get cancer again. Bit by bit it came out that she believed that by constantly watching over him, she could prevent the illness from coming back. She saw the irrationality of this conviction, and we moved to a negotiation of new boundaries and arrangements for John.

I seldom use the word *associations* when I ask for them. Typically only an adult who has been in psychoanalysis knows what that means. Instead I might ask:

- Which other words come into your head when you think of that metaphor?
- Can you let some images appear in connection to that metaphor?
- What feelings come up when you think about this metaphor?
- What does this metaphor remind you of from your past?
- What other experiences come to you when you think about this metaphor?

Sometimes before turning to other family members I also ask circular questions. For example:

- What do you suppose your mother and father are thinking when they hear this metaphor?
- What feelings do you think your sister and brother are having when they hear this metaphor?

Association exploration often requires a pace that is slower than that of implication exploration. There may be less humor and more of a meditative, trancelike atmosphere. Most children 10 or 11 years or older can enter into an association exploration rather well. Even younger children can often find something to say, however brief, when asked something simple like "What does this remind you of?"

FOLLOW-UP TECHNIQUES:
METAPHOR ENACTMENT AND FUTURE PORTRAYAL

A beneficial feature of implication exploration is that it can set the stage for the follow-up techniques of *metaphor enactment* and *future portrayal*.

Metaphor enactment is a form of dramatization (see Chapter 2), but what the family dramatizes is the metaphor.[8] Sometimes the therapist requests a specific family member (or a subsystem) to take part; often he proposes that the entire family do so. In following example, I asked everyone to join, with the father initially setting the scene.

> Mr. and Mrs. Braun's sons are lazy and selfish. Edward, Philip, and Samuel (ages 12, 9, and 8) thought only about themselves and were not learning to care about others, they said.
> I asked Mr. Braun to use a metaphor to depict his and Mrs. Braun's relationship with their sons. Mr. Braun paused and

then replied that he and his wife "ran a hotel." This elicited a big laugh from everyone, the boys included.

After getting Mr. Braun's permission to explore his metaphor, I used implication exploration, asking him, "so if you work in a hotel, what is your position?" He said he was the "concierge, running the front desk," as well as the "bellboy." Mrs. Braun, he continued was the "maid, cook, and waitress." The children were "free guests who never paid their bill."

Mr. Braun then added that the guests were "rude" and "always wanted more." They would "place their orders with room service" and then "criticize how the food was prepared." If they left toys out after playing with them, they expected "the maid to pick everything up." They "never said thank you or gave a tip." At this point, Philip remarked, "Parents are supposed to do all these things for their children." Edward and Samuel continued to find the whole account hilarious but basically accurate.

Seeking to keep all five family members engaged, I then chose to move to metaphor enactment. In response, Mr. Braun brought two extra chairs into the center of the room. He then placed the feet of his children, who were sitting, up on these chairs. Handing Philip the telephone, he told them they could call room service, order food, and demand that the maid clean up. He gave his wife a book to use as a tray.

The boys were clearly delighted with the game. Philip called room service and ordered French fries. Edward threw a book and some toys on the floor, telling Mrs. Braun to get busy cleaning up. Samuel insisted that Mr. Braun get his Game Boy, which he had left downstairs.

After a few minutes I asked each child what he really thought about the hotel. The mood suddenly shifted. All three children said, in diverse ways, that although their parents did a lot of these things for them, in reality they were not so nice about it: Mr. Braun, they said, frequently screamed and called them names. This would upset their mother, who often ended up doing what Mr. Braun had asked the boys to do in an effort to calm him down.

A rather sober discussion ensued. I pointed out to the boys that they seemed to be paying a high price because of the current state of things, and they agreed. The parents were rather taken aback at hearing how much emotional discomfort their behavior had been causing their children. After this session, the Brauns managed to make major changes in their home life. The hotel metaphor, often invoked with humor, remained a central point of reference for them.

The other follow-up technique, *future portrayal,* can be employed in a number of ways. The first step is usually simple: You request a family member—normally the person who first produced the metaphor—to change the metaphor or find a new one. The altered or new metaphor should correspond to this person's wish concerning how the family might shift. For example, a son who describes his father as "bulldozing" him might later say that he would like his father to "use a forklift and lift him up instead of crushing him."

The new metaphor does not have to remain in the same semantic concept field as the original metaphor. For instance, I had a 9-year-old client who said her mother was a "bomb exploding." When we reached the point of imagining a future relationship, she changed the metaphor to "a mother deer with Bambi."

Once the altered or new metaphor is in place you can then explore it in turn. Any of the usual procedures are possible: You can begin a new implication exploration, or ask for associations, or do an enactment of the new metaphor, and so on.

USING METAPHORS TO UNLOCK IRRESOLVABLE CONFLICT

Sometimes a family finds itself locked in what seems an irresolvable conflict. Often this has to do with an impending decision or a major life choice affecting one or all of the family members. Should we have a second child? Should we move to a new home? Should we invite Grandfather to live with us?

Typically when a family can't make this type of decision, we see *polarization* or *ambivalence*. Polarization is especially common. Two members, or two subgroups, each maintain hard-line opposing positions. Each person is convinced she is right. Each is convinced too that her hard-line position is the sole viewpoint she believes in; she sees the situation in black and white, with no gray zones, no nuances. The more they argue, the more entrenched the family members become.

Shifting to the level of metaphor is one of the most effective techniques I know for getting beyond this kind of struggle. Metaphors can bring out the hidden ambivalence—there is almost always *some*—in each party. Then, with the circulation of these new representations, the dialogue can move forward.

This technique normally requires a requested metaphor. Before asking for the metaphors, however, I often use a scaling question. I might ask a family member to identify on a scale of 1% to 100%, how much of himself is committed to the position he has been expressing and what percentage reflects the part of him that would prefer the opposite position. Usually to everyone's astonishment, this person will report a number anywhere from 90%/10% to 50%/50%. Only rarely is a 100%/0% split reported.

In some cases I then ask other family members to identify their "percentage." I might even proceed by using circular questioning, wherein family members guess what the others' percentages will be and then check the accuracy of their guesses. Circular questioning can highlight how each member represents the other's polarization.

I then request a metaphor for *each* of the two (or more) choices, or, in some cases, for each of the two (or more) relevant "parts" of the person. This kind of metaphor technique also can be done with younger children, starting, in my experience, at around age 6. Although a child of 5 years can usually handle simpler metaphor explorations, this type, with its language of "the part of you that . . . and the other part of you that . . . ," is cognitively a bit harder.

Once these metaphoric representations have been found, exploration continues. There are several options for conducting this exploration, as the following case illustrates.

Mr. and Mrs. Market brought their 13-year-old son, Alexander, to family therapy. They desperately sought a solution to what appeared an impossible family impasse. Because of Alexander's aggressive behavior and poor academic performance, the private school he had been attending had informed the family that they would not let him continue. Alexander and his parents each had sharply different opinions regarding what to do about this. Mr. Market wanted Alexander to be sent to a well-reputed boarding school where he could spend the schooldays and nights and return home for weekends. Mrs. Market insisted on the local public school, which would have to take him. Alexander had his eye on another private school in the area. Some of his friends were already there, and the schoolwork was reported to be minimally strenuous. Both parents agreed that this was not an option. Alexander flat out refused to consider either his father's or his mother's ideas.

I chose right in the first session with this family to use the metaphor technique. In response to a scaling question, Alexander said 80% of him felt his own wish was what had to happen. Fifteen percent of him could "relate" to his father's proposal, and 5% to his mother's.

I next decided to work with empty chairs, a step I often use to structure the metaphor exploration in this kind of situation. I put three chairs next to Alexander, explaining that one chair represented the 80% of him that wanted the new private school, another chair represented the part of him that felt sympathetic to his father's proposal and the last chair represented the part of him that felt he could accept his mother's proposal. I asked him to pick which chair was which and then to sit in the 80% one.

It was then time for the first metaphor. I ask Alexander to find a metaphor—an object or event or activity—to represent his own choice. He thought a moment and came up with "a football." I asked him to associate to the football, to explore what it meant to him. He said it meant having friends to play with and being able to do lots of sports and very little schoolwork. It meant being able to enjoy his life.

Next, at my request, Alexander went to the second chair and picked a metaphor for the school his father wanted: "a big heavy book." When I asked him to say some more about this, he began to cry. He said he was very afraid of becoming lonely, as he would be so far from his friends and the family. He was also afraid that he would not be able to keep up with the schoolwork, and he didn't want to fail again.

For the third chair, Alexander's metaphor was "his mother's smiling face." Going to the local public school, he explained would primarily be pleasing to his mother, as she would then have him around more. This was followed by an association in which he saw himself sitting like a small child on his mother's lap, an image he disliked.

The identification of these metaphors immediately changed the tone and direction of the session. Mr. and Mrs. Market put their belligerence aside and spoke calmly. Mr. Market discussed his discomfort with Alexander's being in what he saw as an "overprotected" family nest. He said that he hoped the boarding school would help Alexander to grow up. Mrs. Market admitted that she probably did "too much for Alexander."

Another turning point came a little later. I asked Alexander, as I often do in these situations, to think about what and where he wanted to be at the end of high school, and then to sit in the chair that he thought would be most likely to make this possible. To his own surprise he crossed over to the "heavy book" chair. He said he realized he couldn't play football forever, and he really wanted to succeed. Going away frightened him, but he thought it might be good for him to get out of the home. Before the end of the session, Mrs. Market said that she, too, was willing to go with this option.

The family eventually implemented this plan, and the new arrangement turned out to suit Alexander well.

Occasionally, a family faced with an important decision gets stuck not because of polarization but rather because of a paralyzing ambivalence. They lean one way and then the other way. Both choices seem equally good and equally bad. Exactly the same procedure is usually enough to help them: Scaling questions and finding metaphors for the different possibilities.

Our representational maps portray the world. They portray the world as we think it is, and also the world as we wish or fear it might become.

Only parts of our representational maps are easily available to us in a clear and immediately conscious way. The use of metaphor can give us access to less available parts. We can discover representations that may have been guiding our behavior from the shadows. During such explorations we can also revise our representational maps, filling in details that were lacking or substituting new goals for old ones.

Metaphor is one of the most potent representational devices we possess. I draw on it extensively in couple therapy, individual therapy and family therapy. In work with families it has the added advantage that, thanks to our shared heritage of metaphoric concept fields, it can so easily catalyze an altered "conversation," which is truly systemic.

NOTES

1. I here follow the helpful terminology of Kopp (1995), who grasped the significance of the distinctions I am about to draw.

2. I am not suggesting that metaphor and simile are the same thing. That would be a mistake, as Searle (1979) has convincingly shown. I am saying just that, qua therapeutic instrument, most employments of metaphor, simile, and other figurative expressions are roughly akin.

3. I again follow Kopp's terminology.

4. Papp's important article is reprinted as a chapter in her book *The Process of Change* (1983).

5. For good discussions of this issue see Black (1962, 1993), Lakoff and Johnson (1980, 1999), and Stern (2000). Black (1993), for example, spoke of an "implicative complex" that has an internal "system of relationship."

6. Interestingly, autism constitutes an exception. Both high-level autistic children and adults can seldom make sense of metaphor. An autistic teenager hearing a sibling proclaim that father is a Martian will be genuinely puzzled, and will probably try to explain that father is an earthling like everyone else.

7. As all parents know, children of two or three years can wake up in the night and appear to have had a nightmare, i.e., a dream with a bit of narrative structure. Foulkes' (1999) carefully controlled sleep laboratory studies cast strong doubt on this interpretation, however. It looks much more likely that, once awake, small children simply respond to parents' concerned questions ("Were you having a dream where something scared you?") by collaboratively establishing a minimal story line on the spot. (Of course, as Foulkes fails to note, this lattermost phenomenon itself is of considerable interest.)

8. See Papp's (1982, 1983) couple therapy technique of "choreographing a fantasy."

CHAPTER FOUR

Systemic Art Techniques

● ●

Systemic art techniques are a natural addition to family therapy. They are an excellent means for giving a voice to children of almost any age.[1] Traditionally, in individual child therapy, a child is asked to draw or paint so that the therapist can interpret what he has produced. Family therapists tend to shy away from giving interpretations of this sort, which is doubtlessly one reason why they have ignored art techniques for so long. I share this sentiment about interpretations. But in a systemic context, there is a another way to go about utilizing art techniques: The drawing, painting, or sculpture can be used as a rich representational device that is incorporated directly into the family's dialogic exchange. The family can respond directly to it. They can elaborate a verbal understanding of it. And the therapist can assist from the sidelines rather than taking on an authoritarian role.

This allows the child to verbally speak *directly to his family members*. The drawing is already a representational communication, but with its help the child can more easily move on to verbal speech as well. He may find it easier to reveal things going on in his mind that he had been afraid to express or that he may not have been able to grasp conceptually.

When art techniques are used systemically there are other ways to proceed as well. For example, often I have the family as a whole work together on a drawing or painting. Or I will have some subset of the family do this. Here again the goal is not interpretation. Instead, the therapist helps the family widen their own verbal exchange with one another.

Asking the adults to participate in drawing is helpful for two reasons. First, even for an adult, making a drawing and then talking about it can give access to difficult-to-reach representations. Additionally, an art product stimulates a good flow of discussion in the other direction: Children like to talk about what the adult has fashioned. Adults, however, may sometimes need a little coaxing. The main thing to emphasize is that for therapy purposes the quality of what is drawn is totally unimportant. "It is just a different way for everyone to talk about things," I tell them.

SELECTING ART SUPPLIES

What you need on hand is simple—just something to draw with and draw on. Colored pencils and a pad of drawing paper are enough. However, other supplies are also possible: You can use colored markers, wax crayons, or play dough. I like to have a flip chart in a corner, and a very large pad of drawing paper that can be put on the floor. I use these when I want the family to work on a single drawing together. It is important to have decent, functional supplies, but nothing too expensive or elaborate, which may intimidate parents who can't afford costly things for their children.

It is also important to keep the supplies stashed away until you are ready to begin the art task and bring out only what will be used for that task. This helps the family stay focused on the task itself rather than becoming overly involved with the different materials.

SELECTING A THEME

Prior to bringing out the materials, the therapist introduces the art task by suggesting a theme. How do you decide what theme to propose? It depends on what you want to achieve. One good use of art techniques is to help the therapist become familiar with the family, as well as to get the family accustomed to including the children in the therapeutic exchange. This should occur early in the therapy, even in a first session.

To get this type of information, I ask for the following types of drawings:

- Draw your family.
- Draw yourself and your family doing something together.
- Draw your last vacation.
- Draw a plan of your home. Put the name of each person in the place where he or she sleeps.
- Draw a picture of a recent experience where you and your family had fun together.

These proposals may sound innocuous. Nevertheless, you can count on almost always getting unexpected information. Sometimes the information is surprising for the family, too, as the following example illustrates.

The Golds were a newly formed step family with two sons from the mother's first marriage. They consulted me because the older brother, Theo, had announced that he wanted to move to the home of his biological father. Mr. and Mrs. Gold were certain that this reflected an emotional refusal on Theo's part to accept the stepfather. I requested that each person draw a fun experience that they had recently shared as a family. I was not expecting any particular result.

In response to this assignment, Theo drew a trip to the zoo. As we all looked at his picture, we discovered he had included his stepfather but left out his younger brother. When asked about this, Theo stated that his brother always "ruined things for him," and that this was why he wanted to leave the family. He added that his mother always took his younger brother's side and seemed to prefer him to Theo.

Occasionally the emerging representations are even more striking.

The Mecugni family contacted me because their 8-year-old boy, Anthony, was suffering from sleep disturbance, with nightmares. I had the parents, Anthony, and Vincent, his 4-year-old brother, each draw a picture of their family. When I saw their drawings I became confused. Both of the parents' drawings include a third child. Had I misunderstood the family composition? When I asked about this, they told me that they had once had a third child, but he drowned in an accident 3 years ago. The mother had left Anthony to babysit the child. Anthony was then 5 years old, and the younger child 2 years old. Anthony had gone into the house at the moment the child fell into the swimming pool.

When Anthony saw his parents' pictures, he became very intense. He insisted on returning to his own drawing and putting in a large plant. He said he wanted to add his dead brother to his picture. During the rest of the session both parents came to agree that, for the sake of their two living children's well-being, all four of them needed to let go of this past event and move on. I organized my beginning treatment plan around this need.

Art tasks can also be used to clarify the family's goals for change. When this is the purpose, I ask for the following:

- Draw a wish that, if it came true, would make the family a better place for you.

- Draw how you would like to be, and the family to be, at the end of the therapy.

A third use for art tasks is to represent the problem or an aspect of it.

- Draw the problem in the family.
- Draw how your family has changed since this problem came into your life.
- Draw the accident.
- Draw your last big fight.
- Draw the illness.
- Draw your family since the divorce.

These last suggestions are certain to take the family right to the heart of painful issues, as they did for the Jameses.

The James family sought therapy because their 8-year-old son, Dylan, had become withdrawn, depressed, and refused to speak. His selective mutism had begun 4 months ago, soon after his father was diagnosed with advanced liver and pancreatic cancer. When the parents attempted to discuss the cancer with Dylan, he ignored them. Dylan also refused to visit his father, who was currently hospitalized and undergoing chemotherapy.

During a session with Mrs. James, Dylan, and Dylan's brother, Kevin, I asked the family members each to draw a picture of the family in their home since the cancer had been in their family. Dylan drew a house in black and white with a red cross outside on an ambulance. He placed his mother in the bedroom taking care of his father. His father was hooked up to an intravenous tube, lying in the bed with a sad expression. He drew himself and his brother each alone in other parts of the house.

55

I asked Mrs. James and Kevin to ask Dylan to speak about his drawing. After 4 months of remaining mute, Dylan finally spoke up, saying that since his father had become ill, he had lost both parents. He said that because his mother now had to take care of their father, she no longer played or ate with the two sons. Crying, Mrs. James took her son in her arms. He cried as well and rested his head on her shoulder.

In each of these three cases, I used art techniques early on in the therapy. However, if a family responds well to art techniques—and most do—they can be used occasionally in other sessions as well.

The "Two-Picture" Task

Sometimes I give what I call a "two-picture" task. One type of two-picture task concerns negative developments or changes that have taken place in the family—a crisis, a loss through death, a divorce, an increase in violence. First, each person draws a picture of the family as it is now, since the advent of the loss or negative development. Next, each person draws a picture of the family as it was before, in a better time.[2]

Another version explores representations of expected future negative consequences. This is normally used in the context of a confrontation about destructive behavior. A third option is to draw representations of hope and positive change. Everyone draws the family as it is now, emphasizing the problem at hand. Then all draw the family as they would like it to be.

Other types of two-picture tasks focus on different kinds of polarity. For example, I used this technique with a family in which the father had just been imprisoned for violence against his wife and children, ages 5 and 8 years. My purely verbal exploration of how each had experienced these traumatic events had brought little from the children. "I don't know" was the only answer I received. So I asked each person to draw a place at home in which he or she felt safe, and then, in a second drawing, a place in which he or she had recently felt scared and unprotected.[3] They showed these drawings to one another and discussed them. In so doing, the children were finally able to find words for what had seemed unspeakable.

Family-Generated Themes

In some cases it is beneficial to propose an art task without any theme at all. You ask the family, if they are willing, to "draw something together." Exactly what to draw is their choice. The goal here, of course, is to see how they make the decision together, as well as how they then assign roles, execute the task, and the like. The family's interactions during this process can be very revealing, as I discuss later in this chapter.

USING THE DRAWINGS TO FOSTER VERBAL DIALOGUE

Once the family members finish their drawings, I often suggest they find a title for them. This adds another piece of information and helps the family members begin to bridge from an iconic to a verbal representational modality.

A more extended verbal exchange is, of course, where we go next. The person who has made the drawing is asked to show it to the others and to tell them something about it. If the whole family has worked on the drawing, I ask them to tell me about it. Usually at this point there is little difficulty getting a discussion in motion. Often the main problem is that suddenly *everyone* has things to say, requiring the therapist to direct traffic a little. The therapist must especially keep an eye on any younger children, making sure there is room for their comments and questions.

When a deeper theme emerges, as it frequently does, I help the family zero in on it. Because the exchange may have become quick and lively, it is necessary to make sure that important content does not get passed over too briskly.

I keep watch on affective signals, too. Because it goes so immediately to a deeper representational stratum, an art task can easily elicit strong emotions. This will be evident in a change in someone's tone of voice, a facial expression, or the like. If I see this, I may slow down the discussion and help the person to articulate her feelings for the others.

DECIDING WHO SHOULD DO THE ART TASK

Along with choosing a theme, the therapist must decide whom should be asked to do the art task. I use three different approaches, which I call *individual, parallel,* and *collaborative.*

An *individual* art task involves only one family member doing the task while the others watch. This person is selected for a specific reason. Perhaps a younger child has had great difficulty speaking about a painful topic, for example. The art product is then used to help her communicate with the other family members and, just as important, they with her.

Parallel art tasks involve each family member drawing her own picture, based on the same theme. This instantly creates a great deal of analogic material to explore.

A *collaborative* art task employs a single, large piece of paper. It can stand on a flip chart, or be pinned to a wall, or be spread out on a table or on the floor. The idea here is that the whole family, or sometimes a subset, such as two siblings, cooperates to create a single drawing. An advantage of a collaborative task is that the making itself takes on new aspects. It requires negotiation, collaboration, sharing of space, and the like. This gives the therapist plenty of options, allowing him to focus upon the process as well as upon what is created.

A basic choice when setting up a collaborative art task is who will participate. This decision is normally made by the therapist. Usually the entire family takes part, but not always.

An option is to divide the family into subgroups. In one family where we were exploring gender issues, for example, I had the males and the females split into two groups. In order to explore a change direction in a stepfamily, I asked a young child from the mother's previous marriage to do a drawing with her stepfather, while an older child from the father's previous marriage was paired with his stepmother.

You can also decide to exclude certain members of the family from the collaborative art task. The excluded members are given a role of observation or, in the case of a young child, asked to play or read separately. The decision to exclude certain members is based on various factors such as when the therapist wants to observe how one subsystem interacts without interference from other members.

Ted and Sarah Conlon consulted me because their 5-year-old boy, Joel, had threatened to kill them. The incident had occurred at the height of a furious dispute. The parents also reported that Joel and his brother, Fred, age 10, constantly fought and competed for their parents' attention. This has worsened since the birth of their third child, Ben, now 18 months.

I asked Joel and Fred to draw their apartment together while the parents observed. The boys started in, but immediately began bickering. They disagreed about every detail imaginable, from where the rooms were located to how big each was. When I asked the boys to write the names of everyone corresponding to their bedrooms, Fred wrote "Ted" and "Sarah" on the parents' bedroom, as opposed to "Mom" and "Dad." This was already a wealth of information. More came as I posed a few questions concerning why the children called the parents by their first names. Ted, a professor and theologian with strong convictions about "honoring the ideas of one's children," explained that when Fred first started to call them by their first names, he and Sarah had discussed it. They decided that this must be Fred's natural impulse and that they should honor it. Joel then simply continued in his older brother's tradition.

The drawing thus took us straight into some essential issues about hierarchy. Ted and Sarah had been profoundly shaken by the threat of murder, so it was not difficult to open up a dialogue with them concerning how they could maintain their respect for their children's minds and individuality while at the same time giving the children more guiding structure. Drawing the apartment also brought another matter to the foreground. It turned out that Fred was angry over the current room arrangements, finding it unfair that Ben had been given his own room while the two older brothers had to share a room. The parents had enormous difficulty listening to him talk about this, but they eventually learned how to make a more appropriate communicative space for feelings of resentment and anger.

The biggest difference between collaborative art tasks and individual and parallel art tasks is that the former provides so much to watch. There are plenty of chances to intervene as well, should one so wish. The therapist can bring the family's focus to the process, to the content, or to both.[4]

Here are some of the main things I try to notice:

- How do the family members negotiate in order to get started?
- Whose idea is used?
- As they execute the drawing, who leads and who follows?
- How do they share the space of the drawing?
- How do they share the portion of room space occupied by their own bodies?

- How do they share the drawing materials?
- Who communicates with whom? Who is left out? Who fails to communicate, moving too quickly into action?
- How does turn-taking take place?
- What seems to be the role of each family member during the task?
- Who creates a coalition with whom?
- Does anyone assume a leadership role? How well does the parental alliance function?
- Which family members appear to function independently?
- Which ones appear overly dependent?
- Who gives friendly signals? To whom?
- Who gives aggressive signals? To whom?
- How much competitiveness seems present? On whose part?
- Does someone copy or destroy what another has drawn?
- How do the others respond if someone refuses to participate?
- How is a title chosen? Who has what ideas? How are the ideas discussed?

In some cases I confine my comments to the drawing itself, saying nothing about what I have seen the family doing during the process of completing the art task. But inevitably, whether I mention it or not, I have made a number of observations. At times these prove an enormous help in understanding how the system functions and in devising a treatment plan.

Other times I may comment about the family's process. Usually I wait until the art product is finished, but sometimes I will say something while they are still in the middle of working on the task. My observations, if I share them, are not always about negative factors. Frequently I mention positive things instead, or perhaps both positive and negative.

Sometimes I not only comment on the process but also intervene to change it. This can serve as a first step toward family transformation. Even when it does not work, it will provide useful information about the degree of rigidity of the family's habitual patterns.

> The 11-year-old Arms twins couldn't have been more different from each other. Sean was a shy, introverted boy, whereas Susan was very outspoken and controlling. I gave the twins a collaborative drawing task, but with the requirement that Sean take the lead and be in charge. I hoped to get an impression not only of his leadership capacities, but also of his sister's ability to cooperate and follow.
>
> Each time Sean quietly tried to command, Susan boycotted the art project, going to a corner with her own paper and starting in on her own drawing. I intervened. As Sean had already mentioned to me his strong interest in airplanes, I proposed that they try again to cooperate, and that this time they were to be like the pilot and the copilot of an airplane. Sean was to be the pilot, taking control; Susan was to be the copilot, the second in command. Once I emphasized that a copilot is also very important for an airplane, Susan agreed.
>
> With this notion in place they returned to the art task and now managed rather well. At the end of this session I gave homework along the same lines, and the parents agreed to find a weekly project that necessitated cooperation between the twins.

OTHER USES

There are times in family therapy when the children need to leave the room in order to allow the parents to talk about an issue that isn't appropriate for the children to hear. Having the children do an art task in these cases is a good way of occupying them. It also provides a topic of discussion after the children are invited back into the room.

The three-generation Adler family came to therapy because of conflicts between the parents and the grandparents. These conflicts centered around the family's Friday evening tradition. It had long been their habit to gather on Friday evenings at the grandparents' home for a Sabbath dinner. But now the parents wanted to end this practice, and also to generally have the children see the grandparents less often.

Although the session had barely started, angry, bitter tones were already escalating. It seemed necessary to me that the adults be able to speak openly without worrying about the children's presence. So I took the children to the waiting room and gave them several tubs of play dough, as well as paper and crayons. I requested only that they make something together while I talked to the adults. I didn't give any kind of specific task.

I then returned to the adults and we continued our somewhat fruitless discussion. After about 20 minutes the children knocked on the door. I invited them back in. They proudly brought in an elaborately created Sabbath meal made out of play dough. Setting the food on a table, they explained to all of us each thing they had made, describing how it was used in the meal.

The parents were stunned. And everyone immediately grasped, from this message, how important the Friday ritual was from the children's point of view.

A different atmosphere then ensued. For the rest of the session, the parents and the grandparents productively negotiated about a number of points. The parents agreed to continue the Friday evening visits, and the grandparents agreed to a series of other changes, such as giving up their insistence that the children finish their food. The children stated their emphatic approval of these new arrangements.

More often than not I use art techniques in combination with other techniques. Typically the task is completed and discussed, and then other techniques are utilized in order to further explore the same themes. For example, if an art task highlights factors such as hierarchy, cooperation, and the like, I might move later in the session to a replay enactment of analogous events in the family's daily life at home. It is usually quite easy to make such transitions.

That said, art tasks in and of themselves are often enough. The rest of the session can be spent discussing the art product or thinking about the implications of what has been observed in the process of making it. Most families, and nearly all families with smaller children, can profit almost immediately from these techniques. It is as close as you can get to a sure thing, as long as you are willing to keep the work consistently systemic in nature.

NOTES

1. It is surprising how little has been published in the family therapy literature about art techniques. Even less has been written on how they should be used differently during therapy with a family. Valuable exceptions are Landgarten (1987, 1994), Gil (1994), and Wachtel (1994).

2. Isaacs, Montalvo, and Abelsohn (1986) employed an analogous procedure in their research on children of divorce. They used "drawing a family" to examine children's representations of their families at different points in time after the parents' divorce.

3. An equivalent version is to draw two events rather than two places—for example, a family event where you felt safe, and another event where you felt terrified.

4. This point is made nicely by Landgarten (1994).

CHAPTER FIVE

Externalization

• •

There are many links between a child's representations and her underlying sense of agency. "Externalization" is a technique that directly highlights this connection. This technique was first developed by the narrative therapists, Michael White and David Epston (1990), and has been extended by Jennifer Freeman, David Epston, and Dean Lobovits (Freeman et al., 1997)[1] to work with children. In using it with families I proceed much in the spirit of Freeman, Epston, and Lobovits. The changes I have introduced mainly reflect how I interweave it with the rest of my approach.

With the technique of externalization, everything hinges upon how language is used. The first step is to find a label, a new name, for the presenting problem. This label must appear to absolve the identified client of responsibility and must suggest that the problem is a thing—an outside force, something *external* to the identified client and the other family members. For example, the problem becomes "anorexia" rather than the daughter who does not eat, or "alcohol" rather than the father who drinks. It becomes "hitting," as if separate from the two sons who clobber each other.

Renaming the problem in this way allows the therapist and family to speak about the problem in a manner more free of blame and critique. It also helps the discourse instantly become more systemic. However, a word of caution is required. Vetere and Dowling (2005) warn that externalization may inadvertently downplay the role and responsibilities of adults when a child's symptom or problem is in response to sexual abuse or violence. I strongly agree. We can ask about "when anorexia first entered this family," "the effects of anorexia on this family," and the like. Paradoxically, by offering this illusion of lack of agency ("anorexia" is what is making trouble, not the daughter), we open a new representational space for notions that will end up effectively supporting agency. What I mean by this will be made clear shortly.

Finding the label is not always easy. Time must be taken to get it right, however, as the rest of the use of the procedure depends on having started with a good label. The name must operate as a smooth, simple component inside longer units of language. Nouns, such as "anorexia" and gerunds, such as "hitting," work best, as they fit easily into questions like, "With what other relationships in your family does anorexia also interfere?" Noun phrases, such as "not paying attention," can also work.

The search for a name should be undertaken jointly by the family and the therapist. When a selection is made, it must be agreed upon by all family members and the therapist as well. It must fit as a viable, practical piece of vocabulary. Here is how the search went in one case.

Mr. and Mrs. Scott consulted me because they were concerned about their 6-year-old son, Michael. Mr. Scott complained that Michael was a cry-baby, a coward. Mrs. Scott commented that he was not outspoken enough for his age and other children, including his younger brother, Andrew, pushed him around. Michael looked forlorn and said nothing during these remarks.

I asked them for examples. Mr. Scott explained that the family home was next door to a church. A cemetery surrounded the back of the church. Recently, Michael had developed phobic reactions to the church bells. When they rang, he hid under the table and held his hands over his ears. He also now refused to walk through the cemetery on the way home from school even though it was the shortest way. Both parents insisted that he should be able to cut through the cemetery without being afraid.

I next asked Michael what he would like to change. He replied that he wanted to stop being afraid when the church bells rang, and also wanted to prevent his brother and other children from taking his toys away and from hitting him. He did not agree with the goal of cutting through the cemetery, as the cemetery was "just too full of ghosts and too scary to walk through." We all agreed that a reasonable first goal would be for Michael to stand up to his brother and other children.

We now needed to find the right label for this problem. "Cowardice," suggested Mr. Scott. "Fear," proposed Mrs. Scott. I asked Michael what he thought. He replied that "fear" seemed just right to him. Mr. Scott assented to this too.

As this example illustrates, the label should not be too humiliating. This is what made "fear" a better name than "cowardice."

Once everyone has agreed on a label, it can be put to use. We can employ it to explore the extent of the problem, the consequences of the problem, the history of the problem, and anything else that seems of interest along these lines. The therapist might ask questions like:

- How long has "bulimia" been around in your family?
- At what time of day does "hitting" get worse?

- In addition to at school, where is "not paying attention" causing trouble?
- How have "drugs" changed the relationship between you and your sister?
- What other relationships in the family have changed because of "drugs"?

With the Scott family, questions of this type brought out some more information.

> "How has 'fear' controlled Michael?" I asked. "And how has it affected his relationships with others?" Mrs. Scott replied that she experienced so much frustration with Michael that she held back from doing some activities with him. It also came out that Michael's sleep was often bothered. Both parents also spoke about the need for excessive surveillance of the two brothers, as Michael's brother was "so aggressive" with him.

Having a good label sets the stage for another twist of language as well. The family can be asked what new relation they would prefer to have to the externalized problem. Usually their answer will be expressed as a verb or a verb phrase: "to fight back against drugs"; "to keep hitting out of our home"; "to push away not paying attention." This piece of vocabulary can also be taken over by the therapist.

> I asked the Scott family what they would like to do to "fear," or what kind of new relationship they would like to have to "fear." Michael suggested right away "conquering fear." I asked him to think about what could help him to conquer fear. He said "being brave." This last phrase, "being brave," soon became another much-used phrase in our work.

EXPLORING POSITIVE EXCEPTIONS

The next natural step is usually an exploration of positive exceptions. When do they occur, or when in the past have they occurred? Are there moments or time periods when the problem is absent or less dominant? Such explorations are a staple of much family therapy today.[2] In the context of externalization, such exceptions can be elicited through questions such as:

- When was the last afternoon when you refused to let hitting spoil your playing together?
- What areas of family life have you managed to keep intact, keeping them away from alcohol?
- What are times when not paying attention just does not bother you?

Let us return to the Scott family example.

> I ask for an example of a time when Michael had successfully conquered fear. The family described a recent visit to Disneyland. Michael proudly announced that he went on the haunted house ride, even though he was afraid. He enjoyed the ride a lot.
>
> The parents also remarked that when Michael was watching television, the church bells did not scare him. I asked Michael how he accomplished that. He said that when he saw the television picture he could manage to ignore the bells.
>
> I ask also about personal qualities of Michael that fear had been unable to affect. This elicited information about his positive capabilities, some of which had potential for dealing with his difficulties. Mrs. Scott said he was sensitive and social. Other children liked to play with him. Mr. Scott appreciated his son's curiosity and intelligence: Michael asked lots of questions, and he could already read and write. I suggested that

perhaps Michael could use his intelligence, curiosity, sensitiv-
ity, and sociability to conquer fear and become brave. I did
this as a way to generate motivation. It was a preparation for
more detailed work to come.

As you can see from the example, a discourse more supportive
of agency is put into place. This mostly concerns the agency of
the child, but it also concerns the agency of the parents, who
typically feel helpless and ineffective.

When the Scott family came into therapy, the parents' representations of Michael were as powerless, weak, and cut off
from emotional strength. Michael's representations of himself
were similar. Michael also represented the church bells and the
cemetery as not only dangerous but also overpowering, and
he represented them in this manner both perceptually and
semantically.

Thanks to the externalization technique, the beginnings
of an alternative representational network were established.
In this network, Michael's negative emotional state was newly
envisioned as "fear," an outside force.

This is, of course, a false representation, literally speaking:
It is not true that his state is "outside." Yet once this metaphoric
device has been accepted, the family can move on and develop
new representations that *are* true: that something can be done,
that Michael has ways to struggle against this state, that instead
of a lack of agency, he in fact has plenty of potential power to
act. Once the family shares these new, more positive representations, they are better positioned to function collectively in
finding a different family path. They have begun to differently
represent not only the child's agency but also their own.

Interestingly, another, related side of externalization is that
it can sometimes mobilize humor. Families often kid around,
make word-play, and start to tease one another in a more playful manner. This is a good sign. A different mood enters the

room—one more conducive to creativity and to discovering new directions.

USING EXTERNALIZATION WITH YOUNG CHILDREN

Externalization as I have just described it is easy to use, in my experience, with children of about 7 years or older. With younger children it is more problematic. Some can manage fine, others not. But there are ways of altering the methodology so that it can be used effectively with children as young as 3 years old. The best way is to use puppets, dolls, or toy animals to build up new representations.[3] Most young children are adept at pretend play. If you use externalization with the assistance of puppets or the like, you activate this potent source of creativity.

COMBINING EXTERNALIZATION WITH REPLAY DRAMATIZATION

When using externalization to explore the ramifications of a problem, I often add a replay dramatization. The new language we have established is then put to work in both preparing and executing the replay.

Again, puppets, dolls, and stuffed animals can be used to aid the replay. This is particularly the case with young children, as it engages them more effectively. Even if the children are somewhat older, play props often have a good effect. They lighten the mood. They facilitate optimism and novel thinking. I already mentioned how externalization can liberate humor. Play props amplify that.

> I encouraged the Scott family to do a replay of a recent event in which fear conquered Michael. Just the night before, Mrs. Scott recounted, Michael had let Andrew take his Playmobil away, and Andrew had broken it. When Michael complained, Andrew hit him. Michael agreed this account was accurate.

71

I asked the Scott family to recreate the scenario by acting out what happened with puppets. Mrs. Scott picked a dinosaur, and Mr. Scott a rat. Michael selected a snail that could be manipulated to retract into its shell. Andrew took an alligator.

They put their hands inside the puppets. The alligator then bit the snail, prompting the snail to hide in its shell. The dinosaur told the snail to come out and fight back. The rat told the alligator to stop biting, but the alligator continued.

Frequently in the middle of such replays I shift to a future positive dramatization.

I now suggested that they choose new animals that would represent who they each would like to be. Mrs. Scott selected a green, glistening chameleon. Mr. Scott chose an owl. Andrew wanted to remain the alligator. Michael picked up a gray dolphin. He explained that dolphins have sonar and can tell when other animals approach.

The dolphin picked up a plastic airplane and started to play with it. The alligator promptly tried to take it away. They battled. The owl and chameleon encouraged the dolphin to persist. The dolphin dove up and down, made scary sounds, and held onto the toy airplane. When the alligator attacked, he fought back. Eventually the alligator gave up. Everyone laughed, and Michael was thrilled.

I then asked the family to discuss how they could support the dolphin in its struggle against the alligator. They all had some ideas, even Andrew. Michael asked to borrow my dolphin until the next appointment, and I agreed.[4] In the next session, Michael proudly announced how he had stopped both his brother and other children from hitting him. He had also not let anyone take his toys away.

COMBINING EXTERNALIZATION WITH ART TASKS

Art tasks can be easily combined with externalization. Draw "fear." Draw "anorexia." Draw "not paying attention." The drawing gives a supplementary nonsemantic version of the outside-force representation.

One option is for the child with the difficulty to draw the problem. Often, however, I have everyone draw it, with each family member using a separate piece of paper. This creates an animated exchange about the similarities and differences in their representations.

At times the child who is having trouble is unable or unwilling to draw the problem. A good step here can be to have a sibling or a parent give a hand. It gives yet another implicit message that systemic answers are likely to provide the most help.

Art techniques can be used at many points in the therapy. Examples of one or more moments when the problem is especially bad can be drawn. How the family will be when the problem is no longer there can be portrayed. A drawing can be done of a positive exception moment, when the child or other family members successfully prevented the "outside force" from causing its usual trouble. Sometimes, with a young child, it can even be useful to have the child make art products that can serve as weapons or magic tools to help defeat the "outside force."

> Clementine, age 5, had trouble sleeping through the night alone. She had terrible nightmares in which "monsters tried to eat her alive." In a session with Clementine, her parents, and her sister, Jessica (age 7), I suggested that Clementine draw one or more of the monsters. She said she was too afraid. I asked Jessica if she would be willing to help Clementine. With Clementine at her side giving directions, Jessica drew three monsters—a ghost, a shark, and a zombie.

Clementine then commented that even though just now she was scared, normally she could draw quite well. The others confirmed that Clementine drew beautifully. I asked a little more about this talent. Then I asked if she would be willing to draw some things she might use to fight the monster or to scare them away. She seemed to immediately like this idea. She also asked if she could draw them at home, with her own crayons, instead of doing it here. We talked more about it. She made a plan to draw a gun for fighting the ghost, a dolphin that would help her against the shark, and a fire that would scare the zombie. We arranged to have her keep these drawings near the bed when she went to sleep.

COMBINING EXTERNALIZATION WITH COGNITIVE AND BEHAVIOR TECHNIQUES

Cognitive and behavior techniques can also be effective when interwoven with externalization. My use of them is perhaps where I depart the most from White and Epston's employment of externalization. I sometimes make specific suggestions about how the child with the difficulty (and perhaps other family members too) might do things differently. For example, in combination with externalization I often use thought substitution, self-talk, self-calming, and time-out.

In one session with Michael and Mr. and Mrs. Scott, I made a brief use of cognitive techniques. The parents had reported that Michael was making good progress with standing up to other children. Michael was obviously pleased by their remarks. He said, however, that he still felt scared of one particular boy at school. I asked him more about this, aware that if the boy was a bully and physically strong, some fear might be appropriate. Michael said he was convinced that the boy was no stronger than he, and that he wished he could be "not so silly" in reacting with so much fear to this schoolmate.

I decided to use thought substitution with Michael. I had him imagine this boy threatening him in the schoolyard. I then asked how the boy appeared to him and what thoughts came to him. I asked this in order to better understand both the perceptual and semantic representations.

Michael reported that when this boy came close to him in an angry manner, it was as if the boy suddenly had become huge. Michael then instantly had thoughts such as "I am too weak to fight him. I will have to run inside. After school I will run right home to avoid him." We explored what positive thoughts he could actively induce instead. He suggested, "I know he is the same size as me, and I am just as strong. I can stay right here. I can keep facing him. I don't need to back away." Michael seemed confident about trying this.

In the same session I used thought substitution with Mrs. Scott, who reacted with visible annoyance when Michael recounted how this particular boy at school made him scared. She explored representations such as "I can't stand it when Michael is such a coward" and how they could be traded in for other attributions, such as "He is intelligent, and he is learning how to decide when it pays to stand up to other children and when it does not."

"SPEAKING" TO THE PROBLEM

At times I have family members "speak" to the problem. After a label has already been found, I ask the family members to choose a physical object in the room to represent the externalized problem: a pillow, a stuffed animal, or a toy. Sometimes I even have each person chose a different object. Then we place this object (or objects) in the middle of the room. Each family member, in turn, can then speak to the represented "outside force." This technique often helps family members who have had difficulty speaking about the problem finally open up and reveal their feelings and thoughts.

KEEPING A SYSTEMIC PERSPECTIVE

I want to emphasize the potential of externalization for a truly systemic mode of intervention. The "outside-force" representation becomes the nucleus for a growing, widening cluster of other new representations. This new cluster usually includes altered representations of family relationships. And these altered relationships in turn support change in the family relationships.

For the therapist, maintaining a systemic perspective means keeping an eye on the broader picture. The key is to remain conscious of this. It requires attention.

> Mr. and Mrs. Hudson were at their wits' end with Bryan, their 11-year-old son, who regularly wet his bed at night. Bryan was an only child. "My son will be a failure," Mr. Hudson complained. "He'll never get anywhere if he continues to wet the bed. He doesn't want to grow up—he prefers being a baby. All he thinks about is playing video games."
>
> I asked Bryan if this problem created difficulties for him. He said right away that it did. He was too embarrassed, for example, to sleep overnight at another child's home. He also wouldn't go on any trips with his school class. He worried that the other children would tease him and make fun of him. I decide to use externalization, and I asked the family to find a label for the problem. This took no time at all: "Bed wetting" was the perfect name.

In this case, we were heading in the direction of a more systemic perspective. The family as a whole had committed to the name of the problem. They had all engaged themselves in a slightly different way, and the door was open for a discourse with reduced blaming and criticism. In giving the problem a name, they were beginning to talk as if the "outside force" was one entity and the child a separate entity.

But a third strategic step was needed to really mobilize the power of the technique on a systemic level. This was to bring the family relationships, their habitual systemic patterns with one another, into the foreground. This is not always easy, and sometimes not even possible. But externalization often provides an excellent vehicle for this purpose.

> Bryan was angry that his father made fun of him by calling him a baby. He also disliked that his mother inspected his bed every morning and openly talked about his wet bed at breakfast in front of his father. This gave me an opening to move more explicitly to a systemic level. I commented, "So if you can win in your struggle to overcome bed wetting, you will get your father to treat you like an 11-year-old. And your mother would respect you too." Bryan agreed and clearly liked the notions.

The purpose here is much more than building motivation, although that is of interest too. More important is that other new representations are beginning to accrue to the "outside-force" representation. Bryan was starting to represent a more complex goal that included a concept of changed family relationships. For the moment it was Bryan alone who was talking that way. But the groundwork was being laid for a similar shift on the part of everyone else.

> We went into this further. Bryan said that whenever he and his father did anything together for fun, his father endlessly nagged him about the bed wetting, and the fun was ruined. Bryan's father teased him too, constantly asking him if he had to go to the toilet. His mother, he added, was often critical. She paid too much attention to what and how much he drank at dinners. She made him angry with her in the morning, which

resulted in his going to school "in a bad mood." In the evenings, he no longer felt like playing a game with one or both parents as he had in the past. Upsetting to him as well was the fact that his father and mother fought about his bed wetting. His father criticized his mother because she changed the sheets herself instead of making Bryan do it.

Mr. and Mrs. Hudson clearly went into high alert as they listened to all this. One good option now was to have them respond directly to Bryan, describing how they were responding emotionally. Another option was to use this momentum to take another step with externalization.

I decide to do the latter. I first asked Bryan, "So as you see it, bed wetting has taken away your possibility to be treated like an 11-year-old. Is that right?" He agreed. I then turned to Mr. Hudson. "In what ways do you see your son's struggle with bed wetting as influencing his being treated like an 11-year-old?" Mr. Hudson made a couple of noncommittal remarks. I went on, "What do you see as the effects of bed wetting upon your relationship with Bryan?" This brought out some more thoughtful replies. He appeared sad as he spoke. I asked if this was so, and he said it was. I then asked Mrs. Hudson what effects she thought bed wetting had had upon Mr. Hudson and Bryan's relationship. She added some good comments. A little later I opened up a similar line of questioning concerning Mrs. Hudson and Bryan's relationship. I also touched briefly upon the parents' own relationship with each other.

Naturally all this is valuable information. The primary advantage, however, is something beyond that. The more we build up these representations of systemic behavior, the better positioned we are to start talking about *systemic* change rather than just the child's process of change.

To both Mr. and Mrs. Hudson I posed the question, "What are the obstacles that you think your son has to face to control bed wetting?" After a little discussion, I asked, "What do you think can help your son win the battle with bed wetting?" As they developed this theme, I listened not only for helpful tips for Bryan, but also for systemic ideas. For example, Mr. Hudson spontaneously came up with the idea of nagging Bryan less.

I jumped on this, telling the family I thought Mr. Hudson had a very clever and helpful idea. "This way you can create the context of having a relationship with an 11-year-old. I can well imagine this will be useful for Bryan. You can create a different context, and he can work on changing to better fit the context." As we continued I looked for further opportunities to nudge the family exchange in this direction. Several more appeared as we discussed positive exceptions.

Embedded in this last dialogue with Mr. Hudson was a technique I call *reversing the conditional*. This technique targets some of the family's "if . . . then" representational structures. In this case the father seemed implicitly to believe: "*If* Bryan would just give up wetting the bed, *then* I would change how I behave with him—I would treat him as mature rather than infantilizing him." I wanted the father instead to begin to play, implicitly or explicitly, with a representation in which the components were reversed: "*If* I change how I behave with Bryan, *then* he will give up wetting the bed." Or, more realistically expressed: "*If* I change how I behave with Bryan, *then* this will help him give up wetting the bed."

The more each member can find this type of new slant on things, the higher the likelihood of both individual change for the child and systemic change for the family as a whole. The two levels of change reinforce each other.

NOTES

1. Both White and Epston occasionally described work with children also. Freeman, Epston, and Lobovits have explored work with children much more systematically.

2. Thanks especially to the influence of De Shazer (1991, 1994) and Berg (1994).

3. Freeman and colleagues (1997) used sandplay in a similar fashion.

4. Opinions are divided about whether or not to allow a child to take an object home from the therapist's office. I sometimes allow it and have never seen any evidence of its causing a difficulty in the therapy.

CHAPTER SIX

Setting Limits

• •

In this chapter I discuss how parents can be helped with set-ting limits with their children, and children helped with accept-ing them. Cognitive and behavioral techniques constitute an invaluable resource for the family therapist. It would be a pity to ignore them. For one thing, these techniques get results. For another, depending on the technique, they are applicable to children of all ages, from 2 years upwards. Also, they are backed up by good research. This means that one can weed out, by fol-lowing the research, which techniques are maximally effective and which are less so.

A *problem* with them is that they are not systemic—at least not in the way they normally have been put to use. For me this means introducing modifications, some rather extensive.

COGNITIVE-BEHAVIORAL TECHNIQUES IN A SYSTEMIC CONTEXT

First, in my approach I use these techniques with the entire family present.[1] Everyone, or at least an entire system subgroup, becomes involved. In contrast, "pure" cognitive-behavioral ther-apy is almost always done with the parents or child alone.

Second, I usually interweave cognitive and behavioral techniques with other techniques, such as dramatization, externalization, and metaphor work. I seldom use a cognitive or behavioral technique in an isolated manner.

Third, in the context of exploiting a cognitive or behavioral technique, I often turn to the past of one or both parents. Suppose, for example, I am working with them about how they formulate limit-setting messages. I might briefly explore their memories of how limits were set in their own families of origin.

Fourth, I frequently analyze and understand a behavioral problem in a more systemic manner than is done from a strict cognitive-behavioral standpoint. For example, rather than looking at a child's noncompliance as an isolated phenomenon, I may explore if there are any secondary gains, or pay offs, for the system as a whole, such as distraction from another, deeper issue. Or, in a dramatization of the conflict situation, I might have the parents and children exchange roles. We would then explore how each perceives the other, and what different emotions are in play beneath the surface.

Fifth, I don't often tell parents what to do. This is probably the biggest modification; certainly it is the most important one. Classical cognitive-behavioral work proceeds almost entirely in a directive fashion. The "right," more productive parental behavior is explained. And implementing it is usually explained as well. This approach has its merits, but I prefer drawing upon the cognitive-behavioral technique repertoire a little differently. I go as far as I can with letting the parents find their own answers. Then I supplement—I prune and add—picking what seems especially relevant from a cognitive-behavioral perspective.

Sixth, I frequently find a simple behavioral change to be insufficient. From a wider systemic point of view, I often see a change in one area as needing to be balanced with change in other areas. For example, many families having trouble with defiant or noncompliant behavior can be helped with behavioral techniques; that is the subject of this chapter. But usually, probing more deeply, one discovers this is only half the story. Beneath the highly visible nasty conflicts lies a less visible but equally important lack of nurturing contact. I believe that working with one side and ignoring the other is problematic.[2] The behavior therapist is right to see the triggering causes (the provocations, etc.). Yet one needs also to address a deeper structuring cause (the contact deprivation). Multicausality is at work. (I take up this issue of the need to increase positive contact in Chapter 7.)

My way is thus a middle way. I try to steer a middle course between the directive, highly normative stance of standard cognitive-behavioral therapy and the open, nondirective stance of approaches such as standard solution-oriented brief therapy and narrative therapy. This lets me help families learn how to articulate their own pathways and ideas. It also lets me put to work some of the rich knowledge and wisdom accumulated through several decades of behavioral and cognitive therapy research.

PRESCRIPTIVE REQUESTS AND RULES

The average family therapist is confronted with one type of problem more than any other. Families come in with children who are "behaving badly": They are aggressive or provocative; they do what asked not to do, and they don't do what asked to do. The parents feel helpless and angry. Some such cases are mild: Perhaps a largely social and warm 3-year-old is obstinate and tantrum-prone in certain situations, like when asked to put away toys. Other cases are severe, and they may involve dangerous physical violence, delinquency, or events at school so disruptive the child risks being expelled.

Cognitive and behavioral techniques can play an important role in addressing this kind of presenting problem. In order to ensure reasonable amounts of behavioral compliance, of course, parents should possess several kinds of skills. Many families need help with most or all of these components.

One distinction useful to have in mind, for example, is that between *established rules* and *prescriptive requests*. Established rules are more general—for example, hitting, biting, and kicking are not allowed. Prescriptive requests are on-the-spot demands: "David, please carry the other bag of groceries into the kitchen for me." Sometimes a prescriptive request mirrors a more general rule. A father might say, "It is getting dark—put the bicycle away right now," when the established rule is that outdoor toys are to be put away before dark.

Another component of effective limit-setting is adequate *follow-up*. At times children's behavior needs to have consequences: sanctions for negative behavior, rewards for positive behavior. *Both* rules and requests occasionally should have consequences.

Still another component is *behavioral commentary*. Upon which aspects of a child's behavior should a parent comment? When and how? Effective behavioral commentary implies that the therapist must gather different levels of information. She needs to find out not only about interactional sequences (e.g., what takes place in the morning when Jack is supposed to dress before breakfast), but also about the implicit wider context: rules, eventual consequences, and the like. These background aspects are important in and of themselves and also, from my point of view, laden with systemic characteristics.

Frequently the quickest entry into the problem is to ask for a dramatization. The therapist has the family portray a heuristic example of the parent-child conflict. This will give plenty of useful beginning insights. Usually it is not enough on its own, however. *The role play will highlight both the parents' and the children's respective styles in dealing with prescriptive requests*, but what occurs with respect to consequences may not show up. And almost invariably, little will be revealed about the more general nature of rules in the family.

The therapist must therefore make some decisions. One concerns how much to ask, at this time, about additional information. The other has to do with which component to take as the target for practical work for the remainder of the session. The interactional style? The underlying rule structure? The use of consequences? Any or all of these may be productive avenues.

Interactional style is already addressed in other chapters. Here, I will focus instead upon underlying rule structure and consequences.

THE RULE STRUCTURE

By rules, I am referring to overt, declared rules. Sometimes family therapists talk about hidden rules that implicitly govern family matters, such as an unspoken rule that no one should openly mention a parent's alcoholism. This is an important topic, but it is not what I am referring to here. Declared rules are openly expressed. They are principles the children have been told to follow.

A rule in this sense has a semantic representational form. One way or another, clearly or confusedly, it has already been put into words. It has been *stated*. Subsequently, it exists in everyone's memory (or at least in the memory of everyone who has heard about it).

Naturally, there may be differences in how it has been understood, and remembered, by different family members. These may be differences in degrees of clarity or in the meaning of the rule itself. Each person, in other words, will have her own representation (her memory and understanding of the rule) of the original representation (what was stated in the speech act initiating the rule).[3]

Families can have too few rules or too many. If too few, the children won't fully grasp what is expected of them. If too many, family life will be forced into an emotional straightjacket. The rules may also be inconsistent with one another. This is an especially pernicious situation if parents espouse different, conflicting rules, or if they have discordant representations of a supposedly jointly held rule.

Rules need to be reasonably consistent over time as well. In a family where the rules are perpetually in flux, changing almost daily according to a parent's whim, there might as well be none at all. Rules can also be overly abstract: A rule that a brother should be "nice to his sister" doesn't give much direction to a 4-year-old unless it is spelled out more concretely. Rules also must be communicated well to the children, in the right moment and with the right tone and language, so that a child can form her own adequate corresponding representation.

Every family has its own "rule culture." Discussing this with a family is not always easy. They may have strong feelings about wanting a minimum of rules or wanting elaborate and highly strict rules. Emotions can run high about these things. It may also be hard for parents to see the connection between their background rule culture and a child's noncompliant behavior. Confusion in the rule culture can operate as a powerful structuring cause. This was the case with the Sarons.

> Mr. and Mrs. Saron brought Benjamin, their 6-year-old, to my office. They had just had a conference with his teacher, who wanted to hold Benjamin back a year in school. He was disobedient and fought with other children, she said. He wouldn't do assigned tasks. The teacher described him as undisciplined and unable to respect prohibitions.

Both parents agreed with this picture. They said he was just as out of control at home. He hit his parents. He hit and pushed his younger sister, Nicole, and destroyed her toys.

The Sarons seemed desperate. Yet when I asked about family rules, immediately they stiffened. Mr. Saron told me they had no rules. They believed, he continued, that rules "crush a child's spontaneity." They wanted above all that their children "be happy," and that the four of them, parents and children, "be friends." There was a challenging note in Mr. Saron's tone. Mrs. Saron nodded approvingly.

How was I to proceed at this point? What I have found most fruitful in these types of situations is either or both of the following tactics: (1) The therapist can initiate a discussion of values. This theme is usually easier to explore. The discussion can then be brought back, as shown in later examples, to the subject of rules. (2) The rule culture of each parent's family of origin can be explored. Often new insight into the present situation will emerge from this. With the Saron family, I used both approaches.

I commented that both the children's happiness, and warm family relationships, seemed to be high-priority values for Mr. and Mrs. Saron. We talked about this further. I then asked about other high-priority values, emphasizing questions about what they wished for their children in the future and about what kind of adults they hoped the children would become. This quickly led to their upset about Benjamin's fighting and his destruction of property. They were worried not only about his getting accepted by the school to go to next year's class, but also about the kind of person he was developing into. I asked how important these issues were for them in terms of their personal value system. Extremely important, they both claimed.

Next, without yet saying anything about the possibility of providing the children with clearer rules, I went to the past. I asked about the child-rearing practices each had experienced in their families of origin. Mr. Saron described growing up in a very authoritarian family with "rules for everything." I asked how the rules were enforced. His mother used humiliation and his father physical violence as punishments. Mrs. Saron, who was an only child, lived in a three-generational family with her grandparents and mother. There were constant arguments between her mother, whose parenting style was permissive, and her grandmother, whose style was strict and controlling. Her grandmother effectively made and enforced the rules.

By the end of this exchange, both parents were ready to look at how they might put into place a more viable rule structure in their present family. I pointed out that this rule structure certainly could reflect their own values, rather than the values of their families of origin, and that how they implemented the rules could also be quite different.

Having too many rules is also problematic. Daily life is overly regulated and surveilled, and subject to constant correction. Punishment and shaming are used to achieve obedience. There is too little room to play or to make mistakes.

Mr. Brandt, a lawyer, and Mrs. Brandt, an accountant, came to me for family therapy with their daughter, Hannah, 10 years, and their son, Joshua, 8 years. The school had referred the Brandts because Hannah's "mind just went blank" whenever she had to take tests in school. Also, whenever the teacher asked her a question, she wouldn't speak. Her teacher described her as a fearful, worried child.

Mr. and Mrs. Brandt thought this assessment was basically right. Mrs. Brandt added that Hannah was just like her in wanting never to make a mistake. Mrs. Brandt felt that she too never relaxed and desired to do things perfectly.

Mr. Brandt described how his children were "largely almost perfect" and Hannah was "the most perfect." He went into detail about how neat she kept her room and how obedient she was. Mrs. Brandt agreed, if with less enthusiasm.

I asked the Brandts to describe a typical day. They went into how everyone had to be out of bed, dressed, with his bed made, dirty clothes in the hamper, hair brushed, face washed, and teeth cleaned by 7:30. Mr. Brandt then inspected both children from head to foot, as well as their rooms. If Mr. Brandt found that something had not been done correctly, he berated the child. Typically he punished them by subtracting from their allowance as well.

The rest of the day continued in a similar fashion. Mrs. Brandt came home 2 hours earlier than her husband. Everything was expected to be in "tip-top" order before Mr. Brandt arrived. If there was a jacket on the floor or shoes in the entrance way, she criticized and punished the offender. Mrs. Brandt also reported regularly becoming anxious about an hour before Mr. Brandt came home.

I then inquired about their respective childhood pasts. Mrs. Brandt had parents who were neglectful and disengaged. They had a bakery and were often both at work, leaving the children alone for long periods. Even when they were home, family life was chaotic. She felt frightened and lonely as a child.

Mr. Brandt in his way felt frightened as well. His family atmosphere and interactions were more akin to the present situation, with a lot of control and regimentation. I asked him what this was really like for him as a child. He acknowledged its unpleasantness and how much it had stifled him. He volunteered that "orderliness" was a good thing to have learned for his present profession, but that there was really no need to force so much of it onto his own children.

At this point I turned to Hannah. Although she had been following the discussion with wide-eyed attentiveness, she proved reluctant to talk. She was willing, however, to think about how life would be for her if there were not so many family rules, and to find a metaphor for that. I worked further with Hannah's metaphor.

I find that this type of indirect strategy almost always works better than the therapist telling the parents that they have too many rules. It circumvents argument and confrontation. By moving into the perspective of values, or by exploring the rule cultures of the parents' families of origin, a different level of reflectiveness is achieved. But this is only the first step. Reformulating the rules, the next step, is critical.

REFORMULATING THE RULES

In my experience, parents need support and guidelines for reformulating their rule structure. First, the therapist needs to go over the main points with them. I usually begin by explaining that reformulating the rules will take some time. Rules need to be well thought out. Each parent should evaluate not only individual rules but also the overall picture. Do they have too few rules, generally speaking? Too many? What types of rules seem truly important to them?

Then they should look at the negative behavior they are concerned about. Do they already have a rule—a declared rule that has been communicated to the children—covering this? If not, what form of rule needs to be put into place? What would be the purpose of the rule? Should it have to do with values they want to transmit? Should it have to do with protection of their children?

If a declared rule relevant to the situation already exists, is this rule an appropriate one? Does it need to be modified in any way? And how explicitly and clearly has it been expressed to the children?

The more frequent situation is that no clear rule has been set into place. If this is the case, the parents need to discuss and agree upon the exact wording of the new rule. This must be in a language the children can understand. If, instead, a rule already exists but requires some reworking, this can now be done. Here too the focus should be upon the exact wording.

Next comes the matter of consequences. What will take place when the rule is broken? Even if a family already has a rule in place, it is common that carefully defined consequences have not been established or have not been explicitly spelled out to the children.

In an overall sense, these steps correspond to a classic behavioral therapy procedure. I prefer, however, to carry them out in a more systemic way. Usually I ask the children at some point to leave the room. The parents can then begin their review of the rule structure in general, of the particular rule needed for the targeted noncompliant behavior, and so on. However, when it comes to determining the consequences, I ask them to develop only some tentative ideas.

Next, when the children are brought back, their ideas about consequences are also solicited. Some give and take, and negotiation, usually takes place, with the parents making the final decision. Needless to say, with very young children this type of negotiation is less possible. But with children 5 years or older it works very well.

I have added this modification for two reasons. First, in my experience, it makes the later cooperation of the children considerably more likely. Second, and more importantly, it gives the family a good concrete learning experience on a metalevel. Systemically speaking, the hierarchy stays in place: It is the parents who, at the end of the exchange, make the final choices. At the same time, the children's perspectives have been given room and treated with appropriate respect. In some cases, especially with adolescents, it may also fit to let the children negotiate the content and scope of the rule itself, separate from consequences.

Granted, this is asking a lot of the parents. On the one hand, they now have to establish the rule boundaries more sharply. This may demand more rigor and backbone than they are used to mobilizing. On the other hand, they need to create a place for their children's voices and give respect to them. For some parents this amounts to tackling two new sets of competencies at once.

For that reason sometimes it can also be helpful, while the children are still out of the room, to let the parents practice how they will talk to the children about the new rule and its consequences. Empty chairs can help with this. The chairs represent the children, and the parents can now practice telling the children (i.e., the empty chairs) the rule. For example, how a parent communicates the rule sometimes reveals his or her ambivalence about the rule, or its consequences. These reactions can then be explored further. Or a parent may need help with her overly aggressive tone, or with the very notion that the child's point of view also needs to be heard.

It also may be useful for them to change chairs and role play the children. They should show how they expect their children to respond. Once a parent plays a child, loopholes not previously thought about may be revealed. A parent may also gain helpful insights into what this coming exchange is going to feel like on the child's side.

Finally, the children can be invited back, and the parents can in reality explain the rule to them. Consequences can be discussed, with the parents eventually making a decision about that aspect. During this entire "for real" discussion, there will probably be moments when some comments from the therapist will help keep the process moving forward.

The family is now positioned to try out, at home, the new rule-plus-consequences package that they have fashioned together. They can find out during the next days what works and what does not, what they can accomplish and what seems still out of reach. At the end of the session, the parents should be told that part of the next session will be dedicated to a review of how this has gone.

I have found that it takes about a month to firmly establish a rule in a family. When parents insist on putting into practice more than one rule in less than a month, they often fail. They underestimate how big a change it is going to be, emotionally speaking, on all sides. They also underestimate how much attention and awareness may be required on their part.

A more sure path is to get things going in a new way with one rule alone. Later down the line, a second rule can be formulated and implemented, and later a third, and so on. Eventually the whole procedure will become more natural for everyone concerned. It is hardest in the beginning.

For work with families with conduct problems, the importance of these steps with rules should never be underrated. I have gained this hard-earned knowledge not only from my own earlier mistakes, but also from supervision experience. One can do all kinds of useful things to help parents change how they interact with their children, in the moment, while the negative behavior is occurring. But if there are serious difficulties with the background rule structure, these changes are not likely to last.

CONSEQUENCES

Consequences also have an essential role. For many parents this is the most challenging part of limit-setting: Either they don't follow through with consequences, or they try, but don't do it in a consistent, effective manner.

One key is that the consequences themselves must be well thought out. Consequences should be realistic and age-appropriate. They also need to be made clear to the child beforehand. As already mentioned, it is a good idea to have the child participate in the choice of consequences. This improves their cooperation. Children 5 years or older can usually hold up their end quite well in such a discussion. Often their ideas are creative. Often, too, their ideas illuminate what might work as a meaningful consequence for them. The punishments they come up with are frequently even too severe!

> Two sisters, Pamela, 10, and Mabel, 11, had been having nasty disputes about who had taken the other's clothing without asking first and about whether or not it had been given back. Their parents decided that the daughters need a rule that would teach them how to respect another person's property. The rule was that you should not take what belongs to the other sister without her permission and that whatever had been borrowed (with permission) should be soon returned.
>
> In the session they told the girls about the new rule. The girls were then asked to propose what should be punishments if the rule were broken. Pamela suggested that whoever broke the rule should lose a privilege, such as watching TV in the evening, and also go to her room for 30 minutes. Additionally, during this time she should write an apology to the other. Mabel thought this was fine. She proposed only the modification that she would prefer to draw a picture for her sister as a way of saying she was sorry.
>
> I suggested to the family that these were excellent ideas. I also said that 30 minutes was awfully long, and that 10 minutes would probably be adequate. I also recommended that going to one's room and writing or drawing an apology seemed enough, and that there was probably no need to add the loss of watching TV. The parents agreed to try it this way. They all settled on the 10-minutes-plus-apology consequence.

Sometimes consequences are too severe. They can result in the children being terrified of making mistakes.

Certain types of consequences are, in my opinion, not to be recommended. For example, I discourage parents from taking away food from children or sending them to bed early. For one thing, a parent will have trouble enforcing these and will be likely to give in. Furthermore, going to bed is a time for a child to relax and sleep. It is better that this moment not be experienced as a form of punishment. There are enough alternative possibilities, such as taking away a privilege, that work just as well.

I also believe that punishing a child by interfering with social and family relationships is a poor idea. This is another point where I disagree with a number of cognitive-behavioral therapists.[4] Forbidding a child to participate in an important social event, such as a friend's birthday party or a planned trip with the family to an amusement park, is not recommended. If these become sanctions, they will work, of course, in that they will help reduce the noncompliant behavior. But from a systemic point of view they unnecessarily interfere with the child's social connections, an area too important for both the child's development and the family as a whole.

Consequences also should not punish the parent more than the child.

Mrs. David, a single-parent mother working full-time, was having trouble with her daughter, Emily, age 10. Emily was aggressive with her younger brother, Gabriel, age 6. I asked for an example. Recently, said Mrs. David, Emily took Gabriel's Game Boy and then deliberately broke it.

As we discussed this further, it came out that Mrs. David had appropriate rules about this sort of behavior. And she indeed tried to follow up with consequences after the Game Boy incident. The punishment, however, was to make Emily remain at home on weekends for a month. This meant that for each weekend Emily was not allowed to go out, she sat in the apartment bored, annoyed, and complaining. It also meant that Mrs. David couldn't go out either, effectively spoiling her weekends in addition to Emily's. After 2 weeks Mrs. David gave in and ended the sanction.

Here the punishment was both too long and carried too high a cost for Mrs. David herself. Also, Mrs. David's giving in after the second week, though probably inevitable, taught Emily that if she was sufficiently disagreeable, her mother would be forced to relent.

Enforcing rules is difficult enough in itself. Anything that adds to a parent's burden is worth circumventing, if possible.

PRESCRIPTIVE REQUESTS

Whereas rules are set up ahead of time by the family and are mutually understood, prescriptive requests are little communication moments that happen all day. Many families require just as much help with these requests. Their use constitutes a basic parental skill. Not only the content of what is said is important, but also the manner and timing. Fortunately, a solid body of behavioral therapy research[5] tells us a lot about what works with children in this regard. I will go over some principles here and then indicate how the therapist can help families in this area.

Prescriptive directives need to be *clear* and *concrete*: "It is time to put your toys away now." The specific behavior wished for should be named.

The language must be *age-appropriate*. The directive should not be couched in words or phrases too complicated for the child to grasp. Or, conversely, in a language that is infantile in relation to the child's age.

Directives are best given *one at a time*, when possible. Instead of telling a 6-year-old, "Get ready for bed, prepare your things for school, and put your toys away now," the parent should simply say, "It is time to get ready for bed now." Once the child has accomplished that, the next request can be given.

A closely related principle is that directives should *target a small enough behavioral step*. This is an extremely useful concept that parents very much need to master. Their commands or instructions are frequently too global. This depends, of course, upon the age of the child and his level of cognitive development. For a very young child (or an older child who is neurologically impaired), "It is time to get ready for bed now" may be too vague. One can say it, but it should serve only as a kind of lead-in or introduction. What the child then often specifically requires is, for example, "First take your pajamas out of the drawer," and so on. The trick is to know, for this specific child, how fine-grained the prescriptive aim has to be. When a parent doesn't know, he can be helped to find out.

Prescriptive requests should be *statements*, not *questions*. They should not be statements mixed with questions, either. "Shouldn't you put your toys away?" should be replaced with "Please put your toys away" or "I'd like you to put your toys away now."

Nor should an "okay?" be tacked on at the end. For the child, any whiff of questions can cause confusion or reduce the impression that the parent means what he says. The miscommunicated implication will be that the matter is up to the child's choice.

Prescriptive requests should also be *calm in tone,* or at least as calm and neutral as possible. A parent's agitation will only stimulate the child's agitation. The more impatience and annoyance can be put aside, the better.

Prescriptive requests should be *followed by a short delay*. A period of 5 to 10 seconds is recommended. After that, the parent can repeat the request, perhaps coupling it with a warning. Usually children need a few seconds before they start to obey.

A time limit can always be added to a directive, by the way. Perhaps after waiting some seconds, a parent might say, "I already asked you to pick up your clothes and put them in the basket with the dirty laundry. You have 5 minutes to do this."

Finally, prescriptive requests should be *followed up by brief praise* if the child does in fact perform the requested behavior: a "good," or "that's right," or "that's the way," or something equivalent. These comments should be delivered with a pleasant tone, if possible.

A quick and easy way to help parents to communicate prescriptive directives is to use a dramatization. You can see more exactly what is working well and what is not. It is also simple to stop the action and explain some aspect of directives right at the point where the explanation will be useful.

In a dramatization, Jane, 5 years, was playing with her Barbie dolls in the living room. Mrs. Evans walked in and said "It's time to go to bed. Get ready, okay?" Jane ignored her and continued playing. I stopped the action and inquired if this was typical. Laughing, both said it was.

I explained to Mrs. Evans how to break up such a request into smaller parts. I also suggested adding time limits and brief praise. They played the interaction again. "Jane, I want you to put your dolls and their clothes away. You have 5 minutes to do this." Jane put the items away. Because Mrs. Evans forgot to praise, I reminded her.

Next Mrs. Evans said, "Now undress and put on your pajamas." Jane pantomimed doing that. Mrs. Evans commented, "Good job. Now go into the bathroom and wash your face and brush your teeth. You have 10 minutes for this." The rest of the dramatization continued to go well.

I cannot stress strongly enough the importance of finding right-sized action chunks. If they are too big (the more common problem), then likelihood of noncompliance is higher. If they are too small, the child will probably become irritated.

The ability to communicate prescriptive requests is an important parental skill in any family. As I illustrate later, it is even more important with children who are hyperactive or whose cognitive processing has been otherwise compromised.

POINT SYSTEMS

A more complex behavioral technique is to initiate a point system. This will not be to every therapist's taste, or, for that matter, to every parent's. It is recommended to begin first with the other simpler techniques in this chapter. If these techniques do not produce results, then the therapist can move to more complex ones. But point systems definitely help some families, and have strong research support.[6]

Simply put, compliant behavior wins points. Noncompliant behavior does not gain points. Some point systems also have children lose points as punishment.

First, the parents discuss which behaviors they want to encourage with the new point system. Second, the parents decide which privileges their child will earn with points. A system is arranged in which set amounts of points are earned by particular positive behaviors.

The parents and children can further negotiate which extra privileges can be earned with bonus points or "saved up" points. That is, in order to have privileges or rewards that the child previously took for granted, he *now* needs points. Examples of privileges are watching television, pocket money (an allowance), playing with a Game Boy or video game, having a special sweet after dinner, and spending time on the Internet. Examples of extra privileges or rewards that can be earned with bonus points are money (something most teenagers want), going to a movie, or a special outing with a parent.

Noncompliant behavior either does not earn any points or results in a limited number of points being taken away. The total points earned over a longer time period can lead to earning bigger rewards or privileges.

It is best to maintain a written chart to record what is earned or lost each day. For children ages 4 to 8 years, stickers can be put on the chart or plastic poker chips can be given.[7] Children of this age need to see what they have earned, and a "point" does not have the same impact as a red token or sticker. I suggest that the children and parents go together to a store, where the child can choose which kind of sticker or chip she would like to use for the chart.

Devising a point system does cost some therapy time, and hashing out the details can be tedious. What one gains for the effort with many families, however, is a rapid move toward cooperation on the part of the children.

TIME-OUTS

Another more complex behavioral technique for help with limit-setting is "time-out." A classic technique, it has been proven effective by considerable research.[8] I use it with children from 2 to 8 or 9 years of age. As with point systems, a family often needs several therapy sessions in order to get time-out really functioning. It also requires explanation and guidance from the therapist.

Here are the essentials. A parent uses time-out as a consequence for behavior that is not desired or for noncompliant behavior. It should be used right away, immediately after the behavior itself.

The child must already have been informed, well beforehand, about both the relevant rule and the time-out consequence. It should be explained that the child will have to go to a specific,

designated place in the home for a specific number of minutes.
He will have to stay there with no toys or other amusements.

I suggest to parents that they first give one warning.[9] For
example, if the child has turned on the television at an hour
when this is not permitted, the parent should simply and briefly
say what she wants done—"Lucas, turn the television off"—and
add what will happen if he doesn't comply—". . . or you will
have a time-out." Just that. If Lucas ignores her and continues
to watch television, she sends him to the designated place for
the designated number of minutes.

How long should the time-out be? A good rule of thumb is
to make it 1 or 2 minutes for each year of the child's age (e.g.,
2 to 4 minutes for a 2 year old, 6 to 12 minutes for a 6 year old,
and so on).

What should be the designated place? Ideally it is a location
that the child basically finds boring and in no way frightening,
such as a corner. Naturally the child must be unable to watch
television, play with a toy, read, or the like.

In one family, the child was locked in a closet for their equivalent of time-out. Another family shut the child in the bathroom. I am against locking up a child anywhere for time-out. It
can be anxiety-provoking, even terrorizing.

Some behavior therapists claim that the point of time-out is
not so much punishment as it is self-quieting.[10] By being alone
for a few minutes in a setting with reduced stimulation, the
child has an opportunity to calm himself down. I think this is
exactly right. The purpose of time-out is to increase agency and
self-regulation. This is an idea I always try to transmit to parents
when we are discussing time-out. It helps them understand why,
for example, they need to use a calm (or at least neutral) voice
when putting a child into time-out. And why nothing should
be said that is disrespectful of the child's person or character.
It also helps them realize why locking a child up in a closet is
antithetical to the goal of the technique.

A good question is whether a child's own room should be used as the designated place. There are pros and cons. The problem is how to make sure that the child doesn't simply use the time for play. If some other place in the home can be found, this difficulty is avoided.

For young children, a timer such as an egg timer can be a help. The child takes it along with him. He can follow how much time has passed and how much is left. Sometimes I recommend that a parent and child go shopping so that the child can pick out a timer he likes.

During the time-out itself the parent should not talk or otherwise communicate with the child. The child should experience these minutes with as little outside distraction as possible.

Once the time-out is over and the child has calmed down, the parent tells him he can now leave the place.

With a young child, it can be good at this point to repeat why the child was sent into time-out. If the time-out was the result of the child's not doing something he should have done, the child must now go and complete the originally requested behavior.

This exchange should be brief, to the point, and without digressions. It is extraneous, for example, to ask the child why he misbehaved. Simply mentioning the rule that was broken and the behavior that the parent desires in the future is sufficient. For this exchange, it is also important that the parent himself has calmed down as well. If he is not calm, he should end the time out but wait a few minutes before speaking about it. Or he may decide not to speak about it at all.

When introducing the time-out technique to parents, I first explain how time-out works. Then we work out the details. Usually there is no need to have the children leave the room at this point. In fact, if the child is 5 years or older, there is much to be gained from having him participate in the discussion. His ideas concerning the designated place or whether to use a timer can be solicited too. Again, involving a child in these choices improves the probability of cooperation afterwards. Of course, the parents here, too, make the final decisions.

Unlike with a point system, I often follow up the introduction of the time-out technique with family practice. They do a future dramatization of what will happen the next time the compliance problem surfaces at home. The child plays his role as well. This step is quite different from how time-out is transmitted in standard behavior therapy. But it has the added advantage, systemically speaking, of emphasizing that time-out is meant to help *both* parents and children. It is not meant to be just a tool of enforcement for a frustrated parent.

Needless to say, in the specific moment when a time-out comes, no child ever wants to have to sit through her time-out minutes. This is what makes it a sanction. However, a good number of children do quickly see a potential positive aspect: Up until now, the parents' attempts at discipline, though ineffective, were highly unpleasant from the children's perspective; by comparison, the time-out looks like a lesser evil.

Not all children will go along with a future dramatization in the session. A minority will refuse, either passively or with open defiance. This is no barrier to continuing. The best thing is simply to let the child not participate at this point and ask the parent, or parents, to role-play both the parent and child. This way everyone, including the child, still picks up a clearer picture of what needs to take place.

Time-out is especially useful for families who are having intense escalations of parent-child conflict. It is, of course, harder to implement in such situations. The child may be having a temper tantrum, screaming and kicking on the floor. Or she may refuse to comply with the time-out itself.

Many parents are overwhelmed at that point. They need to stick with it, however. If the child is small enough, he can be carried to the designated place.

There is a fine line here, however. No punitive violence should be used on the parent's side. Another possibility is for the parent to state calmly that he will leave the child where she is and go into another room until the child calms down. Then the parent walks away. She waits to return until the child has become quieter.

If the child cuts the time-out short or stays in the designated place but continues to yell and scream, the parent can start the time-out anew, from the beginning. Here too (again, to the extent possible!) a calm or neutral voice should be used. If this means starting over a number of times, so be it. The parent's attitude must be: This time-out is going to happen, and for its full time length, no matter what.

> Mr. and Mrs. Simon described their son, Christopher, age 3, as having long, escalating tantrums whenever he did not get his way. Mr. Simon said that he dealt with Christopher's tantrums by first threatening him—"If you keep that up, I will really give you something to cry about"—and then, if Christopher continued, spanking him. Mrs. Simon said that when she was alone, the only way to end the tantrum was to give in to Christopher's demands.
>
> I introduced the family to time-out. The parents' first attempts to use it at home were not successful. In the next session we explored why. It seemed that first of all, Christopher's tantrum had typically already been going on for several minutes before they tried to give the time-out. Additionally, the parents were letting Christopher leave the designated place before the time-out was over. On one occasion, in order to stop Christopher's whining while he was in time-out, they let him draw "to keep him busy." We went over these points one

by one. I helped Mr. and Mrs. Simon understand that time-out must be used immediately after the tantrum begins, or the child may work himself into a state where he will be too upset to cooperate. I also suggested that they be sure to keep him in the designated time-out location and that they ignore any whining while he is in time-out.

During the next two sessions we continued to look together at what was being accomplished. Gradually Mr. and Mrs. Simon became more effective in using the technique. Within a few weeks they reported considerable reduction of the tantrums.

What happened with the Simon family is typical when time-out is difficult to implement. The parents need to come back and discuss what happened, as well as what worked and what did not. The therapist must go into considerable detail about this in order to see exactly where they need further help. The more bitter and entrenched the underlying conflicts, the more ongoing support will be necessary. Persistence pays off. In the vast majority of cases these steps can be taken, and the new family behaviors will become routine.

Sibling Use of Time-Out

Older siblings often find themselves in a dilemma. If a younger sibling is strongly provocative, what should they do? Typically, the older one either impulsively responds with a similar behavior (hitting, kicking, etc.) or passively lets himself be hit and kicked, knowing that if he fights back, *he* will be the one punished. Take the following common scenario: The parent, in another room, hears the younger sibling crying. The younger sibling runs to the parent and presents himself as the victim. Taking the side of the younger one, the parent criticizes the older child, telling him that he "should know better" and "should set an example." The parent may punish the older sibling as well.

This situation is not only unfair but also highly detrimental for the sibling relationship. For this reason, I often encourage older siblings to use time-out. In the face of being hit, bitten, kicked, and so on, an older sibling can say, "No, stop now," and put his arms out to push the younger one away. In other words, the older child sets a limit instead of hitting back.

Then, if the younger child persists, the older sibling can invoke time-out. The younger one is sent to the designated place, and so on. (When there is a sufficient age difference between the siblings, the older sibling himself can send the younger to the designated place. If the age difference is slight, the parent may have to step in and do this.) Both siblings can then calm down.

Of course, this will not work unless the parent gives the older child the support to do it. The parent must also have an eye on whether the older child seems to be using it in a responsible, appropriate manner. If he is, the results can be good. This particular form of sibling conflict will be reduced.

Additionally, the older child will feel proud of being able to utilize self-control and deal more effectively with the problem. At the same time, he will feel that he is being treated with more fairness by the parent.

NOTES

1. Surprisingly few family therapists, or cognitive behavioral therapists for that matter, seem to have attempted this. Two interesting exceptions are Rosenberg and Lindblad (1978), working with elective mutism, and Patterson Dishion, and Chamberlain (1993) and Patterson, Reid, and Dishion (1998), with aggression problems.

2. See Cavell (2000) and Christophersen and Mortweet (2001) for a similar critique.

3. A declared family rule created by an overt speech act is what Searle (1995) called an "institutional fact."

4. For example, Barkley (1997) recommended that parents use withdrawal of social privileges such as visiting a friend. Cavell (2000) suggested that parents use grounding (house arrest) for older aggressive children.

5. For example, Anastopoulos, Barkley, and Shelton (1996), Christophersen and Mortweet (2001), and Forehand and McMahon (1981, 1984).

6. Braswell and Bloomquist (1992) found point systems highly effective with ADHD adolescents and children. Barkley (1997) had similar results both with defiant adolescents and children, as well as children with ADHD. Friedberg and McClure (2002) demonstrated success using point systems with many types of child behavior problems.

7. For some particularly clever uses of chips see Barkley (1997).

8. See, for example, Cavell (2000), Barkley (1997), Friedberg and McClure (2002), and Christophersen and Mortweet (2003).

9. Some behavior therapists, for example Christophersen and Mortweet (2003), believe that parents should not give any warning. The argument is that warnings teach the child that he can misbehave one time.

10. For example, Cavell (2000) and Barkley (1997).

CHAPTER SEVEN

The Restoration of Play

• •

Concerning small children, probably the single most neglected resource in family therapy is play. How does the parent play with the child? *Does* the parent play with the child? From an adult's point of view this may appear to be a minor issue. From a child's point of view it is major.

Systematically speaking, play is an optimal way for a parent and child to strengthen their relationship. In play, the parent adapts to the child's world, instead of the child to the parent's. By operating together in this world, the parent and child can build new shared sensitivities and new modes of mutual recognition. In family therapy literature, Gil's (1991, 1994) excellent writings convey how much can take place in this arena.[1]

The problem, however, is that for many parents and children, these resources are not being utilized. Perhaps repetitive conflicts have poisoned the play atmosphere. Or, because of parental stress and burnout, the parent has retreated from playing. Often the parent simply does not know how to join a child in play. Frequently some combination of these factors is at work.

In the last chapter I discussed limit-setting. Typically when a parent-child relationship is highly conflicted, it has become embittered. Setting better limits is an important part of getting back on track, but opening up more positive forms of connection is essential, too. It is an error to assume that once limit-setting goes more smoothly, positive connection will simply flourish on its own. How, then, after aiding with limit-setting, can a therapist help a family develop more nurturing types of parent-child contact?

Plenty of what has been presented in previous chapters can be of use. One day, during a dramatization, a child may speak more about his emotions; another day, with the help of a metaphor, he may reveal a desire or yearning previously kept secret. As such experiences accumulate, a parent senses better how to connect with her child. Positive play adds something more. It ritualizes and consolidates an everyday, easily available activity, which can render the relationship progressively more satisfying on both sides.

Satisfaction *on both sides* is key here. Implied are two related changes. One is that the parent develops new ways to play, in such a manner that the child feels nurtured. The other is that the parent learns to enjoy the play as well. These are entirely realistic goals, even in more desperate situations where the parent-child relationship appears barren.

This chapter is about how to accomplish such changes in family therapy. It is not about the use of play by child therapists nor about approaches to parent-child play outside the family therapy tradition.[2] I will not go into research about play. I will discuss how to bring the parent and child to center stage and help them strengthen their relationship through play.

A family never comes to therapy with a change of play interaction on their agenda. Play is usually the last thing on a parent's mind. It is not just that they do not see the relevance. Rather, when a family first arrives, the parents often are consumed by negative emotions toward the child. They feel disappointed, helpless, angry, even hateful. Even if they are openly hungry for a warmer relationship, their image of what this might mean rarely includes anything to do with play.

For these reasons, it is a mistake to introduce the idea of play too early. The therapist should first organize her work around the more obvious difficulties. If the parent's goal concerns a child who is out of control with aggressive behavior, for example, this must be addressed at the beginning.

Only after some evident progress with this problem has been made should the therapist introduce the theme of play. By then, the parents will have more trust in the therapy, and more confidence in their own effectiveness. Additionally, they will probably be feeling at least a little less hostile toward the child. (If they *don't*, it is all the more important to move on to play techniques, *as long as* change is underway with respect to the original presenting issues.)

An exception to this rule is when only extremely destructive, negative, aggressive interactions take place between parent and child. For example:

> Zack, age 6, had threatened to kill his mother with a kitchen knife. He also had announced that he wanted to live with another family. His mother, crying, said that she had failed as a mother. I asked the family about pleasurable activities that they did together. Everyone agreed that there were none. Zack said that his mother never played with him.

In this case it was important to introduce play as early as possible, before progressing to the presenting problem. To present the theme of play, I connected it to the parents' own stated goals, as I do with all families. I also emphasized that play would lead to more satisfaction for the parents themselves.

- "If you and Zack can connect in this way, it will motivate Zack to control his angry behavior."

- "This will also give you some new ways to enjoy spending time with Zack. Because of all the troubles you have been having lately, you haven't had the chance to enjoy being a parent."

Usually parents are surprised and a little bewildered by this proposed step. But if the idea is presented in the right manner, they are almost always willing to try. Some parents may react with a bit of fear, however. Perhaps a parent confides that he has seldom played with the child, and feels incapable of it. "Getting down on the floor with toys and crayons is just not my thing, never has been," is a common response. In that event, the therapist should assure the parent that many adults find themselves at a loss when it comes to play, and that the therapist can help him figure out what to do.

EXPLAINING HOW TO PLAY

Once the concept of play has been introduced, the therapist then explains that many families have found it rewarding, and that it is beneficial for the child's development. This is, of course, a relatively directive means of proceeding. But the benefits of play are substantial and normally achieved quite quickly.

Following is a description of the components of what to explain to parents. I should note that when I describe these components, I don't present them all at once. Rather, I offer them gradually so that parents can better digest them. Don't expect the parents to immediately understand all the recommended components of play. A real grasp of how such play functions comes only from doing it.

The first component is *waiting*. The parent lets the child choose the play activity. And then the parent lets the child take the lead in how the play will unfold. That sounds simple, yet it is amazingly difficult for many parents. Waiting requires patience and sustained attention. Hardest of all, it requires giving up a modicum of control.

The second component is *manner of entry*. This involves, first, a choice. The parent can stay on the sidelines, in which case she will only comment on the child's play, in a manner explained later. Or, better, she can join in, adding her own creative input. As will be evident shortly, for some parents the "sidelines" version makes more sense as a first step. They may be so lacking in play skills that it is more effective to minimize demands on them in the beginning.

If a parent does opt for joining in, I clarify that she must be careful about three things. First, she should fit what she does to the play direction already established by the child. Her contribution should support, not conflict with, the child's activity or theme. Second, she joins only if the child implicitly agrees. If the child hasn't explicitly invited her, she should watch the child's nonverbal signals to make sure he is not reacting negatively. Finally, as the play proceeds, she should continue to negotiate her role in a sensitive manner.

The third component is *descriptive language*. From time to time, the parent describes, in short sentences, what the child is doing. "You are drawing a flower, a purple flower." "Oh, you are making a tower with the blocks." An occasional question involving a description is okay. Although these comments can be made frequently, they should not come in an unending, unbroken stream.

Why descriptive language? It serves a double function (Downing, 2003). On the one hand, it helps the relationship. The child feels that the parent is interested in what the child is doing. Additionally, it has positive developmental effects. First, it acts as reinforcement, encouraging the child to maintain a focused play activity longer. Second, it promotes "self-speech," the child's own semantically registered awareness of his action. Both factors are important for building a sense of agency. This is true for any child, but such support for agency is all the more important for a child with developmental disorders or poor concentration.

Notice that this type of commentary from the parent is quite different from the educational mode of speech, which many parents excessively favor. A parent operating in the educational mode of speech might, for example, point to an object or picture and announce, "This is a truck" or "This color is red." Descriptive language commentary is not like that. Instead, the words are linked closely to what the child is involved with—with what is already salient in the child's experience. To play in this way, the parent must learn to put aside didactic and educational speech. Paradoxically, research indicates that when descriptive language is nearer to the child's immediate focus of interest, it is more effective than the educational mode of speech for language learning itself (Meins, 1997).

In the same spirit, didactically intended questions should be minimized. The parent should give up, or least avoid, asking, "What is this animal?" or "What does a doggie say?"

Even more important, the parent should forego criticizing what the child is doing. Suggestions or negotiations are okay, but a criticizing tone should be kept out.

The fourth component is *appropriate scaffolding*. The term *scaffolding* comes from Vygotsky (Vygotsky and Cole, 1978). It means that when a child needs help accomplishing an action, the parent supplies just the right dose of help so that the child can complete the action. Perhaps the child is struggling to fit a plastic figure into a toy car. The parent might comment, "If you open the door of the car, it will be easier." Or the parent might physically show this step, and then let the child put the figure into the car. By such means, the child is not left to wallow in his frustration. At the same time, the parent does not take over the action; it is still the child who carries it out.

Appropriate scaffolding strengthens a child's sense of agency. He learns to persevere with a task or effort. And he learns that new maneuvers can be mastered.

The fifth component is *limit-setting*. Suppose, for example, the child becomes aggressive, hitting the parent, or destructive, breaking or nearly breaking a toy. Or suppose he otherwise goes against a familiar rule the parent has made. This should not be ignored. The parent should intervene quickly, calmly requiring the child to stick with play behaviors that do not cross the line of the rule. Presumably the competencies needed for this type of limit-setting have already been established by previous therapeutic work. Occasionally the playtime might even have to come to an early end if the child does not calm down and end the aggressive or destructive behavior.

The sixth component is *praise:* judicious, fitting praise, given specifically in response to a child's actions or words. The praise can be short—just "good," "fine," or the like. Or a sentence or two can be used, as long as what is said makes an immediate link with the child's behavior. For example, "Good that you kept on drawing the school and didn't give up." At times praise can also be coupled with appropriate scaffolding. The parent provides the bit of scaffolding, the child completes his action, and the parent responds with something like "yes" or "that's the way."

Like descriptive language and appropriate scaffolding, selective praise encourages a child to stay longer with one activity. Again, although helpful for any child, this is especially important with children whose development has been compromised: for example, due to a child with hyperactivity, a concentration disturbance, a pervasive developmental disorder, or some other problem.

DECIDING ON A MANNER OF ENTRY

After these components are spelled out to the parent, the "manner of entry" must be decided. As I noted earlier, the parent should be given a choice: either to comment on the child's play from the sidelines, or to actively to join in. If the "sidelines" mode is chosen, this should be seen as a temporary solution. The eventual goal is for the parent to engage in participatory play.[3]

I think an appropriate goal is for parents to participate directly, preferably from the beginning. My reasons for this are as follows: (1) Once a parent learns how to join in the right way, the children like it—a lot. (2) Competent, shared play is much more satisfying for the parent. (3) By playing together, the parent and child learn a great deal about how to cooperate and negotiate with each other. These are critical skills for other aspects of family life. They are also long-range developmental skills for the child. (4) The parent and child can safely explore, in play, all kinds of variations of their relationship—aggressor/aggressee, nurturer/nurturee, and so on. This widens their mutual emotional range with each other. (5) A child who learns to play well with a parent is better prepared for competent play behavior, later on, with other children.

McElreath and Eisenstadt (1997) took a slightly different position. They told parents that they should feel free to join in *nonsymbolic* play (e.g., with a ball) but not *symbolic play* (e.g., with dolls). I also find this idea odd—and unjustified. It is precisely the greater richness of symbolic play, once a child is developmentally ready, that can foster more complex reciprocal exchanges between adult and child.[4]

I also differ from Cavell, McElreath, and Eisenstadt in my position about scaffolding. They instruct parents not to help out when the child has difficulties. I believe that, on the contrary, it is good for parents to help out in certain moments. Obviously a parent should not help out excessively; this would infantalize the child. From my perspective the question instead is *how* the parent should help and whether the style of help promotes or undercuts the child's development of agency.

PRACTICING PLAY

The parent is next asked to play with the child right there in the session. It is explained that this will be for a timed period of 10 minutes only. The parent can try out these elements of play and then get aid and feedback from the therapist at the end. The therapist puts out some toys or drawing materials appropriate for the child's age. The parent and child then sit on the floor or at a table. The therapist sits near them, also on the floor or not far from the table.

When both parents are in the session, one parent is asked to observe. If there are other children present, they can be given the choice either to watch or to do a separate play activity in another part of the room. Naturally the other children may object, wanting to join in the play. If that happens, the therapist helps the parent to set a limit. The parent explains that this will be a short period in which she will play alone with the one child, and that later at home something similar can be arranged with each other child.

During the 10 minutes, as they play, I say nothing unless they get badly stuck. I just watch. As soon as 10 minutes has ended, I ask them both what it was like for them to do this. (If other family members are present, I have questions for them too, as explained later.)

Then I give the parent feedback, stressing both what she did well and offering one or two suggestions about what to try differently. I don't attempt to immediately bring up everything that could have been done differently. Typically I suggest to the parent just one thing to work on, usually pertaining to one of the just described components.[5] For example: "It could be good also to praise Tom a little when he does something right, or something well, like when he finished the drawing." Or, "It would be better not to ask questions."

Mrs. Stone, a single mother, had come to therapy for help with Anne, 3 years old. Over the course of several sessions the two of them had made good progress. Aggressive, noncompliant behavior on Anne's part had been reduced, and Mrs. Stone reported feeling better about herself as a parent.

When I inquired about their playing together, Mrs. Stone said that she had more or less stopped a couple of years ago. She found that Anne "didn't really enjoy it," and she felt little inclination to play herself. However, she agreed that it might be useful for their relationship to explore this new direction. I explained the recommended play procedures. Mrs. Stone then said she was ready to try.

I put out some toys. They sat on the floor, as did I. Anne picked up some Lego pieces and began to build a structure. Almost at once Mrs. Stone started to tell Anne what she thought would be a better way of going about it. Then she caught herself and laughed, remarking, "I forgot, I'm just supposed to say what she is doing."

She then waited more patiently. Occasionally she commented, saying, "You're starting another house now. You're going to put this one next to the first one." Anne, as she played, appears somewhat self-conscious and stiff. At one point, however, she took a tiny plastic rabbit in her hand and had it walk over to one of the houses. With a nuance of friendly surprise in her voice, Mrs. Stone commented, "A rabbit!" Anne looked up at her and smiled. Mrs. Stone repeated, "A rabbit. He's coming to the house." Anne said, "It's his house." This seemed a genuinely positive moment between them.

After they stopped, Anne said, in response to a question from me, that she liked their playing this way. Mrs. Stone reported that she found it difficult just to wait instead of jumping into instructions and corrections.

I commended Mrs. Stone on managing to avoid correcting Anne. I stressed that it was especially good that she noticed she was criticizing and stopped herself.

I suggested that next time they try this, she might add a word or comment of praise once in a while. I also said that, as they continued experimenting with play at home, she should feel free to join in the play if at any time she wanted, as long as this seemed okay with Anne. I added that if she preferred not to join in for now, and just to observe and comment, this was also all right.

After a parent and child have practiced during the session, we work out together what can be done at home. My usual suggestion is that the parent plan for the next weeks to play with the child, just as in the session, for 5 days a week, and for 20 minutes each time.

Sometimes the arrangement must be for fewer days a week. Perhaps a mother works exceptionally long hours on certain days, or a father travels for part of each week. In that case, one helps the family think through a plan that is more limited but still regular, so that the child knows on which days he can expect the playing to take place.

Occasionally I propose doing only 10 (or sometimes even 5) minutes at a time to begin with. This is easier when play is foreign to the parent and consequently stressful for both parties. Eventually, the playtime can be extended to the full 20 minutes.

In cases with behavioral compliance issues, I usually add a more precise recommendation about how to end the play. The potential difficulty, of course, is that because the play is so new and appealing, the child does not want to stop. So I suggest that 5 minutes before ending, the parent warn the child that there are only 5 minutes of play left. Then, a minute before the end, a similar warning should be given (e.g., "Now our play time is almost over"). This lets the child better prepare himself.

If the child looks clearly reluctant to stop, the parent can say something about that too, such as, "I see you don't want to stop playing." This is another good use of descriptive language: to provide appropriate words for a child's emotional state. Then the parent, calmly, should continue to be firm about the time limit. The parent should also have the child help pick up the toys or materials that were used after the playtime is finished.

In how many subsequent sessions is it necessary to return to the theme of play? That varies. Some dyads manage the shift to play almost at once. The only follow-up they need is a few brief conversations in subsequent sessions about how the playing together at home is going. For others it is a longer road. They may be better off trying another 10-minute segment of play in the following session, or even for several additional sessions. This provides a good deal more feedback and continuing support. Usually it can be accomplished early in the session, leaving plenty of time for other concerns.

WORKING WITH FAMILIES AS OPPOSED TO DYADS

When working with play restoration, the more systemically you proceed, the greater the positive impact. As I described earlier, the therapist asks the targeted dyad to play, with the rest of the family watching. Siblings who do not want to watch can be permitted to play alone elsewhere in the room.

There are a number of advantages to having other family members present during the play session if this is possible. First of all, the therapist will notice how the other family members react *to the proposal itself* that (1) this parent, alone, will now play with this child, alone; and that (2) they (this dyad) will be continuing the same experiment at home. Does the suggestion create jealousy? Do a sibling's verbal or nonverbal signals indicate that he resents the idea or that he himself may be hungry for a similar connection? If the therapist gets a sense that feelings of this kind have been stimulated, it is important to speak about that at a later point. Usually the most productive moment is just after the parent and the child designated for the intervention have actually tried their playing together.

Related issues may surface as the play takes place. Does a sibling interfere? Does the other parent interrupt with criticisms or advice? Does the other parent cooperate by keeping the other siblings occupied with something else, if this seems necessary? Suppose one sibling becomes disruptive. What does the other parent do in response?

At times I suggest that both parents play with the child simultaneously. I might do it in another session, or later in the one being used for the first playtime. Expanding play to include both parents allows for evaluation of the parents' ability to coordinate, cooperate, and repair (see Fivaz-Depeursinge & Corboz-Warnery, 1999). These issues also can be worked with in other ways, but triangular play is a good mode for dealing with them. This is especially pertinent when the parents have strongly differing opinions about how to handle their child, or if they compete to be the better parent.

Once the play stops, I initiate a short family exchange about whatever has taken place. I ask the others to share their observations. I also may give one or more compliments. For example:

- Your two children did a really good job playing alone.
- That was very helpful when you [the father] picked up the baby when she started crying and walked around with her.

I also might underline difficulties that arose. For example:

- I know it was a struggle for you [the father] to keep the other children from interrupting.
- You [a sibling] interrupted many times. It was hard for you to let your father and brother play.

A sibling may have something to say about the parent's play in relation to himself. It is important to make room for this. You may hear, for example, "Mom never plays with me, either. Can we play together now?"

Two types of response are possible. If there is enough time remaining, and if the parent who just played seems in no particular need of further exploration (e.g., of feelings, reactions, or memories from her own childhood), the same procedure (20 minutes of play) can be done now with the second child as well. Or, if time is lacking, the therapist—after making sure that the parent has heard and understood this child's wish—can propose that the child play in the same way with the parent in the next session.

I cannot stress enough how important it is to open the door to this kind of discussion with a sibling. The following case illustrates this.

June, age 10, was described by her parents, Mr. and Mrs. White, as a helpful, responsible, obedient child. Her 7-year-old brother, Ari, was just the opposite. He provoked everyone and was disobedient. At the start of therapy, Mrs. White and Ari had an openly hostile relationship.

In the fifth session I introduced a play sequence in which Mrs. White played with Ari. June did not interrupt. Afterward I asked June how it was for her when her mother and brother played. June said, "What do I have to do to get my mother to play with me? Become a devil like Ari?"

This comment led to a very fruitful exchange between June and both her parents. She expressed her sadness that no one played with her. She felt it was unfair that she was always expected to be "grown up," to help out, and to do whatever her parents wanted.

As little time remained, I couldn't have Mrs. White play with June right then. But we arranged for her to do so the next time. Mrs. White also proposed that she would be willing, on each of the days when she was putting in the 20 minutes with Ari, also to play 20 minutes alone with June.

SPECIAL CASES

Play restoration can be useful with many kinds of families, but for families with developmentally delayed or neurologically disturbed children, these techniques take on an added special importance. Besides supporting more constructive interactions, they help the child with his social and language skills.However, the greater the child's deficits (of cognition, working memory, affect regulation, etc.), the more patience and tolerance will be demanded of the parent.[6] Still, it gives something concrete and effective for a parent to do, especially in situations where parents often suffer immensely from feelings of helplessness.

> Mrs. Trapper was worried about Devin, age 4. He had been diagnosed with pervasive developmental disorder (PDD). His language skills were poor. He had trouble with basic social skills, such as making eye contact. He spoke very little in general. He was easily frustrated, and in those moments he often became aggressive.
>
> Trying out play restoration with Devin, Mrs. Trapper focused on describing Devin's actions in words. She seemed to get the idea quickly. She also paid attention to emotional expressions appearing in his face and posture and supplied language for those feelings. She praised him the couple of times he made eye contact with her. At one point he became aggressive, and she gently but quickly set a limit.
>
> In the next session, Mrs. Trapper reported that she felt less helpless and less lonely when she spent time with her son. She said the play periods were going well, and that they were "letting us find a different way to be together."

Another domain where this approach proves invaluable is when children have been separated from their parents. These children may have been placed in an institution or with a foster family. These cases tend to be extremely difficult in a number of respects. But when play restoration is combined with other forms of systemic intervention, one frequently can obtain very satisfying results. The play procedures can be used with a biological parent, with a foster parent, or with an institutional team.

For example, I have trained and supervised a number of teams that work with parents who have lost their parental rights. In many instances the courts permit contact with the child only if the parents agree to participate in family sessions in a protective therapeutic setting. But exactly what should you be trying to accomplish in these sessions? And how? Most such parents have lost their children because they are considered a danger to their child. Typically they can be psychotic, drug addicted, alcoholic, negligent, sexually abusive, or violent. The children have often been traumatized. This is not easy work.

Initially, of course, you need to address issues of safety. Explicit ground rules and agreements may have to be put into place so that the child is protected. Accomplishing this, however, does not in itself change the relationship; it is only a *preparation* for changing the relationship.

What I have found most surprising in these situations is the strong degree to which the parent often wants to maintain contact with his child. Yet the parent also tends to be quite ambivalent, with feelings of anger towards the child, or even hate. That may sound contradictory, but really it is not. Even though the parent's hunger for connection with the child is strong, usually the interactional skills needed to realize this are extremely weak.

Hence the practicality of the structured play format. This gives parent and child (and for that matter, the therapist too) a concrete direction in which to proceed. Step by step, the parent can discover how to form and maintain a new, positive relationship. He will also be helped to get to know the child, and the child will be helped, in some small ways, to get to know the parent. I have often seen such an evolution even when the contact has been supervised and limited to once a month.

With parents who have such severe problems, the therapist must expect the learning process to move slowly. Play restoration is best introduced as soon as possible. If no structure is provided, the sessions can quickly become tense on both sides. The play procedures, along with regular feedback from the therapist, give the parent a sense of direction.

Such interactions also are calming for the child, who, because of past trauma, may easily be frightened by more unstructured contact. Children in such contexts are usually immensely thankful to have the parent's undivided attention in this way, especially in a safe setting.

Mr. Grando, age 24, was divorced. He tended to be immature, irresponsible, and aggressive. He had lost his parental rights because of alcoholism and serious violence toward both his wife and child. A judge had granted him the possibility to have contact with Océane, age 7, only during sessions with a family therapy team present.

Mr. Grando said he was highly motivated to remain in contact with his daughter. He never missed a session, and often arrived early. He was currently in an alcohol treatment program.

During the sessions Mr. Grando was frequently inappropriate with Océane, treating her like a much younger child. As gifts, he brought toys that would have been right for a 2-year-old.

Though skeptical, he was cooperative and willing when play restoration techniques were proposed by the team. They started out by helping him select play materials that fit Océane's age. Her advice was also solicited.

Once the two of them began, Océane initially wanted only to play what her father wanted to play. Her demeanor was restrained and hypervigilant. Little by little, however, she became more assertive. She began taking the lead and introducing creative twists into their play exchange. Over the course of several more sessions, Mr. Grando learned to follow and to join in as well. He became more constructive in his attitude, using praise and humor. There were frequent affectionate exchanges. Océane eventually came to look forward to these sessions with her father.

Another context where work with play has particular benefits is when a parent is in a psychiatric hospital. I have trained several psychiatric nurses to help mentally ill parents use these procedures.

Mrs. Beretta had been hospitalized for 4 weeks following a schizophrenic episode. Thirty years old, she had a childhood history of extreme neglect by her alcoholic mother and sexual abuse by her stepfather. This was her sixth hospitalization. She was now taking medication regularly and was less agitated than at admittance. Her daughter, Ellen, age 5, had been brought by her mother during Sunday visiting hours.

The psychiatric nurse had noticed that, during the visits, Mrs. Beretta seemed quite lost with respect to relating to her child. This time, the nurse proposed play restoration techniques to Mrs. Beretta, who willingly agreed to try.

The nurse explained the steps. At first, Mrs. Beretta sat at the play table, took a puzzle, and started playing with it herself. She looked visibly content, but did not turn to see what Ellen was doing.

The nurse joined her at the play table. She brought Mrs. Beretta's attention to Ellen and asked her to describe what Ellen was drawing. Bit by bit, the nurse guided Mrs. Beretta in waiting, describing, and occasionally praising. Gradually Mrs. Beretta began to perform these basic components herself.

Mrs. Beretta reported afterward that this let her feel more at ease with her daughter. The nurse continued to help her with structured play during several more visiting times. After Mrs. Beretta's release, Ellen remained in the foster family. Mrs. Beretta continued to use her new skills with Ellen in her own home, where Ellen stayed with her on occasional weekends.

Play restoration also works well in families with high levels of aggression and more than one child. In these cases there may be an almost intolerable, explosive atmosphere as each child competitively vies for a parent's attention. This can be even more pronounced in a single-parent family. Play restoration techniques offer a means of tackling both the aggressive behaviors and the underlying rivalry.

Mrs. Santos was a single parent working full-time. She was originally from Portugal, and the oldest of 11 children. Neglect and systemic violence were a daily part of her childhood. Her parents immigrated to France when she was 5 years old. Mrs. Santos's mother died when she was 13. From that moment on, she had to act as the mother for her siblings.

Mrs. Santos did well at school and, against all odds, managed to become well educated. She now had an excellent job. She supported herself and her two children, Marcos, age 6, and Juan, age 3. Mrs. Santos sought help because she couldn't stand her sons' fighting and disobedience. She said that Marcos was a "devil" and Juan was a "terrorist."

In an early session, Mrs. Santos described her discipline methods as "screaming." Over the course of a month or so, she made substantial changes in this area. She learned how to use time-out, to establish clear rules, and to use rewards and consequences. I also helped Marcos to set limits with Juan when Juan hit or bit him instead of responding with more of the same and then getting blamed by his mother.

In the fourth session, Mrs. Santos said she was pleased with the changes in her family. She reported that she had even given herself some time-outs when she was on the verge of erupting and physically attacking the boys. At the same time, she complained, she still did not really enjoy being with her sons. She said she felt like she functioned simply as a "policeman."

I suggested play as an alternative. The boys immediately liked the idea. Mrs. Santos was more reluctant but agreed to go along. Marcos wanted to play first. I ask him to wait and let Juan play first. I explained to Marcos that, because he was older, he could wait better. He accepted this once it was clear that just as much playtime would be given to him.

Juan wanted to play "catch me" on all fours. Mrs. Santos got down on her hands and knees and gave it a try. She quickly became animated, the physicality of the chase seeming to amuse her. Marcos tried to interrupt. Mrs. Santos nicely set a limit, reminding him that his turn was to come soon. Mrs. Santos and Juan wound up laughing and hugging.

Then it was Marcos's chance to play. He began by setting up two Playmobil figures he had brought to the session. One, he explained, was called "Action Man." This was the one he would take. The other, which his mother was to take, was "Monster Man." He wanted the two figures to have a fight, which, with Mrs. Santos cooperating, they proceeded to do. After a little time Marcos switched to wanting to play "catch me" as Juan had. Another chase ensued. At one point Juan tried to join in, and Mrs. Santos told him he must go play and let them alone. Marcos clearly appreciated his mother doing this.

Mrs. Santos was able in the therapy to continue along these lines. Strong emotions also emerged about having had almost no such play contact in her own childhood. With my support, she let herself go through some weeks of mourning this.

I cannot emphasize enough the utility of using play as a way to strengthen the affective bond between parent and child. The approach presented here offers an effective and rapid way to bring this about.

NOTES

1. Carr (2000), Keith and Whitaker (1997), Schaefer and Carey (1997), Wachtel (1994), and Zilbach (1986) are among the few who have also written about play techniques.

2. An interesting approach to parent-child play outside family therapy can be found in Eyberg (1988), who calls her approach "child-centered interaction." McElreath and Eisenstadt (1997) follow Eyberg in general. Cavell (2000) named his methodology "responsive play therapy." Van Fleet (1994, 2000) and Guerney (1964, 1983) have the parent observe the therapist playing with the child for several sessions, and then the parent plays with the child. My effort has been to approach this issue in a more systemic fashion.

3. Eyberg's (1988) approach is fundamentally different from this: She advocated that a parent *only* comment from the sidelines and not join in the play. Cavell (2000) followed Eyberg with respect to this issue.

4. See Feldman (2003). Greenspan and Wieder (1998) have also extensively demonstrated the importance of symbolic play, done with a parent, for children with developmental disturbances.

5. Eyberg and Boggs (1989) preferred a much more directive role for the therapist. They recommended that the therapist comment on every parent verbalization during the play sequence, thus giving maximum feedback. McElreath and Eisensfadt (1997) were rather similar, giving a lot of ongoing feedback from behind the one-way mirror, with the parent wearing an earphone. I find that a more restrained use of feedback is more effective. Often a parent and child must go through several minutes of awkwardness before they can allow something more to happen.

6. An even more specialized form of parent-child play has been developed by Greenspan and Wieder (1998) for developmentally delayed children. Though technically more demanding for both therapist and parent, Greenspan's methodology has many parallels with the present approach. Greenspan also strongly recommended that the parent participate actively in the play rather than just comment from the sidelines.

CHAPTER EIGHT

Links to the Past

• •

Some family therapists explore the past a great deal; some don't explore it at all. I stand roughly in the middle of this spectrum. Talk about the past is one of my central techniques, and I do use it at times and consider it productive.

The family therapy tradition has plenty of approaches to working with the past, as well as a rich legacy of ideas for how to *think* about the past. Some examples include: Boszorymenyi-Nagy's emphasis upon invisible loyalties, legacies, entitlements, and debts, which operate as secret threads connecting the generations (Boszorymenyi-Nagy & Ulrich, 1981, Boszorymenyi-Nagy & Krasner, 1986, Boszorymenyi-Nagy & Spark, 1973); Bowen's (1976) concept of degrees of differentiation of self; Stierlin's (1975, 1978) idea of delegation, or the implicit transmission of a task from a previous family era; and Byng-Hall's (1995) theory of transgenerational family scripts.[1] I draw at times on all these. Like many therapists, I am also fond of the genogram (Bowen, 1976; McGoldrick & Gerson, 1985; McGoldrick, Gerson, & Shellenberger, 1999), which I discuss later in this chapter.[2]

What I find most valuable about these concepts is that they are highly motivating. They do more than give "insight." Once a family grasps how their current problems significantly reflect a broader historical background, they become more ready to tackle concrete change. They wish to free themselves from an inherited curse. They want to recover their power of agency.

For the therapist, to look at the matter from the perspective of motivation dictates a certain stance at the level of technique. This implies that a focus on the past clearly operates in the service of concrete, already specified therapy goals. It should add a new representational complexity to the "why" of the goals (i.e., the motivational charge, the "why change this"). The goals will thus be more important to the family.

Practically speaking, the therapist adopting this point of view must remain highly flexible. Deciding whether to explore the past depends upon the therapy goals, the working relationship with the therapist, and the readiness of the family members to be motivationally stirred by this dimension. When one *does* turn to the past, the time spent doing so might be brief (e.g., 10 minutes) or longer (maybe an entire session, planned beforehand). This too hinges upon how the reflections about the past are meant to intensify the family's progress toward their goals.

Deciding whether to include the children is also important. There may be some aspects of the past that are more appropriate to explore with the adults alone. At other times, however, the presence of children can heighten the family's motivation. This means, of course, that the therapist must find ways to include them. This too I will discuss.

THE DIFFERENT KINDS OF PAST

I find it useful to conceptualize three different kinds of past. One is the *family past*, the history of the particular family that has come to therapy, including the history of the parental couple's relationship before the children were born. Another kind is the *individual past*, the personal history of an individual family member. A third is the *multigenerational past*, reaching back to the life stories of the parents of each present parent, and even beyond.

The Family Past

I might go into the *family past* for any of a number of reasons. The most common one is to explore how past experiences of the parents are shaping their parenting practices in the present. At other times the focus may be on trauma or loss. Other earlier partner relationships, perhaps involving marriage, divorce, and children from those relationships, may need to be discussed. Sometimes attention is brought to repeating patterns of behavior, or symptoms found in previous generations.

When exploring the family past I often have the family members construct a two-generation genogram. My utilization of the genogram largely follows standardized procedures (as described, for example, in McGoldrick et al., 1999). A flip chart is used. I ask each person to choose a color for himself. Men and boys draw squares; women and girls draw circles. The parents begin, with each writing his or her name inside his or her square or circle. The date of birth is added underneath. Then each child does the same, starting with the oldest child and progressing downwards. (One difference with respect to other approaches to the genogram is that I like to have each person write her name inside the symbol, not underneath. Other options are to write the age of the person inside the symbol and the name underneath. I find the name more important than age. Age changes; names stay the same.) The marriage date is also written in. Children usually become quite animated when a family collectively puts on paper a genogram of this sort. Most of the time I explore the past without a genogram, but I find when I use one the family is almost always responsive.

With or without a genogram, often it is the family's past that needs to be brought into focus. This may include the parents' previous adult relationships, especially if children from previous relationships form a part of the present family constellation.

The full meaning of present conflicts and disagreements may only become clear once this earlier family history is thematized.

> Mr. and Mrs. Connor consulted me because of extreme physical and verbal fighting between Leo, age 10, and Carter, age 8. The boys were from Mrs. Connor's first marriage. Mrs. Connor left her first husband, Owen, when she fell in love with his brother, Jack, who was 10 years younger than Owen. She subsequently married Jack, and Owen returned to live with his parents. Furious, almost lethal encounters had occurred between Jack and Owen periodically over the years. The grandparents had cut off all contact with Jack, Mrs. Connor, and their grandchildren.
>
> The more we explored this history, the clearer it became that this past and ongoing family warfare was an important contributing factor in Leo and Carter's aggressive behavior. Leo and Carter were most likely reproducing the violent arguments between their father and uncle. The boys were only able to learn to express their anger more constructively when Owen and Jack came to therapy, and were able to address these issues and move forward.

Here is another poignant example of how bringing in the past is essential.

> The Meyer family began family therapy after William, 11 years old, threatened to commit suicide. Mr. Meyer lost his first wife in a car accident when William was 6 years old and his sister Emma was 2 years old. After six months Mr. Meyer married again. The second Mrs. Meyer was highly abusive toward the children, and Mr. Meyer divorced her after 2 years. The present, third Mrs. Meyer met Mr. Meyer when she was hired as

his secretary in his medical practice last year. They married only three months ago.

There are many good kinds of questions that can get the parents talking about their relationship history. A few examples:

- Where were you each living when you met?
- Were you in school? Working? Both at the same time?
- What did each of you first like about the other?
- What did you enjoy doing together as you first got to know each other?
- When and how did you decide to live together? And also where to live?
- How did you make the decision to marry (or not to marry)?
- How soon afterwards (or before) did you become parents?

Often one can engage the children as well. For example, before I even start with the above questions, I usually ask the children what they know about how their parents met. Then I encourage them to come in with questions whenever they wish. I also turn to them frequently, inquiring if they were already acquainted with some piece information or whether it is new to them. In some cases the children may have surprisingly little knowledge of the parents' history in this respect. Engaging the children helps the therapy move to a more systemic level.

At some moments I might even have one or both of the adults, as they continue their narrative, speak about it directly *to* the children. This increases the likelihood of the children bringing questions from their side. Another possibility is for the therapist at times to translate the significance of these memories for the children, emphasizing how these events from the past may be influencing their parents today.

Concerning some subjects, however, it may be more appropriate to exclude the children. For example, you may want to explore previous partner relationships, a parent's time spent in prison, or a parent's history of prostitution or drug addiction. If the exploration is intended to be short, the children can be asked to step outside the therapy room for a little. If more time would be fruitful, a separate session for the adults alone can be scheduled.

The Individual Past

The individual past normally concerns the past of one of the adults. Areas of interest may be the adult's childhood history or some period of adulthood prior to the relationship with the present partner.

One frequent indication for an inquiry into an adult's individual past is when loss or trauma appears to have a connection with present-day issues. Another is when previous partner relationships, divorces, separations, remarriages, and the like seem relevant.

In families in which the adults have children from previous relationships, I always inquire about the history of their previous couple relationships. Previous and current arrangements concerning these children need to be discussed as well. Here are some typical interventions:

- Tell me about your previous relationships.
- Did you have children together?
- What ages are they and what are their names?
- How did you decide as a couple what role you would take with each other's children from previous relationships?
- Have these decisions changed over time?
- How does your ex-partner treat your new partner? Is he or she more supportive of your current couple relationship or critical of it?

- How often and in what context do you see your children from your other relationships?
- Do you have financial responsibilities toward your children from a previous relationship?
- Does your ex-partner have financial responsibilities toward you?

A turn to the individual past is almost always indicated when the parents have chronic conflicts about parenting styles. In these cases, you can explore how each parent's beliefs reflect his or her own respective childhood history. Is the parent replicating a parenting style of her own mother or father? Conversely, has she chosen to adopt a radically different style of parenting, based upon negative earlier experiences? Naturally the latter type of decision can sometimes create excesses and rigidities of an opposite kind.

The Rolland family came to therapy with their son, Ethan, age 10, who was diagnosed as having ADHD. Mr. and Mrs. Rolland were perpetually arguing about which of them had the right parenting method for Ethan. Mr. Rolland found Mrs. Rolland too soft and easily manipulated by Ethan. Mrs. Rolland thought that Mr. Rolland was too devaluing and severe. She also was strongly against his hitting Ethan, which frequently occurred.

Mrs. Rolland described her mother as a highly organized, strict parent, and her father as easy-going. However, she could never count on her father to follow through on promises, and he often disappointed her. Mrs. Rolland wanted to be warm, flexible, and relaxed as a parent, but also solid and reliable.

Mr. Rolland described his father as a hard disciplinarian who was physically and verbally abusive to his children. He described his mother as almost one of the children, unable to manage family life. He believed it was his father who, despite difficult historical circumstances, held the family together. He

135

said that even though at times it was painful, he had profited greatly from his father's parenting style, and that to emulate him made perfect sense.

We explored this further. I asked Mr. Rolland to go back more concretely, in his imagination, to how it felt to be hit and insulted so often. Gradually he got in touch with his fear and sadness. He talked about the sheer unpleasantness of his childhood. He then made a decision to stop calling Ethan a "sissy" and a "cry baby," and to stop hitting him.

Mrs. Rolland began to understand that she delegated to her husband the strict parental role that her mother had. Following this exploration, it immediately became much easier for the two of them to negotiate some compromises based on what Ethan needed. They discussed how their differences in parenting tendencies might complement rather than work against each other.

Families in which one or both parents have immigrated bring another dimension to the exploration of the past. It is important that children have some familiarity with their parents' history and culture. As the children mature, they must navigate between the culture in which they grew up, and their parents' original culture. Immigrant parents, because of past trauma or a desire to let their children fully assimilate, often hold back too much about their native culture or country.

Mr. Vincente emigrated from Argentina to France at age 18 for political reasons. Many years later he met and married the current Mrs. Vincente, a French woman. They have two children, age 10 and 14. French, which Mr. Vincente speaks fluently, has always been the language of the home.

I inquire what the children know about Mr. Vincente's country of origin. They say that their father rarely talks about it. Nor have they ever met their grandparents on his side, nor any other relatives. The family decides to plan a trip to Argentina to meet Mr. Vincente's parents and siblings.

I usually turn to the genogram for this form of exploration, particularly if I want to go into the matter in some depth. A more extensive genogram than the two-generation type is required. The parent must add his own family of origin. I might also do this with both parents in the same session, having each in turn draw the family where she or he grew up.

If the children are present when such a three-generation genogram is constructed, I often encourage them to ask questions about grandparents, uncles and aunts, and so on. If the children know, or once knew, these figures, I might ask them as well as the parent to describe the characteristics of these relatives. At times the children may even wish to do the writing-in of the names of these relatives, which is fine as long as the parent whose family of origin it is agrees.

After doing genograms of each parent's family of origin, I often propose that the parent bring photographs from his or her childhood to the next session. Children tend to be especially interested in the photographs. The visual representations give them a mental hook for the narratives being told. Photographs can even be taped to the genogram, each one next to the name of the relevant person, and then used to generate further discussion between the children and the parent whose family is portrayed.

The Multigenerational Past

Here the scope is at its widest. At a minimum the multigenerational past includes the history of each parent's own parents: where these figures grew up, the constellation (siblings, etc.) of their respective families, and the like. The story of the couple relationship between the grandparents may also be thematized: how they met and the twists and turns of their common destiny. Sometimes the focus is extended to generations even further back.

Such an exploration cannot be brief. It takes one or two sessions, occasionally even three. It is usually best to leave young children at home. Their conceptual grasp of multigenerational history is limited, and they find long discussions about it rather boring. Older children can be present or not, depending upon the wishes of the parents.

An encounter with this wider history is particularly indicated when there are illnesses, psychiatric problems, or patterns of behavior that seem to repeat over the generations, such as schizophrenia, bipolar disorder, suicide attempts, self-mutilation, addictions, and antisocial and criminal behavior. Trauma can be another important theme—especially collective trauma, such as when war or political or religious persecution are a part of a family's history. Traditions, rituals, beliefs, and values are also good to explore.

Again, I almost always start with a genogram—typically a four-generation genogram. I have the parent draw in symbols for his or her four grandparents, with dates of birth and places of birth. Then we continue to fill in the family tree, working downwards. Here are a few of the interventions I often employ:

- What are the names and dates of birth of your parents? Let's go through them one by one.
- Where did they grow up?
- What are the professions of your parents and their siblings?
- Please give three adjectives to describe each of these people.
- What were some of the significant life events in your parents' childhood?

- What values and cultural, religious, and ethnic traditions did each of your parents bring into your childhood?
- How [if relevant] did history [the Depression, World War II, the Vietnam War] influence each family?

Questions concerning any siblings of the immediate parents should be posed as well:

- Say a little more about your own brothers and sisters. Are they married? Divorced? Do they have children?
- Where does each of your siblings live now? How far is it from where your parents grew up?

One may wish to go back even further in time. These same questions can be repeated to inquire about each great-grandparent's family of origin. For example:

- What are the names, birth dates, and birthplaces of your grandparents' parents? What were their professions?
- Which historical, political, or religious events must have influenced their lives?
- What are their strengths, their weaknesses?

Completing a genogram takes time. But once it stands there on the flipchart, it allows the therapist and the family to tease out some important patterns very quickly.

Mr. and Mrs. Kaplan, both professionals working full-time and living in Paris, had two children, Aaron, age 5, and Eliane, age 7. They had been sent by their doctor, who was concerned about Eliane's health. Eliane was overweight, and the parents had not been able to follow through on putting her on a diet.

Mr. Kaplan's parents, both in their late seventies, lived in the same apartment building as the family on a different floor.

They took care of Eliane and Aaron at lunchtime and after school until Mr. and Mrs. Kaplan returned from work.

Mrs. Kaplan saw Mr. Kaplan's parents as the problem. She claimed that it was the grandparents who fed Eliane too much. She wanted to find a babysitter instead of using the grandparents. Mr. Kaplan strongly disagreed. He didn't view Eliane's weight as a real problem, and he was taken aback and outraged by the idea of a babysitter.

A multigenerational genogram was created. Mr. Kaplan, looking at the diagram and pointing to his various relatives, talked about the extreme losses and deprivation suffered by both his mother's and his father's families. His maternal grandparents had died in a concentration camp in 1944. His mother was hidden in the French countryside. She had little to eat. After the war she was sent to an orphanage, where again she had not enough to eat. Mr. Kaplan's paternal grandfather was deported and also died in a concentration camp. His paternal grandmother escaped to the countryside with her two children. She too had little to eat, as well as being in constant fear of being discovered and killed.

During the course of his narrative, Mr. Kaplan said that he was having a lot of new thoughts with respect to Eliane. For his parents, food was laden with special significance. The abundance of food at each meal and the pressure they exerted on everyone to eat a lot partly echoed old terrors. Indeed, for his mother, being overweight was a sign of prosperity.

At the end of this session Mr. and Mrs. Kaplan made several new plans. Mr. Kaplan agreed that he would take Eliane's need to stay on a diet more seriously. He also suggested that he would try to communicate this need to his parents, and to insist that changes be made. Mrs. Kaplan expressed sympathy for her in-laws. She said although she had known these stories, she hadn't really absorbed them emotionally.

I proposed that we plan a session with the grandparents also attending. Both Mr. and Mrs. Kaplan agreed this would be a good idea.

In this example, the children were not present during the creation of the genogram. My guess is that this allowed Mr. Kaplan to let himself more fully feel the affective impact of his narrative. There are two sides to this question of the children's presence or absence, however. Frequently some elements of the family history that come to light are elements the children deserve to know. In these cases, the therapist can discuss with the parents whether, and how, and under what circumstances the story might best be shared.

WHEN TO INCORPORATE EXPLORING THE PAST

Normally I wait until a family has established their treatment goals before I suggest exploring the past. In most instances this is accomplished in the first sessions (see Chapters 11 and 12). A move to the past, in that case, might then be utilized in a third or fourth session. If brought in this early, however, it will probably be no more than a brief exploration. The point is to heighten motivation and enrich goal representations.

Such quick jumps to the past during the beginning sessions usually concern either the *family past* or the *individual past*, but not necessarily. If the family has come in because of a suicide attempt, an eating disorder, a psychiatric illness, or an addiction problem, a *multigenerational past* exploration might be warranted right away. This is because research indicates that these forms of difficulty often repeat themselves over generations in families. Plus, motivation for change with respect to such issues frequently is hard to elicit. On the other hand, if the family is now in a crisis, that must be dealt with first. Stabilization may be the immediate need. There may simply be no time available for a discussion of the past.

Occasionally even in a first interview it can be appropriate to discuss the past. This almost always concerns the *family past*:

141

a loss, a traumatic experience, a geographic move. It may be impossible even to articulate initial goals without taking this broader context into account.

What if the family does not want to talk about the past? Barring extreme situations, I never push.[3] Some parents don't want to talk about their own childhoods, let alone the wider generational history. I might inquire about their reasons for preferring to leave these subjects out of the therapy, but I usually do not pressure them in any further way. From the standpoint of my methodology, work with the past can be a helpful supplement. Plenty of other techniques are available to aid the family in changing.

Work with the past, undertaken at the right time and in the right way, can be a strong emotional process. Especially when exploring the individual past and the multigenerational past, family members may feel that they are getting to know one another in an important new way. The charged atmosphere that emerges may reflect another element as well. We are creatures who inhabit historical time. Our era and our generational family influence and shape us deeply, much more than we usually acknowledge.

These are "structuring causes." They do not dictate everything we do, but they work in us and on us in ways that are mostly "invisible." Recognizing these patterns can be disconcerting, yet there is an inherent excitement about the spectacle of destiny weaving its web. With luck, one may also discover previously hidden opportunities for the development of individual and interpersonal agency.

NOTES

1. See Goldenberg and Goldenberg (2004) and Reich, Massing, and Cierpka (1996) for excellent overviews of multigenerational family therapy perspectives.

2. Another technique that I admire is "family reconstruction" as developed by Virginia Satir (Satir & Baldwin, 1983; Satir, Banmen, Gerber, & Gomori, 1991; Nerin, 1986). It is an experiential technique that requires a group setting. Earlier family constellations are "recreated" using family sculpture, psychodrama, and the like. The father's family of origin might be enacted, for example. An interesting variant is Anne Ancelin Schützenberger's (1993) "therapie transgenerationnelle psychogeneaologique contextuelle." She creates a "geniosociogramme," which takes into account historical, cultural, and economic influences on the family over generations.

3. An example of an extreme situation would be when current sexual abuse has been disclosed and one is attempting, through questions about the family past, to clarify when and under what circumstances it first began.

CHAPTER NINE

Video-Supported Intervention

●●●●●●●●●●●●●●●●●●●●●●●●●●●

In this book, I have tried to concentrate on transparent, straight-forward techniques. My hope has been that the experienced therapist will be able to easily adopt that which he or she finds most useful or interesting. This short chapter, however, is an exception to that general approach. Here, I describe a complex therapeutic procedure. Since a thorough exposition is not feasible here, I only sketch its general contours. If you are interested in trying this approach, I have provided at the end of the chapter a simplified version of it, which you may apply to your own practice without further study or reading.

This group of techniques involves the use of videotape or DVD. A short video or DVD is made of family members interacting with one another. No therapist or professional staff of any kind are present in the video. Once the video is made, the therapist watches it with one or more family members. The processes and situations observed in the video provide a starting point for discussion. Such an undertaking can be so productive, and fits so well with the overall model given in this book, that I believe I must devote an entire chapter, even if only a brief one, to video therapy.

Videotape is not unknown within family therapy. Many therapists turn to it regularly for training and supervision, myself included. But to introduce video directly into a therapy session is another matter entirely. This allows the family members to make discoveries and draw conclusions based on what they see on the screen, with support from the therapist. Such an experience has affinities with what I have called dramatization (chapter 2), but the differences are more important than the similarities. A short segment of video can be stopped, played, or replayed as wished, and details can even be examined frame by frame. This allows for a grasp of interaction patterns which no other technique can provide.

We are fortunate today in that there exists helpful background for such a procedure. In two overlapping research traditions, attachment research (e.g., Abrams & Hesse, 2006; Hesse & Main, 2006; Lyons-Ruth, Melnik, Bronfman, Sherry-Llanas, 2004) and videomicroanalysis research (e.g., Fivaz-Depeursinge & Corboz-Warnery, 1999; Fogel, 2008; Rochat, 2001; Stern, 1995; and Tronick, 2007), the use of video to study parent-child interaction has been honed and refined for over 30 years. During the last several years, a small number of therapists have been employing a similar video-driven perspective for intervention purposes.

These clinical innovations have largely taken place in the world of what is often called "mother-infant" psychotherapy. The approaches of Beebe (2003) and Papousek (2000) are especially informative, since both are also leading developmental researchers.[1] A few intervention specialists, such as Downing (2004, 2008a, 2008b; Wortmann-Fleischer, Hornstein, and Downing, 2005), have extended the use of video to work with children of all ages, adolescents included. I myself mainly follow Downing's methodology.[2]

For clinical purposes a video that is ten to fifteen minutes long is usually sufficient. Again, the video should feature only the family members, not the therapist nor any other profes-sional support staff. The filming can be done by the family itself at home, or by the therapist in her office, or by someone else in a treatment center.

The type of scene to be videotaped depends on the family. Often a good choice is a typical problem-related interaction. If a 3-year-old has an eating problem, a video of a meal would be highly informative. If quarrels ensue whenever a parent helps a 9-year-old with homework, then an interaction involving home-work should be recorded. Both could be filmed either at home or in the institution or therapy office. Some situations, on the other hand, such as difficulties getting a child to bed in the eve-ning, can only be filmed at home.

For the intervention itself alternative options are possible (Downing, 2008; Downing, Buergin, Reck, and Ziegenhain, 2008). The video might be used to help the family members build up more differentiated representations of one another, to work more closely with emotion, or to define new behavioral goals. The video might serve as a bridge to a parent's earlier experiences, which can be compared to what has been seen on the screen.

Some therapists worry videotaping will cause the family to behave unnaturally, but this is seldom a problem. The family members may display some self-consciousness, and perhaps the parents will try to function a little better than they normally do. Regardless, usual patterns still tend to emerge on tape. Our habitual ways of operating nonverbally are deeply ingrained and cannot be modified quickly or easily. The therapist certainly should ask if what occurs in the video more or less corresponds to how the family normally interacts. And, the therapist should note whether anything seems very different than what she has already perceived of the family's interactions.

Should the entire family come to the session where the video is to be explored? Not necessarily. The therapist and family together should decide beforehand who will be present to watch the tape. For example, if the situation is explosive between a parent and a child, and if this parent is highly motivated to change his or her own behavior, then it might be best to calmly study the video with that parent alone. Or, suppose that two siblings wish to improve their relationship. They could be filmed by themselves, and then later discuss the video with only the therapist present. Being alone, without their parents, they will likely speak more freely. Of course, in most instances it is fine to have the full family present, as in any session.

Ms. Stark, referred by a drug treatment center, wanted help and support as she sought to reunite her family. Her daughter Jacqueline, age 6, had moved back home with her, after spending 2 years with Ms. Stark's sister and her husband. Ms. Stark's other daughter, Francine, 13, who had been living in an institution, wanted to join them. For the last 2 months Francine had been spending weekends with them. Ms. Stark, after a long history of addiction, had not used heroin for almost a year. The father of the children currently had no contact with them or Ms. Stark, and was unwilling to participate in sessions.

In a first interview both Ms. Stark and Francine agreed that they "don't know how to do things as a family." They seldom played or had other nourishing kinds of contact. When I described how we might work with this by using video, Francine enthusiastically announced, "Yes, we will do that!" Ms. Stark also indicated her willingness, though a little passively. Francine was a highly parentified child, as I would discover in the sessions to come.

Over the course of eight further family therapy meetings, video intervention was used three times. Seeing herself on video was extremely helpful for Francine. She learned to relax more in family interactions and to ease off trying to control everything that happened. Ms. Stark learned how to provide more structure for the exchanges between herself and each of the girls, as well as for the three-way interactions.

With the help of the video Ms. Stark also took steps toward expressing a wider range of emotion. She noticed, as we worked with the first video, how her face, though smiling, seemed unchanging and unexpressive. In that session I also made a point of isolating and showing a couple of exception pictures, where her face fleetingly displayed an appropriate sadness while Jacqueline was talking about something that concerned her. Ms. Stark clearly appreciated seeing these exceptions.

For the third video, a scene in the kitchen with Francine and Jacqueline alone was filmed. Watching this video helped Francine grasp, with my help, how what she did prompted different types of reaction from Jacqueline. For example, each time she became bossy in tone, Jacqueline turned away, or became subdued; when she echoed the playful tones in Jacqueline's voice, Jacqueline stayed engaged. With Jacqueline I also explored how she could not give up so quickly in the interaction, even if she did not like what Francine was doing.

One special advantage of video intervention is that it lends itself so well to family therapy work with problems with infants and toddlers. There exists remarkably little in the family therapy literature about how to treat such cases (for an interesting exception see Cierpka & Cierpka [2000]). Yet many families suffer greatly from difficulties in this area, with babies who do not sleep, infants who fail to form an attachment, feeding problems, or inexplicable developmental lags.

Mother-infant psychotherapy is then sometimes recommended by pediatricians or other professionals. However, in my opinion a more systemic approach is often warranted for such cases. True, the challenges are unique. Most of what occurs in interaction with an infant or toddler and other family members is thoroughly "procedural," i.e., bodily and nonverbal, in nature (Beebe, 2003; Downing, 2004; Tronick, 2007). The therapist is confronted by a family member who cannot speak, or who has mastered only a few words, hence the value of adding video to a systemic approach. Clinical microanalysis can show with tremendous precision what is really taking place on the procedural level.

The Berault family had come for help with Caroline, age 5. Both parents had trouble setting limits with her. Often she did not comply, and at times she was aggressive with them.

In the first interview, however, it came out that the family was facing what they considered a more urgent problem. Their infant son of 9 months, Gerald, cried excessively and slept little at night. The whole family had been losing sleep for months. Advice sought from other professionals had led to no improvement.

Two of the next three sessions with the Beraults were dedicated to video intervention. Two videos were filmed at home. For the first video they filmed themselves together putting Gerald to bed, late in the evening. They set the camera on a tripod, in the room where Gerald slept, and let it run.

As they observed the video in the session, it became clear to them that they were overstimulating Gerald. They were surprised and a little shocked, but were also able to laugh about what they saw.

I explored with them in more detail a number of micro-exchanges in the video. Step by step they formulated a series of new ideas about how they might interact with Gerald at this time of day. We discussed how they were holding and carrying him, their tones of voice, their facial expressions, and the like.

In the second video, shot at the same time in the evening during the following week, I was able to point out considerable positive change. We worked further on how they tended to "double up" when interacting with Gerald, with Mr. Berault often coming in immediately after Mrs. Berault's signal, and vice versa, so that Gerald had no time to organize a coherent response to either of them.

Within a period of 4 weeks Gerald began sleeping much better. We then moved to working on their relationship with Caroline.

Most families quickly become enthusiastic about video intervention. They feel it gives them a new understanding of their interactions as a family. They see for themselves how mutual influence operates from moment to moment, and how human relationships are truly systemic.

I close with a recommendation. Some modes of video intervention, e.g. those of Beebe (2003), Downing (2008a, 2008b), and Papousek (2000), are highly sophisticated in nature. For example, the preparatory scanning of the video is carried out with the help of a research-based conceptual framework. Nevertheless, a much simpler form of intervention is also possible. For the systemic therapist who already has solid experience working with families, it can be enlightening to try this interesting technique.

First, arrange for such a video to be filmed, whether in the office or in the family's home. Have the family engage in any activity which you think might be of interest. A short film of about ten minutes is sufficient.

Second, watch the video once or twice by yourself. Do not worry about refined analysis; simply notice the types of systemic processes you are already trained to observe. In ten minutes of video there will be more than enough to hold your interest.

Third, watch the video in a session with whichever family members you choose to have present. Explore their reactions. Block any excessive criticism; if necessary, instruct each family member to speak only about what he or she likes and dislikes about his or her own behavior. Be sure to mention several positive points you have observed. Move on from the video to a more generalized session, in whatever way works best for you and the family, in your accustomed working style.

If you try incorporating a video-supported intervention, a valuable tool will be added to your practical repertoire. The experience with video intervention will train your eyes to see differently, even when you are not using a video. Eventually you will start discriminating more of the "micro" level of interaction. From this increased information flow, your everyday systemic work is also bound to profit.

NOTES

1. Other useful accounts of the use of video for work with parent-child relationships are those of Aarts (2000), Erickson & Durz-Riemer (2003), Marvin (2003), and McDonough (2004). In the family therapy tradition, Byng-Hall (1995) and Bodin (1977) have described similar experiments.

2. Thiel-Bonney (2002) has a good account of how Downing's approach can be integrated into a classic family therapy setting.

PART II

Putting It All Together

CHAPTER TEN

A Roadmap for the Therapy

• •

Family therapists often feel the pressure of two competing needs: to help the family as rapidly as possible, and to help the family as thoroughly as possible. It's a question of efficiency versus breadth, or quickness of change versus quantity of change.

I suppose every kind of therapy has its version of this pressure, but in family therapy it is particularly acute. Typically there are several people involved, not just one. There are usually multiple issues as well, some obvious at the start and some emerging only later. On top of all that, the therapist must take into account not only the immediate problems of each child but also her developmental needs.

My answer to this dilemma is to organize the therapy into distinct phases. This gives a kind of roadmap, making priorities evident (Gammer & Cabié, 1992) so that clear decisions can be made. If, due to managed care or other constraints, only a few sessions are possible, these sessions can be arranged so that their impact is maximized. If work in more depth is feasible, this in turn can be planned in a coherent manner. A practical sequence can be established concerning which issues are addressed when.

The model comprises three phases: the *resolution phase*, the *extension phase*, and the *intimacy phase*. How they are organized depends partly upon the nature of the family constellation. I will first go over how they function when the family consists of both biological parents, with both living at home, and one or more children. Following this, I will discuss how the phases can be modified with single-parent families and with blended families.

Needless to say, I don't claim that every case will fit these guidelines. There are always exceptions where good reasons present themselves for planning the treatment otherwise.

THE RESOLUTION PHASE

The resolution phase typically lasts between three and ten sessions. Its purposes are (a) an elimination or reduction of the presenting problem that has brought the family in, (b) stabilization of any immediate crisis, (c) the building of a trustful working relationship between therapist and family, and (d) a strengthening of the family's confidence in their own ability to change. In the next chapter I describe how the therapist assists the family in defining and prioritizing their goals for this phase. If the working conditions are such that later on the family will have the option to continue therapy, this future possibility is also clarified. It is explained to the family members that the choice to end therapy or to go on will be discussed at that time, and that if they choose to continue, the therapeutic goals will then be renegotiated.

THE EXTENSION PHASE

In the *extension phase* these gains are consolidated and certain additional goals are confronted. This phase also usually lasts between three and ten sessions. It tends to be longer and more important when the family has more than one child.

As was done at the beginning of the resolution phase, new goals are selected by the family, with the therapist helping them explore what they want. Because they have already been through the resolution phase, they now have a good idea of how therapy functions and what it might bring them. They also are now much more in touch with what is going on in their family, including desires and sufferings that previously had found little open expression.

Direct work with sibling relationships, aiding the siblings with their connection with one another, is often a target. This lays an important foundation for the changes the family has already made, as well as being developmentally significant in its own right. Because attention to the sibling subsystem is so critical, I discuss it at more length in Chapter 15.

Another frequent goal concerns the "non-problem" child. Often families arriving for therapy have long been overly focused on the "problem child": the one who is hyperactive, developmentally delayed, chronically ill, and so on. The other sibling (or siblings) may have taken on a seemingly opposite role: well-behaved, quiet, tending to fade into the background. However, when this child is also allowed an open voice in the therapy, the picture may look different. She may have been hiding her own needs—for example, in order to protect her overburdened parents. When this is the case, therapeutic attention to what might change for this child is warranted. Normally it is work that can be quickly achieved, and it is worth the effort. This child will be less at risk for compromised emotional development and less at risk of later becoming a symptom-bearer herself.

Other extension-phase goals do not depend on how many children the family has. Their exact nature depends upon the dynamics of the family itself. For example, they might include negotiation and problem-solving skills, better regulation or expression of affect, coping with crisis and stress, or age-appropriate mentalization capacities (Steele & Steele, 2005b). Such themes may now be articulated for the first time in the therapy. Or, they may have been already raised but put aside, with an understanding that later on, should the family so choose, there would be an opportunity to take them up with the attention they deserve.

Issues concerning the relations between the nuclear and the extended family also are frequently dealt with in this period. It is sometimes necessary to invite members of the extended family, such as grandparents or aunts and uncles, to take part in a session or sessions. (Occasionally this must be done in the resolution phase, however, as is discussed later.)

THE INTIMACY PHASE

Finally, in the *intimacy phase* the adult couple's relationship is brought to the foreground. A strengthening and deepening of their relationship on a number of different levels is sought. Naturally with this step too it is the family members (in this case the two parents) who decide if they wish to pass into this new phase, and toward what ends. Most of the sessions in this phase are conducted with the adults alone, with children or other extended family members attending only occasionally.

This does not mean that the parental subsystem has not been worked with earlier. Some themes almost certainly will have been explored, if briefly. These themes often include how the individuals function as parents (i.e., how they operate as a team in dealing with the children and with the general tasks of family life). For example, if during the resolution phase one child's behavior problems were the chief focus, probably at some point the parents would have been aided with their negotiations (between themselves) about rules and consequences.

They would have been helped to present a united front with respect to limit-setting.

In other words, aspects of the couple relationship will have been examined, but only in the service of the specific goals of the resolution phase and the extension phase. Barring crises or unusual special needs, other types of work at the couple level are postponed until the intimacy phase. During the earlier phases, the therapist communicates to the parents that, should they so wish, a chance to explore how things are between them will be provided at a later point.

Why postpone deeper couple work, even when the therapy conditions allow it? There are two excellent reasons. One is the flight factor. If a premature turn is taken to issues of adult love, trust, sex, and the like, one or both partners may suddenly feel highly threatened. This was not why they came, at least not explicitly. Plenty of parents find working with their relationships with a child already challenging enough. To confront adult couple themes at the same time can be overwhelming. The risk (and it is high!) is that they will break off the therapy.

The second reason is the systemic disruption factor. For children, sensing their parents' relationship starting to undergo transformation can be distressing. It can feel like unknown, scary territory. They may well resist such a development. Problems may worsen, and symptoms may intensify. Gains previously made may be lost. These heightened pressures may even cause the family to leave therapy.

Respecting the phases reduces the risk of such pitfalls. The combined positive effects of the resolution and extension phases create a more solid base for continuation. Once the extension phase has ended, the adult couple will decide either to go on or not. Should they decide not to continue, plenty of good work with the children should already have been consolidated. If they decide to continue, both parents, however nervous they may be, will be more ready for the shift of focus. And the child or children, having successfully navigated the prior change processes, will be in a better position as well. In addition, the therapist will now have a more developed relationship to all the family members.

The intimacy phase tends to be more variable than the other two in both its length and its themes. Everything depends upon the two adults and the idiosyncracies of their relationship. They might want to explore how they nourish each other; their sexual connection; how they handle conflict; how they support each other during hard times and crises; how one or both might pursue interests—friends, sports, work, creative endeavors, education—that lie outside the realm of the couple and the family; how to draw lines around their relationship to protect it from excessive outside demands; and so on. A couple might choose to address any combination of these or other themes.

Why not just recommend separate couple therapy for dealing with these issues? This of course is the default alternative, and it is certainly better than sweeping all such matters under the rug. Nevertheless, the phase-oriented approach offers some obvious advantages.

First, by the time the intimacy phase arrives, the therapist and the parents have usually built a strong working relationship. This means that concentrated work with the hard issues can normally begin immediately.

Second, some of the issues themselves will already have been defined in the earlier phases. A joint decision will have been made to temporarily shelve them, and now they can be taken off the shelf. As a result, an understanding about the nature and significance of these issues—shared by the parents and the therapist alike—is immediately available. Here again time is saved. The momentum built up in the previous phases can be maintained.

Third, in the intimacy phase of family therapy, as opposed to couple's therapy, it is much easier for all concerned to keep one eye on the state of the wider system. How are things continuing to evolve at home with the children? Are the gains made during the previous phases being maintained, or even developed further? Are the new changes taking place at the adult couple level having any negative ramifications for the children? Naturally, sessions that include the children can be scheduled at any time. In this way the progress of the entire family can be more effectively kept on track.

I turn now to other types of family constellation, and how the roadmap applies to them. I will highlight only a few issues.

VARIATIONS WITH SINGLE-PARENT FAMILIES

Obviously, the intimacy phase does not apply to single-parent families. But a good many other factors typically must be considered with respect to the resolution and extension phases.

Some have to with the unique pressures of one-person parenting. Single-parents often live with tremendous stress, even apart from more specific problems with one or more of the children. (I will, however, refer to "mothers," as this is the more common situation.)

Consequently, during the resolution phase it may be important to look at how the mother can get some kind of outside parenting assistance. This is less of an issue when the biological father has taken over some part of parenting on a regular basis. Should additional support be needed, however, the mother might look to her own relatives, or a friend, or a member of her religious community.

Such a step can lead to involving the exterior person in a session or several sessions. Therapeutic support can be given for the details of this second adult's collaboration. In contrast, when working with an intact nuclear family, attention to the relationship with, for example, a grandparent or one of the parents' own siblings, can usually wait until the extension phase. But with a single parent family the need may be more pressing.

Of course, many single mothers do fine in this regard. Their lives are well organized, and they have help where they need it. I do not mean to suggest that this is a problematic area in all single-parent families.

A similar concern may be how the mother can find some form of outside social contact or activity. Because of time and monetary constraints (e.g., perhaps paying for a babysitter) options may be limited in this direction. But typically every little bit helps. Again, with intact families this theme is usually approached later, probably during the intimacy phase. But if a single mother's mental exhaustion or isolation is strongly affecting her parenting, the issue may well merit being approached in the resolution phase. Naturally here too there are plenty of exceptions. Some single mothers already manage quite well to take care of themselves in this regard.

Another possible special matter has to do with a single mother's relationship to a son, as opposed to a daughter. Research has found that single-parent mothers are more likely to have hostile attitudes and negative representations with regard to their sons than mothers in intact families do (Kelly, 2007). The reason probably has to do with the mother's feelings toward the departed biological father. Understandably enough, her lingering anger spills over, so to speak, onto her male child. This may lead her to be excessively coercive, critical, and unsupportive.

Some close therapeutic attention to the issue therefore can be warranted. If the son is also the child prominent in the presenting problem, this theme should be explored as part of the resolution phase. If he isn't, it can probably wait until the extension phase. However, it deserves investigation at some point. Structured play techniques (Chapter 7), if appropriate given a child's age, can be extremely helpful with this issue. They can supplement direct work with the mother's cognitions and mentalization skills. The parent-child play medium will help the two of them build a new repertoire of mutual positive behaviors.

Limit-setting is inherently more difficult for a single parent. No one else is around to help back up the single mother or father. Additionally, the children's pain and anger about the parental separation, however hidden these feelings are, can give rise to extra recalcitrance on their part. As a result, inconsistency may be visible in the setting of boundaries and limits. Again, for the reasons just discussed, these transactions may be worse with the male child. Consequently, the therapeutic work with limit-setting frequently has to go slowly and continue for a long time. First confronted in the resolution phase, it often remains a much-visited topic during the extension phase.

Feelings of loss on the part of the child are another key issue. When the mother cannot mourn the loss of her partner nor experience the sadness of the loss of her dreams of an intact family, it can be especially difficult for her to learn to respect the child's sense of emotional loss concerning the father. Even a child who accepts or even has desired the separation (the child may have witnessed repeated physical violence, for example) will nevertheless face some inner mourning. Here the therapist can aid with much-needed child-mother communication. Attention must be given to the child's version of events. The mother may require help to grasp that these emotions on the child's part do not represent disloyalty toward her. Vetere and Cooper (2005) have developed creative narrative techniques to help children in these families be heard and develop a sense of agency.

Another pattern encountered in many single-parent families is the parentalization of one child. This too is a natural outcome, if, in part, an undesirable one. I say "in part," because the matter can be complex. It may be appropriate for an older child to help with household tasks or care of younger children to a greater extent than is typical in an intact family. It is a question of degree, however. Are excessive demands being put on this child? And to what extent is he or she being drawn into a "pseudo-partner" relationship with the mother?

Typically the best time to address this issue is during the extension phase (assuming that this particular child is not the "symptom-bearer" who has brought the family into therapy). Once the goals of the resolution phase have been sufficiently met, it will be easier to help the parentified child find a voice in the therapy for his or her anxieties and needs—and easier for the mother to hear them. It will also be easier for both to make a plan for change that addresses the difficulty.

Finally, a particularly complicated matter with many single-parent families concerns the father's continued contact with the children. Perhaps the father has, and exercises, visitation rights. Or perhaps the two parents have joint custody. Either way, with some cases this systemic aspect must also be addressed early in the resolution phase, as ongoing conflict between the two parents may have significant negative effects on the children. You may need to examine what kind of messages each parent is conveying to the children about the other (as these messages may be undermining and destructive), how the rituals of going to and from the two homes are organized, and how the resident and the nonresident parent can better negotiate decisions concerning the children. Naturally such work will be more effective if the nonresident parent can in some way be included.

In some cases, relations between the divorced or separated parents are reasonably cooperative. If so, there is more latitude concerning if and when to include the nonresident parent in the therapy. Often his help concerning a child's problems turns out to be extremely useful during the resolution phase. That said, addressing issues about his relationship to the children or the resident parent can be postponed until the extension phase.

In some cases, his attending one or more sessions may not be required at all.

Overall progress with single-parent families may be slow and gradual, as the resolution phase in these cases tends to be rather thick with multiple goals. Parallel themes, and perhaps a good number of them, must be addressed. It is important that the therapist expect this, and that the family be prepared for its likelihood as well.

VARIATIONS WITH BLENDED FAMILIES

Blended families (stepfamilies) bring their own complexities. A separated or divorced biological parent now has a new live-in partner, who must function as a second parent, at least to some degree. Also, the new partner may have brought one or more of his or her own children into the home, either full-time or on a visiting basis. On the periphery one or two nonresident biological parents may be involved as well. This makes for a lot of relationships which are often highly heterogeneous in their qualities and histories.

Some of the typical issues in these situations mirror those in single-parent families—for example, how visits to a nonresident biological parent should be handled, or a child's need for the resident parent to respect her, or the child's sense of loss about the nonresident parent. But other issues are involved as well.

With most blended families, the sooner the new partner can take part in the therapy, the better; right from the start is optimal, if everyone agrees. However, the biological or the non-biological parent or both may be anxious about this inclusive format. If so, these worries should be articulated and spoken to. The therapist explains that both parents are more likely to see the results they wish from the therapy if they engage in it together. The therapist should also be prepared for the likelihood that, as therapy proceeds, the new partner may require considerable encouragement with respect to his or her continued participation.

Unrealistic expectations are a frequent theme with blended families. The biological parent, the stepparent, or both may have assumed that the child or children would cherish and feel grateful toward the new stepparent. Unfortunately the children's feelings are more often the opposite. Hurt and anger about the original parents' separation may still be very alive in them. Apart from that, they may simply find it hard to place trust in a new adult. They also may experience a loyalty bind vis-á-vis their missing parent. The older the child, the more likely such reluctance. (Very young children sometimes are more welcoming toward a new adult.)

As research about blended families shows, it can easily take several years for children to adjust to the situation (Bray, 2005). The impact of this difficulty should not be underrated. First, the state of the children's relationship to the stepparent strongly influences the extent to which they manage to adjust overall. Second, their own attitudes and behaviors in turn have considerable impact upon the adult couple relationship (Bray, 2005).

Unrealistic expectations must be dealt with early in the resolution phase. The two adults need to accept that positive change in this area, though perfectly possible, may be quite slow in coming. The new partner can then be helped to initiate some specific steps toward building a relationship with each child. The structured play techniques can also be of considerable use here. For older children, other activities can be undertaken, such as joint projects or outings. The nonbiological parent must also learn to understand that a good part of the holding back of the children has little to do with him as a person and much more to do with the surrounding circumstances.

Problems with limit-setting and discipline may need to be addressed from a similar perspective. A typical problem is that the children comply poorly with the new partner's attempts at limit-setting. The biological parent may already have some difficulties in this area, and the new partner may find himself having even more trouble. Perhaps the children ignore what he says, act as if he has no right to set limits, and so on.

This can be a source of conflict and stress for all concerned, including the biological parent. At the same time, the hard reality is that change in this area too will probably occur only gradually and over a long period. With the help of the therapist more extreme manifestations of the problem may be brought under control more quickly, but broader change can be expected to take much longer.

Rules and discipline need to be discussed during both the resolution and extension phases, and sometimes during the intimacy phase, too. The adults must also face that, during a long transition, a certain imbalance is going to be unavoidable and the larger share of the parenting will have to fall on the biological parent. Eventual positive shifts with respect to the nonbiological parent's limit-setting transactions will probably take place parallel to, and as a kind of echo of, the positive shifts in her more overall relationships to the children. As each child allows more trust on a deeper level, acceptance of the situation will favorably affect cooperation with discipline.

Frequently another aspect of work concerns the adult couple relationship itself. With blended families this bond is often somewhat fragile, perhaps more so than either party realizes. Research shows, for example, that the risk of crises and separation remains quite high for the first 2 to 3 years (Bray & Kelly, 1998; Hetherington & Kelly, 2002).

Nonetheless, initial inquiry into this area may be difficult. It may be hard enough to get the steppartner to join the therapy in the first place. Furthermore, both adults may experience little desire to confront themes having to do with their own connection. This is, after all, not usually why they sought therapy.

Ironically, following the usual phase-based structure, in which focus is kept on parent-child and child-child issues during the first two phases and adult couple themes are shelved until the intimacy phase, does not function well for many blended family cases. The couple's resilience as a couple may prove not strong enough. Additionally, the new partner's emotional commitments to the children, and to raising them, at this point may not be particularly deep.

A slightly altered approach is therefore recommended. One tries, delicately, to air couple themes early on. The therapist might attempt this even in the resolution phase if it appears possible. Again, the therapist must do this delicately. For example, she might inform the couple about some of what the research shows concerning blended families. Permission can then be asked for the therapist to pose related questions to each of the partners. With luck this discussion can partially reveal where each of them currently stands regarding the relationship: what is going well, what less well, and so on. For instance, does the new partner often feel that he or she must compete with the children for the biological parent's affection and time? If so, this theme deserves early therapeutic attention. Such an issue can be explored in a tentative fashion during the resolution or extension phases and then worked with in more depth, if possible, in the intimacy phase.

A separate matter has to do with family rituals and routines: mundane, daily rituals such as the typical scenario for meals, as well as the more complex practices belonging to birthdays, holidays, and vacations. A blended family has to find its way in giving a shape to such rituals. Often new shapes must be found, or shapes at least partially new, as the nonbiological parent will bring a sensibility and style different from the departed parent.

Some blended family parents will already have given this dimension the conscious attention it deserves. But others will not have thought much about it or will have underestimated how important it is in the lives of the children. In these cases, it is appropriate for the therapist to introduce the topic. One usually productive way is to have the children share with the parents their feelings about the various rituals, or lack of them. Normally this is a theme that can be left aside until the extension phase.

As I noted earlier, nothing about phasic model sequencing is fixed. The phases should serve as a rough guide only. There are plenty of exceptions. Sometimes things must be arranged differently because of the type of system, as just explained. Sometimes there are other reasons for altering how the therapy is organized.

CHAPTER ELEVEN

Opening Moves: The First Interview

• •

In the last chapter I described a general level of case conceptualization. In this chapter and the next one I go into more detail about the therapy process itself. I discuss how the techniques covered in previous chapters are selected, organized, and put to practical work.

Every therapist has her own style and format for a first interview.[1] Here I describe a structure I have developed over the years, and I highlight what to do with the children.

WHO SHOULD COME?

Like most family therapists, I prefer that all the family members attend the first session. Everyone who lives together is invited. This might include a grandmother or an uncle. It might include an aunt who, strictly speaking, doesn't live under the same roof but often is physically present.

However, I don't take a hard line on this. If the mother and father insist on coming without the children, or they strongly want to bring one child but not a second one, I go along. In the session I try to learn how they came to this decision.

Some therapists prefer to invite a wider social network. Close friends may be encouraged to attend, or people from the referral source, such as school, social service, or probation personnel. I appreciate the reasons for this choice,[2] but my preference is first to meet with the family by themselves. I can then contact others involved with the family for a second or third session if this seems warranted.

Having the family alone for the initial interview provides a better opportunity to begin a rapport with the child or children. Realistically, the more adults in the room, the more the children fade into the background. Also, if other professionals take the trouble to come, their time needs to be used well. This almost always means a quick plunge into a "problem-saturated discourse" (White & Epston, 1990). That can get some important things accomplished, but it gives little chance to create the atmosphere one needs for making good contact with the children.

ARRANGING THE OFFICE

The arrangement of the room deserves some thought. I place the chairs beforehand in a circle. Ideally, there are different-sized chairs for different-sized people. A pile of large pillows sits in one corner of the room. My desk is in another corner. There is a small table, of child-friendly dimensions, in another corner.

Go easy on toys. Your office shouldn't look like a toystore. Have a few available that are appropriate to the ages of the children who are coming. A Lego set in a closed box is always a good bet. Drawing pads, with colored pencils and crayons, might lie on the table. Several children's books can be visible. These might be stacked on the floor or placed on a low shelf. Dolls, stuffed animal puppets, and games can be kept out of sight but on hand in a large closed bag or in a closet, ready to be brought out later if there is a need.

Naturally, in many institutions the just-described ideal is not possible. The room may be cramped, the furniture barely adequate. There may be no toys apart from what you carry in. So you make do. You can easily enough bring, as a minimum, a large drawing pad and crayons, a few dolls, and some animal puppets.

Finally there is the matter of snacks and drinks. Don't underestimate the importance of this if children are going to be present. Have something around. The children will appreciate it, and you will run little risk of having your sessions disrupted by a hunger meltdown. Put the snacks somewhere out of sight, however. They will be eaten during a break.

The moment the family walks in, your younger guests are going examine this new terrain very closely. The more they like what they see, the more disposed they will be to cooperate with you later down the line.

THE FIVE STAGES

I prefer, when possible, a long first session; between 90 minutes and 2 hours is typical. I follow a rough format of five stages. It is not a rigid structure. At times, for various reasons, the interview takes quite another course. If only a shorter amount of time is available, I might take two separate sessions to cover the five stages.

Stage 1: Acquaintance

In the earlier years of family therapy there was a lot of talk about "joining."[3] It was suggested that you dedicate a first half hour or so to making a connection with the family. The thought was that this would help set up a good working relationship between therapist and family.

I think this is a good idea. My emphasis, however, is on three additional aspects. One is making sure that the children of the family experience, right from the start, that their voices will be heard. The other is the uncovering of useful information. A third is discovering resources. For this opening stage it is useful to plan 20 to 30 minutes.

The family arrives. You greet each member in turn. Consider squatting or bending down to speak to small children so that you are at their eye level for at least this one time. Greet babies too, and take a moment to look at them.

Naturally you are already using your eyes and ears with full attention. Half the purpose of this first interview is to give you opportunities to watch and listen. What are the movements, gestures, voice tones, and rhythms? How do the family members negotiate these opening events? They have to move themselves from waiting room to office. How do they choose chairs, get settled in? How do they relate to you at the same time? A vast number of nonverbal signals are traded back and forth. What do you notice?

While everyone seats himself, I usually remain standing. The family members choose their own seats. Nothing is said about where each person should sit. There is a chair for each person. A child might prefer to sit on a parent's lap. I then take a chair that no one else has chosen and decide where to place it. I typically do not place my chair between the parents or in the middle of the children, although later in the session I may have reason to move to another position. When a family member is not present in the first session, I place an empty chair to represent this person. I might ask the family where best to put this chair.

Next, standing up and walking around, I explain how the space in the therapy room is to be used. I show the play space and invite the children to leave their chairs so they can see it. I point out drawing materials, toys, and books. I then encourage the children to come back and sit again. I clarify to everyone that the space where the chairs are is a place to talk and listen.

I add that the other spaces are fine to use for playing, but that toys and the like should not be brought over to the speaking area.

The idea here, of course, is to define some boundaries. This is not only to keep the play activities from interfering with the talk exchange, but also to make explicit to the children that they, too, have a designated place (the chairs) where they are welcome to join in the talk exchange, if they wish.

Who ought to maintain these boundaries during the session? The parents, not the therapist. This is a critical point. Children often do not respect the "designated areas." Some children may even start right in with provocative challenges, bringing toys to their chairs and beginning to play. When this happens, the therapist should ask the parents to ask the child to either go play in the play area or join us without toys in the talk area.

Why the parent? First, because this will give you information about the parent's skills at setting limits, as well as the child's ability to accept them. Second, it establishes from the start that the therapist's role is not to replace the parent or to demonstrate parenting. The therapist's support is given in other ways. If parents cannot seem to maintain this boundary, I empathize with them about how hard it is. If necessary, I ask that the parent ask the child to play quietly in the talking area. I do not want to embarrass the parent at this early point or delve into exploring the limit-setting difficulties.

Before turning to the first topic—what the family members have in mind about why they have come—I give a preview of what will happen in the session. I say that I am going to ask about what has brought them here. After that I will ask each person something about himself and also about his family so I can get to know them all a bit. Then we will explore what they would like to be different in their family. We might even try something different right there in the session. Decisions about whether it makes sense for them to come back again, and when, will come at the end. All of this will take around an hour and a half to two hours. At some point in the middle there will be a pause so that the children can have something to eat and drink. For the parents, a cup of tea or coffee will be offered.

After the preview, I start in with a set of questions. For this round, I recommend that the therapist begin with the children. This signals to the children that you are interested in them and intend to listen to what they contribute. Questions such as the following are useful:

- What do you know about why you are here today?
- What do you think we will do here today?
- Who told you about coming today?
- What do you remember about what they told you?

The purpose of this is to verify that the children understand, at least a little, the purpose of the family having come. If it turns out that no one has spoken to them about it, the therapist can request that the parents explain it to them now.

One then continues with the adults. Here are typical questions:

- What would you like help with?
- Can you briefly tell me what we could talk about here that would be helpful for you?

It is important at this moment to keep the discussion short. The impulse of the parents will be to initiate a lengthy account of the problems at home. The therapist should politely deflect this, explaining that in a few moments there will be plenty of time to go into the details, and for now she just wants a chance to get to know something about the family members and family apart from the problems they have been struggling with. Sometimes a family member may not resist holding off on describing

175

problems. In these cases, I empathize with the family member's concern and then gently redirect the therapy again, as is illustrated in the following case.

> Mr. Tyson was a foreman at a construction company. He had taken time off from work to come to the session with his wife and his two sons, Joseph, age 9, and Aidan, age 12. Mr. Tyson told me that he wanted to get down to business right away and tell his view of the problems Joseph was having. Mr. Tyson did not want to present himself or have me take time to get to know the family.
>
> I responded by saying that I was glad that his son's problems were so important to him that he had taken time out of his busy schedule, and that I appreciated the fact that he was a person who did not like to waste time. I then restated that I could be more efficient in tackling these problems if I first got to know the family briefly.

One turns then to the next round of questions, casting a wider net for a few minutes. The therapist wants to find out about personal strengths and unique individual qualities. Information about family values and strengths will also probably emerge. Any of this may prove useful later in the session.

As for whom to address first, a good rule of thumb is to begin this time with the parents. This reassures the family that you respect the age hierarchy. I typically ask who is the oldest parent and start with him or her. This usually elicits a laugh from the children. With the children, I begin with the oldest and work down to the youngest.

I generally spend about 3 to 4 minutes with each person. Exactly what to ask varies from family to family, from person to person, and from age level to age level. Here are a few typical questions to choose from (you wouldn't have time to ask every one of them):

- Tell me a little about yourself.
- What are some of the activities that you most enjoy doing?
- What are some of the things that you are most interested in?
- What do you do well?
- Tell me what is special about you.

Questions more appropriate for the adults might also include:

- Tell me about what you do.
- Tell me more about what you like or don't like about being a housewife and mother.
- What qualities do you bring to your job?
- What do you like about your job? What don't you like about it?
- Did you grow up around this area or do you come from somewhere else?

> With Mr. Tyson, I asked how many people worked underneath him. Ten people, he told me. I reflected that he was often responsible for others. I asked him if he liked this, and he said he did. He felt he was good at getting others to do their work well.
>
> Mrs. Tyson told me she was "just a housewife." I asked what she liked and didn't like about being a housewife, and about what she did well and what less well. I inquired about her interests and hobbies and about what she did before she had children.

Children might be asked:

- What school do you go to?
- What grade are you in at school?
- Which subjects do you like? Which don't you like?

177

- Who are your friends? What are their names?
- What do you like to play with your friends?
- What do you like to do when you are not in school?

It is important to pay attention not only to what the child says, but also to his developmental level, including (given his age) his social and contact skills.

With each person I try to include at least one question designed to elicit information about positive qualities and capacities.[4] Often for this I use circular questions too.

- What makes your mother special?
- What do you like about your brother?
- What do you appreciate about your daughter?
- Tell me about one of your proudest moments as Joseph's father.
- What are some of the qualities of your daughter that you most admire?
- If I knew your son/daughter, better, what qualities in him/ her would I most admire?

Circular questions have the advantage of eliciting two kinds of information at the same time: what the positive qualities of the family member are, and how the other family member represents those qualities. These questions also reveal a lot about the family's skills with messages of appreciation.

Circular questions can also work in the opposite direction:

- Tell me what other people in the family like about you.

This question may elicit a response along the lines of "I don't know." In that case, the therapist can usually move to a second family member, asking what they find special about the first person.

Another option is to choose one member of the family and then ask each other family member, in turn, to tell this person what he or she appreciates about the person or what is special about the person. Note that younger children are not likely to grasp abstract concepts such as "specialness" or "qualities." Make what you ask more concrete:

- What is your father especially good at doing?
- What does your brother do that you like?

Give special attention to what you begin to learn about the sibling relationships. (The importance of this dimension is discussed in Chapter 14). Start forming your impressions now.

One more step remains for the acquaintance stage. So far all the questioning has been about individuals. Now the therapist elicits some information about the family as a whole. This is done partly with more questions and partly via other means, which will be discussed shortly.

Questions about the family as a whole are designed to give a further glimpse into the family's beliefs, values, priorities, role divisions, and the like. Keep in mind the family's cultural background, religious orientation, and economic status, as this will help guide how you listen and choose questions. The concept of "family developmental stage" is also useful. A young couple whose first child was born a month ago faces one set of typical tasks and stresses. A family with two adolescent children and a third who has left for a university elsewhere in the country faces different ones.[5]

Naturally the age of the children, and their level of verbal skills, will influence what you ask. Again, younger children can speak most easily about behavior and concrete doings.

- What do you like to do together as a family?
- How do you spend your weekends?

179

- How do you spend evenings?
- Describe a typical school day from waking up to going to sleep.
- Tell me about your last vacation.
- How do you celebrate birthdays?

With children, one surefire topic is pets. And as a source of information, it is not to be underrated! Even when a family does not have any pets, inquiring about how they came to the decision not to have pets can create a lively discussion. Here are some questions you can ask:

- Do you have pets?
- What are their names?
- How did you choose their names?
- How old are they?
- How did you get them?
- Who takes care of the pets?
- Where do they sleep?

In this part of the session, I also like to begin mobilizing representational resources beyond linguistic ones. For example, I may introduce a brief art technique. This is always productive, regardless of the age of the child. Her level of engagement will rise at once.

One easy art technique for a first interview is to have all the children draw their home together, in what is called a "collective" art task (Chapter 4). I use this technique even with teenagers. It seems to be an excellent icebreaker. They seem especially to enjoy drawing their home; I ask where the computer and television are. The parents are asked to observe. As the drawing progresses, I ask to be shown where in the home the family members eat, do homework, play, conduct hobbies, and so on. I ask that names be written in the rooms where people sleep.

This kind of information can prove useful, as it did with the Tyson family.

> Mr. and Mrs. Tyson watched as Joseph and Aidan drew their apartment on a large paper together. The boys drew four rooms. Joseph put two doors in each room. He explained that both doors were always open, except for in "his mother's bedroom." I asked the boys to explain.
>
> She had her own bedroom, they said. Mrs. Tyson added, "I got tired of picking up my husband's clothes, so I decided to turn the living room into my bedroom." Inquiring more about this, I learned that the family now had no living room or space where they could all be together, except when they sat around the kitchen table.
>
> Joseph then wrote his father's name in the bedroom at the farthest end of the apartment from his mother's. The two boys' bedrooms were in the middle. Joseph remarked that he never slept alone, however. He either went to Aidan's bedroom and crawled into his bed, or went to his father's bedroom, where he slept on the floor.
>
> I asked where the television and computer were. Mr. Tyson told me that Mrs. Tyson had recently thrown the television in the garbage because she got fed up with the upsetting images being transmitted and because the boys did not respect the rules they made around watching television.

Another quick and useful art technique appropriate for a first session is to have each person, including the parents, draw something that he or she likes to do with the others. Or have them draw an event that they recently did together and that made them feel happy. Such "parallel" art products can then be explored systemically (see Chapter 4).

The Therapist and the Children

As you have probably noticed by now, one of the main goals during the acquaintance stage is to make the therapy child-inclusive from the outset. One of your primary tasks is to build a relationship between yourself and each child. This is not going to happen by itself; you have to make an effort. This is why I advocate spending the initial minutes on acquaintance instead of turning immediately to goals. Much more is going on than just the creation of a pleasant atmosphere. The children are finding out that they have a place here, that they will be responded to, and that their input counts.

At the same time, don't overdo it. Be careful about trying excessively to please the children. The last thing you want to do is push the parents to the background. You need cooperative adults on hand even more than cooperative children.

In the same vein, watch your behavior for any overtones of competition with the parents. A fine line must be maintained. You want to model appropriate adult-to-child relating, but try to do it in a way that doesn't suggest that you are demonstrating the superiority of your expertise. Keep an eye on how the parents appear to react to how you conduct yourself in relation to the children.

Next, there is the question of discipline, of setting limits and boundaries during the session. As already mentioned, it is best that you not take that over. Motivate the parents to take charge. This is empowering if you do it the right way. And even if a parent has difficulties in the execution, that is something with which you can work. The risk, if you take over the disciplining, is that you may send a message to the parent (and to the children too) that, in this area, she or he is incompetent. Similarly, it is better if a parent assumes responsibility for taking a child to the bathroom or quieting down a sibling fight.

Basic traffic control concerning who speaks and who listens is another matter. Mainly the therapist should take care of this. Above all, when a child is speaking, one must keep the adults and the siblings from interrupting or trying to speak for him. In these moments, keep in mind the usefulness of mirroring back a person's constructive intentions—for example, "Mrs. Jones, I know you want to help your son express himself better. I prefer that he try to tell me, even though it is hard for him."

Stage 2: Goal Determination

Now comes a shift. The struggles and difficulties that brought the family in are discussed. An increase in everybody's tension and anxiety is likely.

The first step is to clarify how the family came to contact you or your institution. Who referred them? Why? What other professionals have they seen about this issue? There are many different ways that families can land in a family therapy session. Perhaps friends or relatives who know you, the therapist, have sent them. Perhaps a professional—a doctor, teacher, or social worker—told them to get help. Perhaps one family member is already in individual therapy or seeing a psychiatrist for medication, and this person suggested family therapy.

Here are some typical questions:

- Whose idea was it to contact me [or our institution]?
- Did this person give you my name specifically, or just the name of the institution?
- What did this person tell you about me [or our institution]?
- Did this person who referred you suggest family therapy?
- If this person suggested family sessions, did she or he explain why?
- Has anyone in your family seen a psychiatrist or psychotherapist previously?
- Is anyone seeing a psychiatrist or psychotherapist now?
- Are you satisfied with the therapy?
- Have you seen any other kind of professionals for these problems before?

If other professionals have been involved with the family, you need to know:

- What did [the professional or team] tell you about the possible causes of these difficulties?
- What did he or she advise you to do?
- Did these suggestions help?

Often it is appropriate for you to contact the referral source yourself and to hear what they have to say.[6]

The next step is asking about the specifics of what the family wants to change—or, more specifically, about each person's representation of what most ought to change. It is worthwhile first to give a quick overview of what is coming. For example: "What I want to do now is to have each of you give your views on the problem that has brought you here—what you think is the problem, and your ideas about how it can be solved." More specific questions should then be directed initially to the parents. For example:

- Often in families people have different ideas of what could change in a family. What would you like to be different?
- What do you think are the problems in your family?
- How could your family change so that you feel happier (e.g., better, less upset, more comfortable) in your family?

These questions are rather hard for children 7 years or younger. The following classic intervention from child therapy is a good substitute[7]:

Imagine you are a magician and you have a magic wand. If you had a magic wand and could change three things in your family, what would you want to change?

I actually have a wand in the closet of my office. I give it to a child to hold when I use this intervention. It's corny, but children like it. Normally they take the game surprisingly seriously (as a way to make a serious statement, that is). This bit of theater with a real wand is also an old technique.

A "good fairy" version of De Shazer's (1994) miracle question is also possible:

> Imagine that there are good fairies. Now imagine that one of them visits your home while everybody is sleeping. This fairy can make miracles. She can make problems disappear. You wake up the next morning. What will be different after the good fairy has visited?

In one family, a 5-year-old answered the wand question with, "We would have a big bag of money appear so that Mommy and Daddy would not worry anymore." In another family with two children, ages 4 and 8, the eight-year-old responded that his wand would make his brother disappear! We got to central issues quickly in both these sessions.

Don't be in a rush, however, with these wand and magic fairy questions. Be prepared that a child's first response may be, "I don't know" or "Nothing." Encourage the child to think a little more about it. If still no definite reply is given, just move on. Pushing is likely to provoke the parents to try to answer for the child, or to interrupt in some other way to protect him.

After hearing the family members ideas about change, the therapist helps the family examine them more closely. Their representations of desired change often need to become more precise or more realistic. The family members also may or may not be in agreement about what they wish. Negotiation may be necessary.

In determining goals with the family members during this stage, I mostly follow De Shazer (1982, 1985, 1991, 1994) and Berg (1994). One wants to end up with goals that are specific, workable, and realistic. Also, goals stated in positive, not negative, terms are usually best.[8] Some concrete new behavior is usually defined in the goal. Broader, more open goals can be redefined into smaller, concrete change steps. This reshaping of the representations of goals normally doesn't take long, but it lays a critical groundwork.

It is common for family members first to express their goals in negative terms. "He hits everyone," says the father. The therapist can translate this type of statement back in positive terms: "So you would like him to express his anger in words." Or perhaps, "You would like him to learn to treat people in a more respectful way." A mother complains that her daughter's "tantrums are horrible when I say no to her." One could respond, "So you would like her to be able to accept 'no' in a calmer way." Worried about a son, the parents say, "No one likes him. He has no friends. No one wants to play with him." This could be restated as, "You wish that your son would be liked by other children, and that they would invite him to play with them."

The therapist also must notice whether some expectations are too high for the therapy. When this is the case, the therapist assists the family in breaking up these wishes into realistic smaller goals. For example:

> The Washton family had come to family therapy because of severe violence among their children. Gabby, 11 years old, asked me if maybe I could help stop the screaming and fighting with her sister, Janine, age 7, and brother, Nicholas, age 4. They bit and kicked her as well as took her personal belongings. She showed me the scars on her arms from being bitten. Her brother showed a scar on his leg from his sister Janine's bite. They agreed that the most important first step would be to stop the biting.

What about the interactions in the moment, which the therapist, of course, is attentively observing? Should one comment on these as well? For the most part my leaning is not to do that. I try to notice all I can. For example, how are the bodies positioned vis-a-vis another? What happens in the flow of gesture, movement and facial expression? More globally speaking, how does each parent respond to the children's ideas? Do the parents speak for the children? Which parent do the children turn to when they want assistance? What coalitions—the stronger and weaker connections, the inclusions, the exclusions—seem to exist?

Occasionally I will speak about something I see. But in a first interview, it is better, as a general guideline, not to share such observations. Family members can easily feel criticized and self-conscious when these observations are put into words. Some of this can be done in later sessions, when the family is more ready and when there is a specific reason to point out such phenomena.

Frequently a major intervention in a first interview is reframing. The goal is to offer an alternative representational perspective for a problem, a recent event, a personal characteristic of a family member, or the like. Reframing can be positive or negative. In the majority of situations, positive reframing is used. For example, a parent describes her child as too aggressive and demanding. The therapist might say to the parent, "Your child can really stand up for himself." Or, "Your daughter knows what she wants and is willing to fight for it."

Negative reframing can also be useful, however. It is best used when a serious problem or event has been minimized by the family.[9] In one case, a teenage boy hit a psychiatric nurse on the head with a glass soda bottle. She was hospitalized for a concussion. The parents later described what their son had done as a "normal, typical thing that boys do." His intent, they insisted, was not to hurt but to tease her. The therapist reframed the boy's actions as a serious act of violence toward a staff member. Eventually, during this session, the parents came to see the danger in what their son had done.

As noted earlier, family members may articulate multiple goals, some of which may be contradictory. Here, the next step is a negotiation among themselves. The therapist helps family members to set priorities and to work out a compromise. Any final decision needs to be made by the parents, of course. The children are encouraged to give input, but under normal circumstances they are not given a "vote."

At the same time, a child's wish or goal should not be fully ignored, especially if it is a realistic and appropriate goal (e.g., "that Daddy not yell at me so much"). Suppose the parents decide that the child's goal is not a first priority. Here the therapist can either suggest to the parents that perhaps the child's wish can be worked on at a later point in the therapy, or can find a way to have the child's goal integrated into the parents' preferred goals, if this is possible.

One family I worked with, for example, set goals concerning their anorexic teenage daughter. But in the first interview her younger sister, age 5, expressed a strong desire that the mother spend more time playing with her. The family decided to adopt this as an additional goal and to begin to do something about it at once. (I showed the mother play restoration.) Another possibility would have been to take up the younger sister's goal at a later point.

Some families, at this point, present a staggering list of genuine problems and crises. A therapist can easily feel overwhelmed. You must remember that you can't solve their problems. Maybe *they* can't solve all their problems. The more dramatic their situation, the more important it is to help them think through which difficulties need to be addressed first and which can wait.[10]

Once the family has agreed upon a goal, and the goal has been well-defined, the therapist can begin teasing out additional information about their thoughts and beliefs about it. For example:

- When did you each notice that the problem first began?
- Did you notice anything recently that could have made the problem worse?
- What are each of your ideas about what could have caused this problem?
- What solutions have you tried?
- Which solutions do you think helped? Which did not?
- What do you think would help the problem to go away?

It also may be that the problem behavior has been triggered by a recent event or change in the family. This is what I refer to as a "triggering cause." To discover possible triggering causes, it is important to explicitly ask whether there have been any recent changes in the family. A move? An illness? A death? Someone exiting from or entering the family? An economic change, such as a parent losing or changing his job? By recent, I mean in the past 2 years.

Mr. and Mrs. Rios came to therapy with their son, Miguel, age 11. After an initial getting acquainted, Mr. and Mrs. Rios described Miguel's "bad behavior." He had repeatedly threatened to kill his mother and he had recently tried to run away from home. As the discussion continued, Mrs. Rios mentioned that Mr. Rios had been very depressed and irritable at home.

I asked whether the family had been through any important changes during the last 2 years. Mr. Rios recounted that he was fired from his job a year ago and was still unemployed. The family had been forced to move because their apartment belonged to his employer. They were facing yet another move at the end of the school year, in 2 months. Miguel's angry outbursts began during the months following Mr. Rios's job loss. They had gotten worse since Mrs. Rios had returned to work full-time to help support the family.

Scaling questions can also be useful during this stage, though admittedly they are not essential. I like scaling questions because they create new representations, as well as new semantics for those representations. An old staple of behavior therapy, scale-related interventions have been developed in creative ways in the solution-oriented therapies.

I utilize scales with both adults and children, and the way I bring them in is very similar to Berg (1994) and De Shazer (1994). Typically, a family member is asked to quantify her own perceptions. The therapist asks the client to imagine a scale of 0 to 10, with 10 signifying the highest imaginable point and 0 the lowest. For example: "Ten is as angry as you can possibly be, and 0 is you are feeling no anger at all." Then the therapist asks the family member to situate himself on the scale. "So right now, where are you?" The reply will be something like "at 7" or "somewhere around 3 or 4."

What exactly do these numbers signify? In a sense, the therapist will never know. What is operative are other factors. First and foremost, scaling questions help foster better discriminatory capacities. Instead of just sensing "I am angry," the family member learns to appreciate nuances. Second, the family member learns to communicate about these experiential nuances. Third, she learns a new way to represent a change process. Now she can begin to think about, for example, "What might help me bring my anger down from an 8 to a 5?" In this way, scaling questions generate a stronger sense of agency. Moreover, they have additional advantages when children are present, which I will discuss shortly.

Scales can be useful in many contexts. Following are three which I often turn to.

The first is for evaluating the severity of the problem. I call this "the state of the problem scale." The therapist might, for example, ask, "On a scale of 0 to 10, with 0 being that the problems that brought you here are completely solved, and 10 being that the problem is at its worst, where would you put things right now?"

The second is for evaluating the level of optimism about whether or not the problem can be improved or made to disappear. I call this the "hope scale." One version goes like this: "On a scale of 0 to 10, with 10 being that you are fully hopeful that this problem can disappear, and 0 being you believe that the problem will never get better, where would you put yourself today?"

The third type of scale represents the degree of effort a family member is ready to invest. I call this the "motivation scale." For example, "On a scale of 0 to 10, with 10 being you are ready to work really hard to reach this goal, and 0 that you are so tired or fed up that you have no energy to work on the problem, where would you put yourself today?"

Scales are also one of the best ways I have found to mobilize young children to connect more strongly with the therapy process. Some changes are usually necessary, however. Scales basically are a form of spatial metaphor. For children, one can make the publically-shared representation *directly spatial,* the way a thermometer is spatial.

For example, for a "state of the problem" scale, the therapist can draw a line on a flip chart with an arrow at one end. The therapist puts a 0 at one end of the line and a 10 at the other. The child can then be helped to choose a metaphoric symbol for each end of the scale, and to draw these in. She might pick a smiling face for 10 and an unhappy face for 0. (Some children choose animals for the ends of the scale. Some like colors.) Next she writes in the numbers between 0 and 10. Finally I ask the child, "Where is the problem now?" or "Where are you now?" and have her mark that point on the scale.

A piece of rope laid on the floor can be used in a similar manner. Each end of the rope represents one end of the scale. The intermediate numbers are not bothered with. The child is asked to place himself on the scale by walking to the point on the rope where he feels the problem or problem state is at the moment.[11]

With both adults and children, scales can also be used to have the person guess what she thinks others might say about where she is. Perhaps a child has been exploring a scale "where 10 means having very big problems in school and 0 means having no problems in school." The child has already shown her own sense of where she stands. The therapist might then ask, "Where would your teacher or mother, father, . . . friends etc. put your school problems?" In other words, scaling questions can be circular,

Plenty of other maneuvers can be done with goal representations, scaling questions, and the like. In a first session, however, one has to budget the time. Goal representations will be further addressed in coming sessions. What is now more urgent, in my approach, is to strengthen the level of commitment and involvement throughout the system as a whole.

Stage 3: Goal Exploration

So far I have been proceeding, for the most part, along classic brief therapy lines. But at stage 3 with my approach there now comes a fork in the road. A typical solution-oriented continuation would be to begin exploring exceptions to the problem. "When are things better with the problem?" "What is going on then that makes it better?" "How could you do more of that, or create conditions like that, at other times?"

Exploring exceptions is a powerful, effective technique, and I use it at certain times (see the discussion of stage 4). However, one faces a major potential difficulty with it if one is working with a family with children. Once the therapist and the parents start heading in this direction, the children usually tune out. Their interest wanes, and they become bored. Suddenly the dialogue turns into an affair of the adults.

This is true almost universally with smaller children. But even an older child may not stay on board. A hyperactive older child, for example, will rarely bother to follow the twists and turns of exception-discourse.[12]

For these reasons, my model moves at this point to techniques more likely to activate the interest of the children. I see this as an essential consolidation of what has been done up to now.

The best such techniques for this next step are dramatization, systemic art techniques, and externalization (see Chapters 2, 4, and 5, respectively). These three techniques have something in common. Both dramatization and art techniques move beyond language, mobilizing alternative representational resources. Externalization easily can do the same. One can mix an art technique with it.

The therapist needs to understand her purpose here. The point is not to amuse the children or to show that the therapist can be nice to them. The aim is to engage the children more thoroughly in the therapeutic process of change itself. The best way to accomplish that is to alter and enrich their representations. This will heighten the chance of new modes of systemic cooperation at home.

For a first-interview dramatization, you want a specific, concrete example of the main problem or symptom. It is easier when the family chooses an example that has occurred as recently as possible. This way their memories are fresher.

Systemic art techniques are also an easy means of helping children participate in the first interview. As already mentioned, an art technique can often bring out unexpected, valuable information. One can propose a drawing of the home or have family members draw something they like to do together, for example. During this stage, an art technique can also help to further illuminate each family member's representations of the problem, of the context, and the like. One might explore how things were before the problems came or what the future will look like once the goals are reached. This information can then be incorporated into the family's exchange.

Externalization techniques in the first interview allow the therapist and family to immediately establish a discourse about the problem that is free of blame and criticism about the child's personhood. As was described in Chapter 5, the key is to have the family choose a label, a new name, for the presenting problem that frees the child of responsibility. This name portrays the problem as something "external" to the child. Once it has been chosen, the therapist can use this label to get the family talking about the consequences of the problem, the history of the problem, the extent of the problem, exceptions when the problem does not happen, and so on.

The advantage of dramatization, art techniques, and externalization is that they are highly active procedures. However, for some families so fast a start is not appropriate. In these cases, I open up a slower-moving conversation about the selected goal, about relevant background information, and the like. I do this even at the price of losing the involvement of younger children.

I take this approach with families that seem particularly scared, rigid, secretive, or overwhelmed by some current crisis. I also do it when their motivation for having come is extremely low or almost nonexistent (such as with a mandated family, for example). In all such instances, if I manage to get as far as having a well-defined goal on the table, I choose to be highly cautious about what comes next. It may make more sense to keep the pressure on the parents as low as possible.

Another reason to forego such techniques has to do with the type of goal and the related problem. Substantially more factual information may be needed, for example. If, for example, the family's problem has to do with a medical issue or a recent trauma or loss; or if there are multiple problems so interconnected that discussing one necessitates discussion of two or three others as well, the therapist will need to spend plenty of time accumulating details.[13] One may have to go over the known psychiatric disturbances of several family members, or hear the story of where and why the family has changed residences four times over the last 2 years.

If one does opt for a slower-moving discussion, it is still possible at moments to bring in circular questions. If one hears that the father has recently changed his job, is very stressed, and often comes home late, the therapist could ask the 8-year-old daughter, "What have you noticed that is different about your dad since he changed jobs?" Or, "How has your dad's being away so much changed how your mom is?" There can be opportunities, in other words, to draw the children into the conversation.

THE PAUSE

When to pause? Do it whenever you think fits, but if there has been no strong reason to take the pause earlier, a good time to do it is between the *goal* exploration stage and the *change* elaboration stage 4. By now, smaller children may have to go to the bathroom and may be hungry.

It is also often the best time for your needs, which are, at this point, to be thinking about how to help the family make a specific new step in the direction of change. This is the theme of the next stage.

Some therapists do first interviews (and perhaps even later sessions) with the support of a colleague team who watches from behind a one-way mirror.[14] If that is how you work, this is a logical moment to consult with your colleagues (the other most fruitful time is after stage 4).

To introduce the break, I usually say something like: "Now we will take a 10-minute break. There are drinks and snacks, if you would like your children to have them. Feel free to stay right here in the room or to step outside."

A therapist working with a consulting team might want, of course, to announce a longer pause. If you are working solo, on the other hand, it can be interesting to pay attention to the family interactions during the pause. How do they go about sharing the food and drinks? What other events, if any, happen?

Occasionally after the pause I talk about what I have observed, but only when it fits with the goal with which we are already working. This was the case with the Washton family, introduced earlier in this chapter.

In the first session with the Washton family, Janine (7) had been described as selfish and as jealous of Nicholas (4) and Gabby (1). During the break I saw Janine open the package of cookies I had put out. Before taking any herself, she offered some to Nicholas. His reaction was to grab the package out of her hand and run to the other corner of the room with it. Janine strode over and took it back. Nicholas began crying.

Mr. and Mrs. Washton were talking with each other in the waiting room and did not seen what happened. Returning to the therapy room, they discovered Nicholas crying. Both started criticizing Janine for not sharing. They told me this was exactly what she always did at home. Janine protested.

I focused on what had just happened. I asked Janine to do a brief dramatization showing her version of what happened with the cookies. Nicholas refused to participate, so Janine played both herself and her brother. She showed how she offered him the cookies and he grabbed them and ran away. I then verified the accuracy of what she demonstrated in her dramatization. Janine spoke openly about how she felt unfairly treated when this sort of thing happened. The parents listened and began to understand.

STAGE 4: CHANGE ELABORATION

Here you keep the momentum going. If you brought in an active technique during the goal exploration, you can usually continue with it. If you have been working with dramatization, you can suggest that the family now experiment with dramatizing a new behavior (see Chapter 2). If you were working with art techniques, you might suggest that the family make a drawing of how they would like things to be in the future (see chapter 4). If you have used externalization, you can focus still more closely upon how they can combat the problem the next time it appears (see Chapter 5). During this stage the atmosphere often becomes markedly optimistic. Playfulness and humor may easily emerge.

This stage tends to unfold more rapidly. Often around 15 minutes is long enough. If time constraints are not particularly tight, you can spend more time on these techniques. For example, if you are doing a future dramatization, you might have the family begin with one person's version and then try a second person's. Another interesting procedure is to have everybody tell his or her notion of how things could be and then put these ideas together a single combined version. If, on the other hand, time is short, a single possible future dramatization may be best.

In general, the therapeutic purposes here are (1) to make the representations of change still more detailed and vivid, (2) to augment motivation, and (3) to continue to keep the children closely connected with everything that is emerging. You want to stay as systemic as possible.

It is also worthwhile, to the extent you can, to let the family members be the ones who generate the ideas about change. This point has been discussed in earlier chapters. The more it is they who come up with the ideas, the more likely they will be to implement them at home.

An exception to having the family find their own solutions is when the therapist perceives a need to introduce behavioral or cognitive techniques, such as setting limits, making rules, using a point system, or working with play restoration. The therapist can propose such steps by saying that they have been found effective by other families for the same type of problem and also have (in most instances) solid research support.

The restoration of play can also sometimes be used to explore change during a first session. This can be especially productive with young children.

If you chose *not* to use active techniques during the goal exploration stage and instead stayed with a more straightforward discussion of the goal, it is best to stay in this mode during the stage of change elaboration. You reflect together about what one or more initial steps toward change might be. Future-oriented questions can be helpful (Selekman, 1997):

- What could be a first, small step each of you might take to do things differently?
- What do you think you could change that would help your daughter reach her goal?

Circular future-oriented questions can be brought in too.

- What would your sister say you could do as a step toward helping you both fight less?
- What would your son say you would be doing differently the day after the good fairy visited?

An investigation of exceptions to the negative behavior is also possible. Both circular questioning, and the examination of exceptions, are almost always feasible as long as a family has first managed to agree about a specific goal.

STAGE 5: CONCLUDING

In this stage the therapist does some summarizing, makes treatment arrangements, and perhaps suggests a task to do between sessions. Often these items can be covered in 10 to 15 minutes.

A good initial step in this stage is to share your own impressions and evaluation. It is helpful to begin with the strengths and positive qualities you have discovered in the family. For example, the family might first be addressed as a group and given a general compliment. Then you might turn to each family member and mention one strength you have observed in this person—a strength that will help the family to move in a direction of change.

A brief reiteration of the family's goals and priorities can also be important. As before, goals are stated concisely, concretely, and, so far as possible, in behavioral terms.

If a family has come in with multiple problems or with more than one goal, they normally will have already clarified their priorities by this point. However, in some cases the engagement and change exploration stages will have raised more questions, and everything may look different after having taken a closer look at practical realities. If this has occurred, take a moment to review the situation, and, if warranted, to introduce another short negotiation.

Sometimes the therapist will also want to recommend that, in addition to continuing the family sessions, the family seek some additional type of evaluation or consultation—a neurological evaluation of a child, for example, or further testing of speech or intellectual development. These suggestions are brought in now.

This is also one of the most common times for a parent to ask the therapist for her opinion about what caused the problem. Each therapist will have her own way to deal with that question. I tend to be very hesitant about offering any specific hypotheses concerning etiology, systemic meaning, and the like, as the family members can easily end up feeling blamed. If I give an answer, usually I simply offer a small palette of alternative possible explanations. I then shift quickly back to a focus upon the prospect of change.

I do encourage families at this point. I emphasize that their goals are reachable. I try also to be realistic in how I phrase this. I mention the hard work it will take, the step-by-step process, and the need to accumulate a series of small changes in order to arrive at a bigger change.

Then we take up the specifics of a therapeutic contract: where to meet in the future, how often, and the like. (I discuss the issues of session frequency and site options in the next chapter.) The fee is discussed if a therapist's work context is such that families pay him directly. I give an estimation of what I think would be a reasonable number of sessions. Often I suggest three to four sessions for the specific defined goal, with part of the fourth session being dedicated to evaluating together if the therapy has helped the family move toward their goals. If we decide at that time to continue, we can set up more sessions. If only a limited number of sessions is permitted due to limitations established by the treatment institution or insurance provider, this too can be discussed now.

Although I quite often continue the therapy after the fourth session (for example) has been reached, I do prefer that a first short block of therapeutic work be openly defined and agreed upon. The goal is transparent, and the number of sessions in this block is clear. Carefully delimiting the scope of this first phase of work has several advantages. It communicates an optimistic message: that the family probably *can* attain their agreed-upon goal. It communicates a "hard work" message: that progress, and what has to be done at home to achieve it, is expected. And it underlines that any continuation of the therapy, if that occurs, will result from the family's own decision and wishes.

Often the thorniest part of working out a contract is settling on who should participate in the sessions. In the early years of family therapy, fathers were often very resistant to participating. Fortunately this has changed over the years, but it still can be a sticking point for some families.

Reluctance may also be expressed about the idea that the "other" children, those not labeled as having a problem, be brought in too. The therapist must be prepared with good grounds to offer. I mention reasons like the following:

- All the other children are also affected by the problems, and they need to be able to express how this affects them.
- Each child's perceptions and ideas can be very helpful to me, as they all can offer another perspective in addition to yours as parents.

Whether or not all family members should attend all of the sessions is of course a point of dispute among family therapists. Everyone has his own position. Mine is fairly flexible. I openly state my preference to have all family members present, and as often as possible. Nevertheless in practice I am ready to work with whomever shows up. If someone is consistently absent, I bring that up as something to be examined in the therapy.

Sometimes for a special purpose, however, I might suggest that the parents come alone for a session or two, as I discussed earlier, or that a child come alone with a parent (see Chapter 12). At other times, additional people who are closely involved with the family might be invited to join in, such as a grand-parent who frequently takes care of the children, or an impor-tant aunt or uncle, or a professional from another institution.

In some cases I get the impression that a family member in attendance at the first session is reluctant to participate in future sessions but is not openly admitting this. In these situations, I might explore this with indirect questions. For example:

- Who inside or outside the family is hopeful, in a positive way, about these family sessions being a help to you?
- Who inside or outside the family has negative expectations about the family sessions being a help?

The other last step is frequently to suggest a task. I may say that during the course of the therapy I expect the family at times to do "homework." I explain that this kind of "homework" is dif-ferent than that at school. We will decide together upon specific new actions to experiment with at home. This will give them the opportunity to profit to a maximum degree from the family sessions. Today too, I add, I may provide us with an opportunity to choose such a task.[15] (Sometimes I give no task. Usually this is when a family is unsure about whether they want to continue and needs more time to think it over.)

Most typically, possible tasks will have emerged during the change elaboration stage, when the family came up with spe-cific ideas of how things might be different. Now the therapist's role is to refer again to those ideas and to help the family decide what an appropriate, realistic first step might be. With respect to organizing a task in a first interview, however, two further pieces of advice are worth mentioning.

First, keep it simple. A problem with first interview tasks is that you don't yet know this family very well. You have little practical feeling for how well they are likely to manage with an implementation of new behavior. One can be fooled. A seemingly highly motivated family may have more hidden resistance than you think. A family who appears to show little drive toward change during the session may later, at home, work diligently at doing something different. So the safe thing is to assist the family in finding a task as uncomplicated and straightforward as possible. The therapist is better off not pressuring himself or the family to be overly creative.

Second, pay attention to how you communicate about the task. Check that what you say is really being understood by the family members. You might have the children repeat what they think is to be done. Or you might have the parents explain the task to the children. I have done a lot of live supervision of first interviews, and I have often seen therapists explain tasks with what they think is crystal clarity, only to later discover that the family did not understand what was meant.

To summarize, a rough time schedule might look like this:

Acquaintance stage, 20 minutes

Goal determination stage, 10 minutes

Goal exploration stage, 30 minutes

Pause, 10 minutes

Elaborating Change, 15 minutes

Concluding, 10 minutes

Thus, a first session will last from 1 hour and 30 minutes to 2 hours.

These are not meant as rigid guidelines. Often one of these stages may need more time, or will proceed more quickly. You only need stay with this outline if it fits. Should the session end and, for whatever reason, you have not gone through all the stages, then in the following session you simply pick up where you left off.

When a first session goes well, family members leave with a sense of optimism. They have clearer pictures of what they want, what they have to do to get it, and how, systemically, they have to cooperate to make this happen. Their sense of their own strengths and resources is clearer. Hopefully they also feel that they have been treated with respect, support, and transparence.

NOTES

1. Much has been written on how to conduct first interviews. For good discussions see Carr (2000), Cierpka (1996), and Berg (1994).

2. See, for example, Carr (2000).

3. See Minuchin and Fishman (1981).

4. Freeman et al. (1997) have used similar questions, although later in the session. However, they asked only about the positive qualities of the child with the problem, and not about the parents or other siblings.

5. See Walsh (1994), Carr (2000), and Schneewind (1991) for overviews of family developmental levels.

6. See Carr (2000) for a good account of dealing with referral issues.

7. No one I have been in contact with seems to know the origin of this clever technique in the child therapy tradition. Virginia Satir seems to be one of the first to import it into family therapy.

8. De Shazer and Berg have insisted that goals *always* be couched in positive terms. I have a slightly different picture concerning this, as explained shortly.

9. See Minuchin and Fishman (1981) concerning the occasional usefulness of negative reframing.

10. Referring agencies and institutions may also have an agenda that needs to be taken into account. See Berg (1994) and Carr (2000) for a good discussion.

11. This technique was developed by the team of Norddeutsches Institut für Kurzzeittherapie in Bremen, Germany (Cabie & Isebaert, 1997).

12. He will do better with it, however, when he himself is being asked about variations in his own behavior and experiential states.

13. For instance during an initial session with one family who had two children and a father with an ADHD diagnosis, I had to devote

most of the session to an extensive discussion of the implications of ADHD.

14. As was done for example by the Mental Research Institute team in Palo Alto (Weakland & Fisch, 1992), and Selvini-Palazolli et al. in Milan (1978), and is still done by Andersen (1991) using a "reflecting team", in the Ackerman Institute group in New York (Papp, 1983), and the Milwaukee group (De Shazer, 1985, 1994).

15. See Carr (2000) for an excellent discussion about homework.

CHAPTER TWELVE

Continuing

● ●

What do you do after the first session? From the standpoint of the present method, three principles are recommended: 1. Give a high priority to homework follow-up. 2. Maintain a clear focus, session by session, on well-defined goals. 3. Continue to keep the children actively engaged. When these guidelines are carefully followed, the family is most likely to receive maximum help at minimum time and cost.

For continuing sessions (all meetings subsequent to the first interview) I have a loose structure that I usually follow. There are plenty of exceptions, naturally, for various reasons. But often this structure provides an organized flow to what one does.

The typical parts or stages of the session are: (1) *warming up*, (2) *change inquiry*, (3) *goal determination*, (4) *goal exploration*, (5) *change elaboration*, and (6) *concluding*. Mostly this parallels the sequence suggested for a first interview. However, the warming up stage replaces the acquaintance stage, and the change inquiry stage, which has to do with asking about home tasks, is new.

I normally plan on 90 minutes for such a session. If there are institutional or insurance constraints and the session must be shorter (say, 50 minutes), that can be done. One trims and economizes in each stage, while keeping the same overall organization.[1]

The usual occasion for jettisoning this structure is when the family arrives in a crisis. Perhaps there has been a death, or an outbreak of violence, or an alcoholic parent has had a relapse. The entire session will probably have to be given over to dealing with this new situation, forgetting niceties such as warming up and a homework discussion. Even in these cases, however, one does try to arrive at a consensus by the end of the session about immediate concrete goals for the family to tackle in the coming days.

Similarly, families may sometimes bring up a new theme that preoccupies them even if no crisis is involved. Perhaps the mother has just been offered a new job that involves working full-time, and she wants to discuss the impact on the family before she accepts it. In these situations, how to organize the session should be negotiated. The family members and the therapist might agree that this matter should take precedence and that all or most of the session should be devoted to it.

In most cases, though, roughly following the stage structure outlined here works well. Many professionals who have worked with me have found it useful.

WARMING UP

Many adults are perfectly capable of sitting down and starting right in on their therapy agenda for the day. Children, however, generally need at least a short transition.

A few minutes of light social exchange can accomplish this. The therapist might comment on a toy a child has brought, or a runny nose, or even how cold the weather is. If the therapist knows that some sort of event occurred during the week, such as a birthday party, an athletic competition, or a school test, she can ask how it went. The idea is to convey that you take an interest in the family members, separate from their struggles and problems.

Normally this stage is extremely short. Five minutes is enough. If you discover that 10 minutes have passed and you are still in a conversation of this kind, take the initiative to move on.

CHANGE INQUIRY

This step is a crucial core element of the method I am proposing. Assuming that one or more homework tasks were agreed upon in the last meeting, that task is now thoroughly discussed. One of the biggest problems I have run into when doing supervision is an underestimation on the therapist's part of the value of this exploration.

It is a good idea, however, to open up this stage not by asking about the *task* but rather by asking about the *change*. For example:

- Have you seen any changes, even small ones?
- What is new since the last time we met?
- Have you noticed anything that is different since the last session?
- Give me examples of any changes you've seen. Anything, even very little changes.
- What did you do as a family that seemed to help since the last session?

I ask about the change rather than about the task because change may have occurred even if the family didn't do the task. By beginning with these change questions, you increase the likelihood of getting news about any actual shifts.

Notice too the emphasis upon "even small changes." This reflects a couple of aspects of how families generally tend to change. First, an ongoing change process often begins with rather minute, seemingly unimpressive new steps. To keep the momentum going, it is critical to support these. Second, there is an important distinction between the *reality* of change and the family's *representations* of change. They are not the same. And there can be discrepancies between them. Usually the discrepancy is that although the family is indeed changing, on a representational level they have not yet noticed it. Hence the purpose of such exploration is not just to bring the information (about a change) to the therapist, but also to bring the information to the family members themselves, in the sense of conscious, accurate discrimination, together with appropriate language for them.

Scaling questions can fit in well, too:

- How have things been during dinner? Remember that scale where 10 means a nice dinnertime and 0 is an awful dinnertime? Where on the scale has dinner mostly been?
- Last time we met you said that Jason was having tantrums several times a day, and most days at a level of 9. How often have the tantrums been occurring lately? What level have they mostly been?

Needless to say, when the therapist asks about change without mentioning the task, the family may themselves bring up the task. This is fine. The therapist can discuss the task and the change together. But he must remain clear in his own mind that he needs independent information about both.

If the family does *not* mention the task, the therapist should bring it up after a few minutes. For example:

- Let's talk about the homework. How did it go?
- Who thought about doing the task?
- How did you decide whether to do the homework or not do the homework?

After this has been discussed, where do you go next? It depends upon what I call the "task outcome." There are four possible versions.

Task Done, Change in Progress

The most common outcome is "task done, change in progress." The family has done the task as planned, or a part of it, or a version of it reasonably close to what had been suggested. And some positive change has taken place, however small.

The therapist now explores both the doing of the task and (if this has not already just been discussed) the related change.

- How did you make the task work?
- What did you notice about what your father did that was different?
- How did you get yourself to do the task?
- Tell me some things that the task helped you to do differently.
- What was it like for you when the task worked?

Remember as well that the purpose of the questions is not just to support and reinforce. This is a significant form of work with representations and with discrimination capacities. The family is learning how to perceive the change process, as well as how to conceptualize it. Of course, reinforcement, which the therapist can provide through an occasional compliment, is desirable too.

Normally at least one question is directed to each individual family member, including all children. From a child you may get only a mumble. But often you will receive interesting input.

Task Done, No Change in Progress

A second outcome possibility is "task done, no change in progress." The family reports that they accomplished the task but it failed to help them. For example, the parents successfully implemented a reward system using points, but the 9-year-old girl's oppositional behavior remained as bad as ever.

A first step, of course, is for the therapist to question further. She must make absolutely certain that no change has occurred. Often a shift has indeed taken place, but it is so small that the family has not discerned it. Questions like those described earlier, which probe for slight degrees of change, are used.

Suppose, however, that the family's first impression seems right. If, after investigation, it appears that no shift has taken place, the therapist should explore why this result occurred. For example:

- I appreciate your trying the task, and your willingness to work on the problems. When you did the task, did you run into any difficulties?
- What are your ideas about why the task was not helpful?
- This task did not lead to change. What do you suppose could be a task that could make some slight difference?
- Do any of you have new ideas about what could help more than this task?

Normally questions like these elicit useful information. What is learned can then be used, later in the session, to design a new task. For example, the therapist may see that the problem needs to be renegotiated into still smaller steps, or that some other smaller goal should be tackled.

Task Not Done, Change in Progress

As mentioned earlier, sometimes change occurs even when the task was not done. This is a curious homework outcome, yet it does happen.

The Black family decided that, for a task, Amanda, age 7, and Lauren, age 6, would limit their arguing and fighting from 5 to 7 o'clock every day. Mr. and Mrs. Black also agreed not to intervene during this time unless one of the girls was getting hurt.

At the next meeting, the family reported that they forgot about the arrangement. The task was not done. However, the girls were fighting less and settling their fights more independently, without calling the parents to intervene.

Naturally, when this type of result occurs, the therapist gives the family positive feedback. But it is just as important to find out, in detail, what actually has transpired. For example:

- How do you explain that this positive change came about?
- I appreciate your decision as a family to do what fits you instead of what was decided on in the session. What led to your doing this?
- Maybe you have done something different that led up to this change—something you forgot about or did not think was worth talking about here. Think about this and tell me what you did differently.
- What did other family members see [Mom, Dad, child] doing differently?
- Did you think about your [son, daughter] differently since the last session? How?

As he pursues such questions, the therapist tries to tease out why the new shift took place. For example, perhaps something that happened during the previous session—an emotion, an increase in empathy, an inner decision—led to change at home. Doing the task would have been superfluous. Equally possible is that one or more family members created their own different task. This task may have been more appropriate. Or it simply may have been something the family member was motivated to do.

In some cases, merely *thinking* about the task leads to change by stimulating new representations. For example, a child may become more aware of his own agency after realizing that there are more options about how to act and react differently. Or, a family might begin to see what happens at home as systemic in nature rather than attributable to a single "problem" family member.

Task Not Done, No Change in Progress

A fourth potential homework outcome is "task not done, no change in progress." The family "forgot" to do the task, or there "was no time" for it. Or they simply decided not do it. And no positive shifts appear to have taken place with respect to their goals, even after an in-depth exploration about possible change has been conducted.

In this situation, you must first check for your own countertransference responses. Disappointment and annoyance are common. If these reactions are not well managed, they can lead to a very typical therapeutic error: to forego an exploration of why the task was not done and jump into negotiating a new, "better" task. Of course, discussion about a new task may prove appropriate later in the session, but not yet. What one needs to do now is slow down and acquire more information.

- Who in the family did not want to do the task? Who wanted to do it?
- How did you decide that this task would not be helpful for you?

A variant of "task not done, no change in progress" is that not only is there no positive change, but things have gotten even worse. A detailed exploration of this result should be undertaken.

- How do each of you explain that things have gotten worse?
- I am impressed that you have come back to another session even though things have gotten worse. What motivated you to come today?
- Are there any exceptions when the problem got a little better, although for a very short time?
- Can you think of anything you did before you began therapy that led to even the smallest change that you can begin to use again now?

Exactly what such questions tease out will be very different from family to family. Sometimes the explanation is that one family member (or more) wanted to do the task, but another (or more) did not. What took place was a power struggle, open or covert. The power struggle was resolved by ignoring the task.

Or, one family member (or more) may feel despair regarding the very idea of change. He believes, with profound hopelessness, that all roads are barred, that nothing can shift. Such a representation will easily undercut any impulses to try something new. The expected disappointment is avoided.

With some families the issue is more one of trust than hopelessness. For one reason or another the family, or one member, distrusts the therapist. This often reflects previous disappointing experiences with another therapist, social worker, or personnel from child protective services.

Once these reasons or feelings have been clarified, it is essential that the therapist help the family move beyond them, at least to the degree that the therapy can go forward. Plenty of times, however, the family decides that the original task suits them just fine. The barrier was not the task, but some other factor. In other instances a different task may be warranted. Usually the final decision about which task to try next is left for the last part of the session, however.

GOAL DETERMINATION

In the first interview, the determining of a goal, and subgoals, was an essential step. But that does not mean discussion of goals stops in subsequent sessions. The question of what the family wants from the therapy is regularly reviewed and revised.

There are two important reasons for this. One is to continue to strengthen each family member's sense of agency. The other is that the therapy process itself will give family members more clarity about what they desire. They are learning better who they are and what they want.

The therapy goals exist in a kind of hierarchy. Usually the first interview establishes an "umbrella" or main goal. For example, perhaps the consensus of the whole family is that Ian should become more cooperative and grown up. Typically this umbrella goal also was loosely divided into subgoals. These several subgoals might respectively reflect the separate domains in which "cooperative and grown up" behavior is wished for, for example at school as well as at home.

During the goal determination stage of a *continuing* session, which sort of goal is talked about—umbrella goals or subgoals? It depends. Usually the umbrella goal remains the same, with little revision, throughout the first three to five sessions. In these sessions the subgoals are more extensively discussed, reexamined, and perhaps called into question. That is what allows a marshaling of coordinated techniques in order to reach the umbrella goal quickly, or to at least make significant progress toward it.

Once the initial main goal is attained (or nearly attained), the therapist engages with the family in a fresh discussion about what to do and where to go. It may be that a new umbrella goal is selected, and the therapy now becomes organized in the service of that goal.

For now I will stay with what should happen when subgoals alone are called into question. Later in this chapter I will go into how, at an appropriate moment, umbrella goals can be reexamined.

Frequently, if the earlier homework inquiry has been thorough, the question of which subgoal to focus upon for the rest of the session will already be clear.

> Mr. and Mrs. Richards had set as a goal to have their daughter Nancy, age 6, become less afraid when she had nightmares. They wanted her to be able to sleep through the night and stop having to wake them up to help her.
>
> The homework was for the parents and Nancy to create a monster-fighting kit so that Nancy could conquer her fear when she had nightmares. They did the task successfully, and Nancy reported that she felt much less scared. However, she was still waking her parents up each night so that they could help her fall back asleep. The family agreed that the next goal was to help Nancy develop skills so she could both control her fear and also fall back asleep again without waking her parents.

The same is often true when the homework was done but did not lead to change. A clear subgoal warranting immediate further work may have already emerged.

> Anna, age 9, could not accept a "no" from her parents without having a major tantrum. In the previous session, Mr. and Mrs. Lambert and Anna had agreed to set up a point system as a homework task. They made a chart on which points earned by Anna could be written down every day. They also decided which extra privileges and rewards Anna would receive in exchange for the points.
>
> In the current meeting they explained that they did the homework. They drew a table, set up a point system, agreed

on rewards, and followed through on implementing it. Anna, however, continued to have several "meltdowns" each day. She had earned 0 points. The homework did not achieve the goal.

With this in mind, we decided to explore two new subgoals: first, how Anna could begin to express anger "like other 9-year-olds," and second, how Anna could better control her "meltdowns" instead of letting them control her. As a core part of this exploration, we focused on what happened during the parents and Anna's interactions that did not encourage Anna to calm herself down. We also decided to try relaxation techniques that Anna could use when she got upset.

Questions such as the following are helpful when it is not obvious which subgoal should now be given priority.

- What do you imagine is the next step we need to work on to achieve your goal?
- How can I be helpful to you today?
- What would be important for you to go home with today at the end of the session?
- Can you give me a concrete example of an event that happened since our last session that is typical of what you want to change?

GOAL EXPLORATION

In this stage a problem behavior or situation is examined in more depth. Techniques such as dramatization, work with metaphor, art techniques, and externalization are frequently used. The implementation of such techniques is largely the same as in the first interview.

However, there are differences. One is that many families tend to become more lively in continuing sessions. They feel more comfortable with the therapist, and they are better grasping what family therapy is all about and how they can use it. As a result, family members tend to share more and more willingly bring in other aspects of their lives. In an overall sense this is quite positive, but it does require the therapist to give increased attention to structure. Choices will continue to have to be made about which themes to take up when, about how much time to give to them, and the like.

Another difference is that the more open atmosphere will permit new kinds of input from the therapist. More observations, and more soft confrontation, often become appropriate. For example, perhaps the therapist has already observed, as early as the first interview, that often the mother and child exchange disparaging looks when the father shares his ideas. At that time she said nothing about it to the family, however. In continuing sessions, sharing such an observation is more possible.

Still another difference from the first interview is that techniques of exploration of the past might be used. The therapist can go to any of the four pasts: the family past, the adult past, the childhood past of each parent, and the multigenerational past (see Chapter 8). An exploration of the past might be as short as 10 minutes—or as long as an hour. Doing a genogram of each parent's family of origin, for example, can take a lot of time, requiring other parts of the session to be somewhat abbreviated.

CHANGE ELABORATION

In this stage new behavior is explored and representations of what the family would like to be different are amplified. A future dramatization might be tried. A metaphor might be sought for a desired state, or a picture of it drawn. Change elaboration unfolds in a continuing session much as it does in a first interview.

The main difference concerns the amount of background information the therapist brings to the process. He will have a better idea now of the gains and losses involved in change for each member of the family. He will also be more acquainted with their flexibility or rigidity, their willingness (or lack of it) to take risks, and their style of humor. All of this informs what he proposes as a possible experiment. With one family he may be highly cautious; with another, more challenging.

In contrast to a first interview, during this stage in a continuing session I occasionally suggest a ritual.[2] In a sense rituals are a type of task, if they are to be done between sessions. However, unlike more usual tasks, detailed planning of the ritual is usually done during this stage rather than during the concluding stage.

Here is an example of how a ritual can be planned during a session:

> The Marston family had trouble with organization, thinking ahead, and making plans. The parents often missed appointments with teachers and doctors. Birthdays were sometimes forgotten or celebrated only at the last minute. The last vacation, planned at the last minute, disappointed the children because the trains were booked. The family was even usually late for family therapy sessions.
>
> The grandfather's 80th birthday was approaching. He had lived with the family since the grandmother's death. I suggested that, as practice, the family plan, during the session, a celebration for the grandfather. The children were thrilled to participate in this exchange. They planned a surprise party, thinking through each detail and step in turn.

THE PAUSE

The pause is the same as in the first interview. A break lasting from 5 to 10 minutes is recommended. The chief difference is just that the children know the pause is coming and look forward to it.

Another small difference, in ongoing sessions, is that the children may now seek out the therapist and want to speak with her. They feel less shy, and the pause seems like a good chance to pose questions with their siblings and parents not present. I am often asked questions like, "Do you have children? and "Do you live in this place where you work?" The therapist may have to think about how much she wishes to respond to such questions and where she needs to gently set a boundary.

CONCLUDING

Most of the time, this final short stage also proceeds largely as it does during a first interview. The differences tend to be minor.

One difference concerns tasks. Normally this negotiation goes more quickly, as the family now has a better understanding of what the homework idea is all about. And the therapist will have a far better notion of what they are capable of and what they are not.

In many instances the discussion of the homework from the previous session (done during the change inquiry stage) will have functioned as a preparation. For example, it may now be clear to everyone that the same task as last time should be tried again, or that a similar task incorporating some new steps would fit well. Even when it appears that a quite different task would be appropriate, the family may be more active giving suggestions from their side.

Another difference, in most cases, is that it is now assumed, all around, that the family will be coming back. The only remaining question is when they will return. This is normally arranged quite quickly. Should a family not wish to continue, that usually will have been aired earlier in the session.

Some therapists and institutions prefer regular scheduling. Other institutions and therapists, myself included, prefer flexible scheduling. The choice of frequency is complex, as several factors are involved. In my experience, the younger the children, the closer the meetings need to be spaced. Young children forget things easily, and time for them is much longer than for adults.

Another factor is the interval necessary for the specific goal being worked on. For some goals the family will need relatively frequent ongoing support. Once every week or 2 weeks may be more appropriate than once every month or every 6 weeks, for example.

Another factor is the family's own pace and style of change. Some families want and need more time to accomplish a task. Others can change faster and may therefore wish for shorter intervals between meetings.

Geographic factors may play a role too. Some families I work with have to travel a considerable distance. They may prefer to do extra-long sessions spaced far apart (e.g, every 6 or 8 weeks).

With flexible scheduling, both the family's and the therapist's opinions must be taken into account. Often I try to follow the family's expressed wish for the interval between the second and third session. Then, in the third session, we evaluate together whether or not this length of time was too short or too long. This gives a rough idea of how best to proceed.

WORKING WITH MULTIPLE GOALS

More needs to be said about negotiating with the family whether to stop or to continue the family therapy. I am all for sparse, fast-moving intervention, as has been evident throughout this book. My modus operandi is designed for rapid change. But in Chapter 10, I explained why I also believe in helping the family lay a more solid foundation for their future, if possible.

On a practical level this can at times mean negotiating with the family to extend the therapy to work with a second or even a third or fourth main goal—*if* it seems warranted and *if* the family wishes it. The time investment is small, and the gains can be tremendous.

At times a therapist prefers her work to be brief or a therapist is forced by external (institutional) constraints to limit herself to 3 or 4 sessions. One simply confines the work to the initial goal of the resolution phase (the first phase). The therapy is ended after this is attained.

Suppose, however, the overall time frame is more open. Both therapist and institution are willing to do more, if it seems warranted. Assume, too, that the initial sessions (typically four to eight meetings) of work with a family have gone well. The main goal they defined in the first interview has been attained or neared. What then? My recommendation is to review with the family where they stand. The therapist helps the family look as clearly as possible at the choices available to them. Should they end the therapy now, or should they continue? If they wish to continue, for the sake of what specific new goal?

With some families, desire for an additional goal has already been thematized in an earlier session. Perhaps a family came for help with a child with hyperactive behavior. But in the second meeting, the father brings up an important difficulty concerning a second child and requests aid with this situation, too. The typical response from a therapist working with the present model would be to confirm the father's wish but suggest (given that no crisis is involved) a postponement of this new proposal. Several sessions from now, the therapist would explain, once things are going better with the child with hyperactive behavior, the goals for the therapy can be renegotiated. The father's wish can then be evaluated by the family as a whole. They can decide at that point whether or not they want to undertake some further work along such lines.

With other families no such additional wishes have been expressed in earlier meetings. In these situations, once the initial goal has been attained, the therapist spells out the possible choices for the family. Here is a typical intervention:

> You have worked successfully together and Nancy has conquered her fears at night. Nancy, it is very good that you now control your fears and sleep alone. We could end the therapy here, if you as a family so desire. Or we could continue. This is your choice to make.

It is useful and appropriate for the therapist to also give input. If she sees what might be a valuable possible continuing avenue, she can point this out and share her reflections about it.

> A next goal could be to focus on helping Nancy with developing social skills. Nancy, you have already said how much it hurts you that you are not asked to play with other children and not invited to birthday parties. And you two [addressing the parents] you have expressed concern that Nancy is too serious and does not play very much. If it interests you, we could now discuss what might be involved if we were to make this a focus for the therapy. Then you could make a decision about whether it fits.

Such an intervention should be prepared ahead of time. The therapist has to tread a careful line. There is a responsibility, I think, for the therapist to share her own insights. The family has a right to make an informed decision. On the other hand, suggestions can be counterproductive if they are "too far ahead of the client," as Berg (1994) nicely stresses.

The transaction should also be a highly transparent one—nothing indirect, in my opinion. Once again, it is not only the goal itself that counts. The process of deciding should also be conducted in a way that confirms and strengthens the family members' sense of agency.

Of course, this implies that, should the family opt for ending at this point, the therapist accepts this choice with goodwill, and comes in at once with appropriate support (barring a few extreme situations, such as when the safety of a child is a concern).

Naturally, when families do terminate after reaching an initial goal, the therapist underlines that in the future they can return if they ever feel the need. Some families return for further help with the initial problem; others may return for help with an entirely new one.

A more complicated situation arises when one parent wants to continue and the other does not, or a child wants the therapy to go on and the parents do not. If this happens, the therapist can encourage the family members to negotiate a decision during the session, making sure that the various opinions are expressed and heard.

Another possibility is for the therapist to suggest to the family that they discuss their differences at home and come to a decision. The family then informs the therapist of their decision in a subsequent session. My preference, however, is for the family to negotiate during the session. This allows the therapist not only to hear the various ideas but also to encourage each person to state what he or she wishes, so that no one is left out of the negotiation process. When the therapist is present, she can also help the family perhaps find a solution that is acceptable to both parents, as they have the final decision making power.

If the parents do decide to go on, the new goal they have chosen is immediately explored in detail. The investigation is largely similar to how goals are examined in a first interview. Goal representations are rendered concrete, subgoals are thought about, and the like. Art techniques and metaphor may also be used. The children are brought into this process as much as possible, just as during a first interview. In the language of phases, a transition is made from the resolution phase to the extension phase.

What kinds of new goals do families typically select when the question is opened up in this fashion? Let me give a few examples.

A common extension phase goal concerns the same child for whose difficulties the family first came in.

The Valentines were a new stepfamily. Mr. and Mrs. Valentine had been married for 6 months. Mrs. Valentine's two children from her first marriage, Gracie, age 9, and Patrick, age 7, lived with them. Mr. Valentine's son, Richard, age 9, stayed with them two weekends a month and during school vacations.

The family's initial goal was to have Patrick attend school regularly. Patrick often was quite late for school or got ill just before going to school. This especially happened on the Mondays after weekend visits to his father. Typically Patrick had stomachaches that began on Sunday evening and continued into Monday.

A month later, the family reported that Patrick was doing much better about getting to school. He had been going every day, usually on time. Mr. and Mrs. Valentine were pleased. Patrick, however, said that what he was doing was hard for him. The stomachaches were just as bad—he simply forced himself to get to school anyway. He added that sometimes he concentrated poorly at school because of the pain.

Mrs. Valentine agreed with me to adopt a new goal: to help Patrick to feel better when he went to school on Mondays.

We explored in more detail exactly what happened when he visited his father and when he returned home again.

It came out that Patrick mostly enjoyed the time spent with his father. He liked being home again as well. The transition itself, however, was terrible for him. When his father brought him back to his mother, the two parents rarely spoke. They handled the transition with rigid muteness. Or, if they did talk, their exchange quickly escalated into a nasty dispute. I proposed a new ritual, given that the father was willing to go along. When the father brought Patrick back, he and Mrs. Valentine would sit down, share a cup of coffee or tea, and speak together about Patrick for 15 minutes. The exchange would be friendly, or, at worst, neutral—no "hot" topics were to be brought up.

Additionally, I suggested that Patrick, Gracie, and Mrs. Valentine spend an hour together on Sunday evenings without Mr. Valentine. They could play a game together or talk. Afterwards, Mrs. Valentine and Patrick could prepare his school things for Monday.

A month later I heard that this goal had been achieved with success. Patrick was having almost no stomachaches. He liked the new transition arrangements very much. His father had proved quite willing to cooperate once it had been explained to him what was at stake.

Another typical extension phase scenario is that the therapeutic focus shifts to a second child whose problems are important enough to warrant attention.

Mrs. Newton, a single parent working part-time, came to family therapy with Isabella, age 10, and Daniel, age 5. She wanted help with Daniel, who was anxious about separations and who often acted fearful with other children. Daniel quickly made new steps. He began acting more courageous, defending himself when other children hit him, and had less trouble with separating from his mother.

As we evaluated where we were, I raised some concerns about Isabella. Mrs. Newton had previously described her as a great help at home and a "terrific assistant parent." Indeed, Isabella's relation to both her brother and mother seemed caring and positive. But I brought up the fact (which had emerged previously) that Isabella was rarely invited to play with other children. She herself had said she preferred to stay at home or to be "with adults." I expressed appreciation for her good qualities, and then wondered whether she was too grown up and serious for her age.

Isabella became visibly sad. Mrs. Newton agreed that Isabella was sometimes missing out on being a child. We decided that the family would adopt as a new goal that Isabella be helped to take steps toward developing social connections with peers and playing with her mother.

Sibling themes (a topic I discuss in Chapter 14) are one of the most frequently chosen continuation scenarios. Often it is the children themselves who push for this; perhaps they want less fighting and jealousy and more sibling loyalty.

Harry, age 3, was brought to family therapy for his low tolerance for frustration and refusal to accept limits. His siblings, Olivia, age 6, and Ozzy, age 7, participated in all the meetings.

A number of times I noticed a quick, silent exchange between Olivia and Ozzy while their parents were talking about Harry's behavior. Eyes were rolled; fleeting grimaces, ironic in manner, appeared and disappeared. At one point I inquired, teasing them a little, about what these looks could signify. Olivia and Ozzy spoke about how their mother protected Harry, how he "got away with murder," and about the resulting degradation of family life from their point of view.

After several sessions Harry was controlling his temper more. The parents were more competently setting limits.

Pleased with this shift, the parents declared they were ready to stop therapy.

Just as the parents announced this, a flash of looks went on between Olivia and Ozzy. I commented on it and asked them to say more openly how they were responding. They both talked about their immense dissatisfaction with Harry. He often entered their rooms when they were not there and took their personal items (toys, clothes, school supplies). Sometimes he lost, hid, or even destroyed their things. Olivia and Ozzy retaliated by refusing to play with Harry, by hitting him, and by taking his toys in revenge and deliberately breaking them. By the time both of them were finished speaking, both parents expressed their willingness to continue the therapy.

Certain more complex forms of goal renegotiation can have great importance during the extension phase in cases involving children placed in foster families or in institutions. Often these are children who have experienced violence, abuse, or neglect in their biological families. The amount of human suffering can be considerable. Systemic therapeutic interventions need be very respectful of the children's wishes and needs. The requests of foster parents, of biological relatives other than the parents, of the institution staff, and of agencies such as child protective services must also be taken into account.

Eric, age 6, Melanie, age 4, and Sandra, age 2, had witnessed their father brutally murder their mother. Immediately afterwards the three children were placed in different institutions.

The coordinating agency arranged a series of family therapy meetings, which I supervised. The children were highly traumatized. Sandra screamed or cried most of the day, every day. Melanie was very frightened. Eric could not play or talk about what happened, and he acted hostile and aggressive.

The goal was that the children be helped with these symptoms and behaviors.

Two months later both the family therapist and the staffs of the institutions felt that this goal had been reached. The children were doing markedly better. It was tentatively proposed that the meetings be ended. The children themselves, however, wanted to continue seeing each other. The coordinating agency, as well as the separate institutions, decided to support this wish. A new goal was negotiated: to support and strengthen their bond with one another. Continuing meetings with the family therapists were held.

Six months later the three children were able to move into the home of their mother's sister. That arrangement worked out well and proved durable.

Seven years later yet another goal was undertaken. This was arranged by the same coordinating agency and, fortunately enough, with the same family therapists. The father, released from prison, had expressed a desire to see the children. The judge had granted him permission to do so in a professionally supervised setting. The children wished to see him as well. The specific negotiated goals for this new series of family therapy meetings were, first, for the children and the father to get to know one another, and, second, for the children, through discussion with the father, to better understand what had taken place in the past.

Other continuation scenarios have to do with the adult couple relationship. Here the therapy progresses to what I have called the "intimacy phase." I discussed this phase in Chapter 10, but I will briefly review it again here.

It is extremely common for two parents to begin family therapy because of a problem concerning a child and then, after one or two sessions, want help with their own connection as a couple. One of them may bring it up, or both. How should the family therapist respond?

Opinions vary. Some therapists regularly advise the parents to begin couple therapy somewhere else, parallel to the family therapy. Other therapists immediately begin working with the couple relationship themselves.

As described earlier, I prefer a third way of handling the situation. With some exceptions, I usually propose that such a focus is in principle possible in the context of our work together, but that the couple would be better off to wait a little. I point out the advantages of first reaching (or nearing) the goal for which they came. I emphasize that this should not take long (assuming I see it that way). At that later point, I suggest, we can renegotiate. We can set up new goals, if the couple still wishes, with a focus upon their own relationship.

This allows, to my mind, a more truly systemic form of treatment. The child's problem, for which they first came to therapy, is not forgotten. Everybody receives his due. Some families, after having reached their initial goal, decide during reexamination that they want to focus on a new goal also having to do with one of their children rather than turning to their relationship. Then, after a few sessions given over to that area, we move to a focus upon the couple relationship.

This makes for a very practical sequence, with transparency for family and therapist alike. We know where we are at each point, and know where we are going. Additionally, systemically speaking, we have gained an important advantage: The focus on the couple can take place in the context of an improved family atmosphere. Because the parent-child relations have gotten better, the couple work will be systemically less at risk for interference or sabotage "from below."

In some cases, however, addressing the couple relationship at the outset is best—for example, if the couple is in a crisis. Perhaps they are considering separating, or one has just discovered that the other is having an affair. Other exceptions are blended families. As discussed in Chapter 10, couple relationships in step families are fragile since the couple has had little time alone without the responsibilities and stresses of being parents.

Much more can be said, of course, about the details of working with couple relationships, whether this takes place in the intimacy phase or earlier. I use many of the techniques already presented in this book, and some others as well. However, the emotional climate tends to be different—more intense—than with regular family therapy work. As this is a subject outside the purposes of this book, I will not go further into it here.

In principle, I also have nothing against other modalities of therapy being recommended. Like many family therapists, I occasionally suggest that a parent get individual or group therapy with someone else, parallel to or after the family therapy. Or I suggest that a child get additional individual or group therapy. At the same time, I believe in a form of family work that, though moving rapidly, is dense and can reach as many different points of the system as is appropriate. The journey is short, but the effects can be long-lasting.

NOTES

1. What such a shortening of the session mostly affects is the amount of exploration in each stage, as well as the choice of techniques. Some techniques, such as dramatization, require more time than others.

2. Extensive literature on the use of rituals in family therapy includes See Imber-Black, Roberts, and Whiting (1988), Davis (1988), and O'Connor and Horwitz (1988).

PART III

Special Themes

CHAPTER THIRTEEN

Children With Hyperactive Behavior

● ●

Almost everyone today who works directly or indirectly with children is confronted by a growing demand for help with children with hyperactive behavior and attention difficulties. How can the developmental potential of these children be maximized? And how can the parents and siblings meet the challenges of living with a child diagnosed with attention-deficit/hyperactivity disorder (ADHD)?

Medication may be warranted, along with school-based interventions, special tutoring, individual or group therapy for the child, and a support group for the parents. Family therapy can provide an optimal framework within which these different treatment aspects can be coordinated.[1] The family members can jointly determine how best to meet the needs of such a child, while taking into account the needs of everyone else as well. Solutions that are a good collective fit can be found.

The presence of ADHD has a massive effect upon a family. Not only does the child have schoolwork and learning difficulties, but he also can be unpleasant to be around, at least some of the time. Most children with hyperactive behavior have marked social deficits. They have trouble waiting their turn. They interrupt, and they often speak without thinking. They have difficulty playing quietly and often make a lot of noise and extraneous sounds. They misperceive others' social cues. They are easily frustrated and often moody. Such behaviors mar their relations with not only parents and siblings, but also peers and teachers.

For a significant number of such children it is even worse. On top of the other difficulties, they have problems with discipline and aggressiveness. Temper tantrums, oppositional behaviors, and fighting are frequent events.

In the classroom as well, the child often irritates teachers and other children. He cannot sit still in his seat. A short attention span causes trouble with finishing tasks. Instructions are poorly heard. Information about homework is not remembered. Books and items to be taken from school to home, or home to school, are forgotten or mislaid.

For parents, the special needs of such a child are extraordinarily demanding. Parents show up for therapy exhausted. They feel incompetent, frustrated, and guilty. Some argue in endless circles about what to do or what has gone wrong. Marriages can be very stressed; separation and divorce are frequent.

Sibling relationships suffer, too. Often this child's impulsiveness and aggressiveness lead to excessive provoking of a sibling. Siblings may also feel embarrassed by the child.

> Stefanie, 11 years old, did not want to go to the same school as her brother François, age 8. She described him as "blabbing private things" about her to other children. The day she began menstruating, François told his entire school class all the details. She felt humiliated by his behavior. She was angry that her mother protected François and made excuses for him.

As if an ADHD child were not difficult enough, one in three families with an ADHD child will have *more* than one child with

ADHD (Biederman, Faraone, Keenen, Knee & Tsuang, 1990). And in one in two families with an ADHD child, one or both of the parents has adult ADHD (Biederman et al., 1995). These are general epidemiological statistics. My informal guess is that, among families seeking clinical help, these statistics are probably even higher.

RESEARCH ON ETIOLOGY AND DIAGNOSIS OF ADHD

This chapter focuses on a systemic family approach to ADHD, with emphasis on treatment matters and techniques. First, however, I will go over a few preliminary points concerning research and diagnosis.

Etiology

To date, it appears that the largest risk factor for ADHD is genetic.[2] Large-scale twin studies suggest that 80% of childhood ADHD can be accounted for on the basis of genetic factors. If a parent has adult ADHD, there is a 57% probability that one or more children in the family will also have it (Biederman et al., 1995).

Alcohol consumed during pregnancy has been found to increase risk (Barkley, 2000).[3] So has direct exposure, during pregnancy, to cigarette smoke. Exposure to lead is also suspected. Complicated pregnancy, low birthweight, and brain injury during birth also pose a risk for symptoms of ADHD (Barkley, DuPaul & McMurray, 1990; Breslau et al., 1996; Whitaker et al., 1997). Childhood head trauma injury is thought to occasionally play a role also (Amen, 2002).

What about family interaction? This is not completely clear. To date, the most cautious assumption appears to be that family dynamics in themselves play no etiological role. On the other hand, they obviously can have considerable influence, good or bad, upon the child's developmental progress.

Brain functioning

Neuroimaging has shown abnormal brain activity and slower brain growth with ADHD children. The orbital-frontal region, especially the striatum and its connections to the caudate nucleus, displays underactive functioning. A deficit of dopamine may be one reason. The same parts of the brain have also been found to be smaller in ADHD children compared to non-ADHD children.

These brain regions play a critical part in the control of behavior, motivation, and emotions. Some researchers have persuasively suggested that ADHD therefore can best be viewed as a problem of "executive function" deficits, rather than just a problem of inattention and impulsivity (Barkley, 1997, 1998, 2000; Castellanos, 1997; Pliszka, Carlson & Swanson, 1999). This hypothesis also more neatly accounts for the ADHD child's impaired working memory and poor sense of time and planning.

Diagnosis

A firm diagnosis of ADHD should be made by someone specialized in this field.[4] For most family therapists, it makes sense to refer out for a diagnosis.

The topic of diagnosis is too large to cover here. I will mention only two important points. One is that some children display inattentiveness and distractibility, but not combined with hyperactivity. Currently this is called attention-deficit disorder (ADD).[5] Children with ADD share some traits with children with ADHD: a short attention span, distractibility, trouble getting organized, forgetfulness. Frequently their social skills are poor too, as they can be unobservant of social signals. At the same time they lack the motor agitation and impulsiveness of children with hyperactive behavior. They tend to be more distractible and passive in quality, rather than energetic. They are also less prone, statistically speaking, to oppositional and aggressive behavior (Barkley, 2000). Because many treatment issues are the same for children with attention-deficit disorder (ADD), I will mention where similar techniques can be used with them as well.

A more complicated issue is comorbidity. Research suggests that 50% or more of ADHD children meet the criteria for oppositional-defiant disorder, and 35% for conduct disorder.[6] But some children with ADHD also meet the criteria for anxiety disorder (25%), obsessive-compulsive disorder (10% to 33%), and major depressive disorder (25%); (Barkley, 1998; Pliszka et al., 1999).[7] To the extent such comorbidity is present, the family therapist must weigh the pros and cons of parallel individual or group treatment for the child.

Medication

Central nervous system stimulant medications are the drugs most typically used for children with ADHD. Stimulant medications can be of great help.[8] At the same time, medication remains controversial. Some parents are against giving it to their children. Furthermore, about 20% to 30% of children may display no positive response, or even worsening behavior in response to medication (DuPaul et al., 1998). Many children (estimates suggest around one half) suffer from side effects also. These vary from mild to severe. The most frequent side effects are decreased appetite, insomnia, stomachaches, and headaches. With a tiny number of children, stimulant medications also produce tics, an effect that ceases once the medication is stopped.[9]

Stimulant medication is *not* recommended for children under 5 years of age. Children under 5 are less responsive to it. Furthermore, there are very few research studies looking at the effects in this age group (DuPaul et al., 1998). Contraindicated as well is prescribing for children who have a history of tics, Tourette's disorder, seizure disorders, or psychosis, as their symptoms can worsen with medication (DuPaul et al., 1998).

Should comorbidity imply multiple medications? For example, some psychiatrists advocate prescribing stimulant medication together with antidepressants. There can be situations where this is necessary, but I am for avoiding it whenever possible. When you work directly with families, you see how much practical trouble is created when they must deal with multiple medications and their multiple side effects.

Another problem you may encounter is a family showing up for treatment with a child who is taking stimulant medication prescribed by a family doctor, but who has not had a diagnosis by a specialist. These are generally children who are aggressive and have behavior problems. Insist on a diagnosis at once. The child may not have ADHD at all.

When recommending medication, therapists must also emphasize to families that it can help, but it rarely makes all the problems disappear. Even when medication is effective and the side effects tolerable, basic difficulties remain, such as the child's organizational and preparation skills (e.g., getting ready for school in the morning), his social skills, and problematic sibling relationships, hence the value of therapy combined with medication.

If medication is used, it is important for the family therapist to stay in touch with the prescribing psychiatrist. It is the family therapist who is more likely to hear, for example, that sleeping has become more difficult, or that because of the child's loss of appetite, meals have become a struggle. Questions about dosage and when the medication is taken may need to be discussed between the family therapist and the psychiatrist from time to time.

A SYSTEMIC APPROACH TO TREATMENT

For several reasons, I strongly recommend family sessions with the parents and all children present from the beginning.

First, this approach provides invaluable information. The therapist doesn't just hear about how the child with hyperactive behavior and the rest of the family interact. He actually witnesses the interaction.

Second, the therapist will receive considerable input not only from the parents, but also from the siblings, about what goes on at home. Count on the siblings' having a lot to say. Moreover, as therapy gets underway, their input will include much useful information about what is and what is not changing at home. At times they see this more clearly than the parents.

Third, life in a family with one or more members with ADHD creates a lot of hard-to-tolerate feelings—for everybody. Family sessions can give recognition to these feelings and offer support and aid for how to deal with them.

Fourth, important questions concerning how to reorganize family life (e.g., with respect to meals, homework, or evening activities) will be confronted in the therapy. Collective exploration of such questions allows answers that are more fitting.

Fifth, the parents, the child with hyperactivity, and to some small extent the other children, can undergo a joint learning process. They can be helped to build certain new reciprocal procedures. These procedures have to do with practical matters where both parents and child need to be involved, such as the monitoring and completing of homework. By introducing these procedures during family sessions, considerable economy is achieved. The parents and the child learn about them at the same time. Better still, they can practice them, together, on the spot. Emerging frictions and difficulties can be resolved right away, either through mutually negotiated solutions or by feedback from the therapist. This is perhaps the most important advantage of a family therapy setting.

Excellent cognitive-behavioral therapy techniques have evolved for dealing with ADHD. My approach incorporates a number of them. As elsewhere, I have modified the techniques to render them more functional for a systemic setting. For ADHD, as for most disorders, cognitive-behavioral treatment normally separates the parents and the child. The parents receive their "training," for example in a parents' group, and concurrently the child is seen in either individual sessions or a group.[10]

One interesting exception, much nearer to what I advocate, is the work of Everett and Everett (1999), a team of cognitive-behavioral therapists who conduct some sessions where the family is seen together. Their methodology is largely different from my own, however, because for a significant part of the therapy they see the child and the parents separately. The family is not invited to attend together until the tenth session or later.[11]

Virtually every technique described in this chapter can be used in different contexts for non-ADHD children. I highlight them here simply because I have found them so effective for dealing with hyperactivity in family therapy. Similarly, many of the techniques I have discussed in previous chapters also work well with ADHD children. For example, discipline and compliance are pressing issues for many ADHD families. As I have already thoroughly covered these techniques, I will not discuss them here. The same is true for sibling issues, which are bound to be significant in any ADHD family with more than one child. The interventions for sibling issues are discussed in Chapter 14.

Overall, therapy work with a family with an ADHD child is similar to that with any family. Much depends upon the idiosyncrasies of the family itself: their particular wishes, their inner struggles, and their distinct personalities. The two main differences are the pace of change and the level of psychoeducation.

The pace of change may well be slow. These families can be helped a great deal, but the process frequently takes more time than equivalent work with another family. More effort may be required on everybody's part, including the therapist. In this respect, work with ADHD families is more akin to family therapy with eating disorders.

Considerable psychoeducation is also necessary. Specialized information must be supplied by the therapist. This will also lead to a certain interplay between the psychoeducation and the family's goals. As the family better understands what they are dealing with, they will probably modify some of their goals and establish a few new ones as well.

BEGINNING THERAPY WITH ADHD FAMILIES

There are different ways in which family therapy with hyperactive children is likely to begin. The most frequent, for the usual practitioner, is that the family comes because of problems with the ADHD child but are unaware of the ADHD condition, because the child has not yet been diagnosed. It is the therapist who forms the hypothesis, however tentatively, and who first speaks about it.

How does one best proceed in this situation? My recommendation is to move in parallel directions. On the one hand, you can focus upon the family's initial goals in the usual manner. These may have to do with school problems, organizing daily tasks, disobedience, social difficulties, and the like. The family is helped to zero in on their desires for change, just as would be done in any first session (see Chapter 11). Priorities are set, goals are more concretely defined, and so on.

Along with this, however, the possibility of an ADHD diagnosis can be openly discussed by the therapist. Therapists accustomed to working with hyperactivity may spot the signs right away. The hypothesis takes shape as the therapist notices the child's behavior in the session and hears information about behaviors at home and at school. But however well-grounded the hypothesis is, it is better to communicate it only tentatively. The therapist can explain some basic facts about ADHD and then propose that the child be taken to a specialist for a precise evaluation.

For many families, the first reactions are simultaneous shock and relief. The upsetting part is hearing that, if the diagnosis is confirmed, there will be no quick cure or easy solution. The reduction of guilt on their part, however, brings relief. The therapist explains that, as far as we know, hyperactivity is caused by genetic and other neurological factors, not family doings. The hypothesis also lets parents immediately begin developing new ways of thinking and speaking about their child. Some of the more extreme negative attributions ("He is lazy, selfish, and irresponsible") may start to be replaced by a more understanding point of view.

The therapist can also emphasize that once more certainty has been obtained about the child's condition, a better and more comprehensive treatment plan can be orchestrated. It may turn out, for example, that in order to attain their wished-for goals, they may want to consider medication, special school needs, and the like. The therapist adds that all these details can better be discussed once the evaluation has been made.

The second possibility is that a family comes to family therapy with concerns about one child, without ADHD, and before long brings up difficulties they are also having with the child's sibling, who turns out to have ADHD. The direction of the therapy can then be negotiated with the family. Should the problems with the ADHD child also be addressed now, during the resolution phase? Or does it make more sense to wait until the extension phase? In many cases the latter is preferable.

Another, more infrequent variant of this scenario is that the parents are so focused on the "identified patient" that they have failed to notice the struggles the ADHD child is having. In this case it is appropriate for the therapist to share his own concerns, and at a minimum suggest an outside diagnostic evaluation.

A third possibility is that a family arrives with a child (or more than one) already diagnosed with ADHD. They know what they are facing, at least to a degree, and want help with it. The referral may have been made by a pediatrician, psychiatrist, school, or hospital service for children, for example. Often the family will already have received much of the essential information about the nature of ADHD and about intervention options. The child may even already be in group or individual therapy. Naturally, in this situation, the therapist can turn immediately to the family's concrete goals for change.

ADDRESSING PROBLEMS WITH TIME MANAGEMENT

One group of complaints you are likely to hear from parents with an ADHD child follows:

- She is never ready when she is supposed to be.
- He can't get up in the mornings without my nagging him.
- He starts playing in the middle of getting dressed for school.
- I have to remind him 20 times before he does his homework.
- She is so easily distracted she never finishes anything.
- He is thoughtless and selfish. He didn't even care that the rest of us were sitting in the car waiting for him.

These problems relate to *time management*. In one version or another, they are an inevitable sore point in family life with one or more ADHD children (or with an ADD child; the issue is pretty much the same).

We speak about "distractibility," but arguably the deficit is more complex than that. Such children seem to have difficulty with the very representation of time and temporal passage. They are poor at making plans. They are poor at orienting themselves toward a delayed reward. In the middle of doing a task, they are prone to misrepresenting how much time has passed, causing them to take longer than others to complete an activity.[12] Their representations of time are weak and lack internal detail and structure. Much of what Barkley and others call an "executive function" deficit can be understood from this perspective.

Futilely, parents often try to *take over* the registering and representing of time for the child. "It's been 10 minutes now." "It's been 15 minutes." "If we don't leave in 5 minutes, we'll never be at the school on time." They nag and cajole. This may resolve an immediate conflict or obstacle, but it doesn't change anything internally in the child.

The family can better crystallize their picture of the change they want if the therapist explains this issue of poor representation of time. They can also be helped to find a more neutral label for the problem. Usually the parents are caught up in highly negative ascriptions. A name like "the time problem" can be introduced by the therapist. Another option, of course, is to generate a more blame-free label by using the technique of externalization (Chapter 5) in the first or second session.

The therapist then helps the parents explore how they can aid the child in strengthening his representational capacities concerning time. A practical means of going about this is to use auxiliary representational devices. Typically these include both time devices (a clock, a timer, a radio) as well as a pictorial or written representation of a desired behavior. I will explain how these are to be used in a moment.

For this initial step, it is best to select an everyday task that must be performed at the same time each day—for example, getting dressed in the morning, or doing homework from 4:00 to 5:30 in the afternoon, or cleaning one's room at 6:00 in the evening, or before dinner. The parents first need to discuss with the child, there in the session, exactly what it is they want: what specific behavior, performed at what time. The therapist must make sure that they very explicitly communicate this, with all the necessary detail, and that the child is taking it in. (Remember, the concentration difficulties of a child with ADHD or ADD make following and understanding instructions more problematic than for most children.)

> Colin, age 10, had been diagnosed as having ADHD. His parents said he was often late for school. Mornings had turned into a battle. Mrs. Gell would wake him up "at least 10 times" before he finally got out of bed. Getting dressed required much prodding. Mr. Gell drove Colin to school on his way to work. He threatened and screamed at Colin, and told him that he would be a failure.
>
> In the session, a new routine was worked out to deal with the morning time-management problem. Mr. and Mrs. Gell negotiated with Colin that he was to be out of bed by 7:15, dressed by 7:30, finished with breakfast by 8:00, and ready to walk out the door by 8:15. Colin agreed, finding that this time sequence was in principle a realistic one.

The choice of auxiliary devices should be explored next. The idea is to change the child's environment so that more cues of a more vivid and salient nature are there to aid him.

One set of cues operates as a reminder of the task itself. It can be useful to have the exact steps of the task written out on a piece of paper. The child himself should do the writing, not a parent. The therapist can explain that the child is creating something that is to serve as an aid to himself. The child should also choose where at home the paper should be stored.

> Colin wrote down the desired behavior, in all its parts, on a large piece of paper. I suggested that he title it. He wrote at the top, "Solutions for the Time Problem." He decided that, in the evening just before going to bed, he would put it at the center

of the desk in his room. At other times it would stay on the desk, uncovered by other papers, in the far left-hand corner. He also had the idea to put it in a clear plastic folder so that it would stay intact.

The next step is to arrange for cues about time itself. This can be a cellphone, a mechanical egg timer, a small electronic timer (usually found in kitchen-supply stores), a large clock with big numbers, or a digital clock. Multiple cues may also be used. The right prominent location for it must be decided upon.

Mrs. Gell declared that she would prefer not to wake Colin up anymore. I supported this, as the entire purpose of what we were setting up was to have Colin become autonomous with respect to organizing his morning time. They all brainstormed.

Colin liked the idea of a clock radio that would play music. The parents readily agreed. I suggested getting one that did not shut off by itself, so that Colin would have to shut it off. Collectively they thought through where it would go in the room, who would set it the night before, and so on. Everyone decided that it would be placed on the far side of the room so that Colin would have to get out of bed to shut it off. Colin suggested that his father help him remember to set the alarm in the evening. Mr. Gell was willing. Mrs. Gell said she was pleased that her husband would have an active role for this part.

Colin and both parents decided that a digital timer would be an additional help. At 7:15, the egg timer could be set for 15 minutes so that it would ring at 7:30, the time at which Colin was supposed to be dressed and moving on to breakfast. Mrs. Gell agreed that once Colin was out of bed, she would set the timer and hand it to Colin.

At breakfast, Mrs. Gell would reset the timer for 8:00, the end of the breakfast time, and then at 8:00, she would reset it for 8:15, the time to leave home. I arranged with her too that at the beginning of each time block, she would repeat once, in a calm voice, what was to be done in that time block. I had Colin go over his understanding of all this to confirm that he grasped the details.

Consequences should be negotiated as well. The therapist should not underestimate how much sheer effort will be involved for the child with ADHD or ADD to learn to register time more clearly. Motivation is an important aspect here—so important, in fact, that I advocate that *both* negative consequences and positive rewards be used. (With other kinds of children, either a negative or a positive consequence alone often works fine.)

If a point system (Chapter 6) is used, it is good to set it up with poker chips or some other token system rather than merely with written points. Stronger visual and tactile cues are better, especially for children under 7 years old.[13] The idea with point systems such as these is to reinforce, as immediately as possible, not just the external behavior but also the registration of the time intervals itself.

Mr. and Mrs. Gell decided on a token system, using plastic poker chips as rewards. Directly after the successful completion of each short time block, Colin would receive a chip in his hand. One chip would be for getting out of bed and shutting off the alarm at 7:15. Another would be given for being dressed at 7:30, a third for eating breakfast by 8:00, and a fourth when he was ready to leave at 8:15. A system for trading chips in for more substantial rewards was negotiated. As usual, I encouraged the parents to also give Colin praise, such as a smile, a hug, and a "nice going."

It took several weeks for Colin to manage the entire morning sequence by himself. He eventually decided that he wanted to set the digital timer himself each morning. His parents gave him an extra daily token for adding this element.

What about generalization (the transfer of the new skill to other contexts)? Unfortunately, in much work with children with ADHD and ADD, this too is more difficult. The therapist should not assume that it will take place automatically. This means that once a child like Colin has achieved better time management in one daily domain, he may still need help acquiring it in another.

> I helped the Gell family target a new context for time management. This, they decided would be Colin's getting himself to bed on time in the evening. The idea came from Colin himself, who now was enthusiastic about becoming more in charge of his life. He also saw that it would be easier to get out of bed in the mornings if he made it to bed on time in the evenings and then got a good night of sleep.
>
> They set up a similar program with the timer and poker chip rewards. Colin made this shift more quickly. A week later I heard that getting to bed was going better.

Colin's increased interest in getting help for a new area is also fairly typical. The child discovers that he likes the strengthened sense of agency. He also likes the decrease in family uproar and nagging.

ADDRESSING PROBLEMS WITH SCHOOL HOMEWORK

Homework can be another nightmare for the entire family.

Homework must be carefully completed to do well in school. But children with ADHD and ADD usually require more practice at home than other children to keep up in school, and they require more help from a parent or other adult. At the same time, they are even less inclined than other children to do their homework. They possess neither the patience nor the concentration abilities, nor can they listen well to a helping adult. Mutual stress and ongoing arguments may become par for the course.

Matters are not helped by the child's distractibility at school. She may fail to listen carefully to the teacher's instructions about a specific piece of homework, or not bother to write down what she heard, or forget the book or handout she was supposed to bring home.

About 25% of children with ADHD also have learning disabilities (Frick et al., 1991; Sermud-Clikeman et al., 1992). Typically, 18% have trouble with reading, 30% with math, and 21% with spelling (Power et al., 2001).[14] Needless to say, add learning disabilities to ADHD, and the homework situation risks becoming even more of a battleground.

In part, homework problems are a matter of time management, and they can be dealt with as such in the therapy. Like getting ready for school in the morning, homework is a daily task regularly undertaken at a certain time of day. This means that virtually all the technical steps just described for time management can be useful. At the same time, however, doing homework is more complex. The child genuinely needs monitoring and scaffolding for the very doing of the activity. This necessitates some additional aspects of therapeutic intervention.

A good first step can focus upon the prologue at school. A new notebook can be bought for the child if he doesn't already have one or if he dislikes the one he has. This notebook is used uniquely for writing down homework assignments. Should no homework be assigned, the child is to write "no homework" for that day, and bring the book back home all the same.

The child is to show this book to the parent after school every day. This means the parent too must remember to ask to see it! This is a point worth emphasizing in the session, I have learned.

Of course, it is important for the parents to meet with the child's teachers once a clear diagnosis of ADHD has been made.[15]

Having the teacher briefly check the notebook just before the child leaves school at the end of the day is optimal. Of course, this is possible only if a high level of cooperation exists between the family and the teacher. The teacher ideally gives the parents daily feedback on the child's performance and behavior. Specific behavioral goals for school are chosen conjointly by the teacher and parents. Then the teacher's reports on the child's progress are translated into consequences and rewards at home.

A next step is for the parents and child to establish details concerning the homework itself. Specific, regular times to begin and end, and a specific place, should be negotiated. If on certain days this is not possible—for example because of a sports activity—then the family should schedule a time for the homework on that day. The idea is to maximize regularity and ritualization.

Pay close attention to the discussion concerning the place. Make sure the family chooses a location with a minimum of distractions—no background music, no TV or computer on nearby. It is also better not to have siblings present in the same room during homework time, if at all possible.

Milo, age 8, had trouble with doing homework. He and his father, Mr. Koch, addressed this by first buying a notebook for Milo to keep track of his assignments. They then discussed when and where the homework would be done. They decided together that homework would be finished an hour before dinner so that the two of them could play a game before dinner or, if it was still light, play ball outside. Their playing together was to be contingent upon Milo's completing his homework. They budgeted 45 minutes for the homework.

Milo suggested doing the homework in his father's home office. Mr. Koch agreed. He added that he would set up an additional small table in his office so that Milo could have his own workspace there. While Milo did his homework, his father would do his bookkeeping, ready at any time to help Milo with the homework.

Breaks should be planned too—perhaps three or four in an hour, for example. There are two methods of organizing them, and this should also be decided upon. Breaks can occur either between different homework assignments or at the end of a specific amount of time.

The breaks should be short—5 minutes is good, for example. A timer can be used to measure both the break itself and each work block (if it has been decided that the work blocks will have a defined time).

Be sure, too, that the overall time allotted for the homework is realistic in length. There are limits to what a child with ADD or ADHD can tolerate. It is also important that, once the homework is finished, there is time left over, before dinner or before going to bed, for the child to play or run around. A hyperactive child needs to release pent-up restlessness.

As with other such types of arrangements, I often suggest that the child write down these details on a large paper. This paper can be hung up on a wall somewhere physically close to where he does his homework.

Homework also requires certain supplies—paper, pens, pencils, eraser, scissors, a calculator, perhaps a timer. Another useful shared project for parent and child can be to prepare a homework "supplies sack." I like to have the parent and child discuss what belongs in the sack. Then they can plan when they will go out together to buy it.[16] They can also work out where to keep the homework supplies. As these children notoriously lose things, it is usually best for the parent to put the supplies away and then give them to the child at homework time.

A point or token system is definitely recommended for getting children with hyperactivity to better cooperate with homework. Having the parent break down the homework ritual into little steps, with rewards given after each step is accomplished, is also useful.

Homework monitoring is frequently a burdensome chore for a parent. Even when it goes smoothly, it is not pleasurable on the adult side. Although family therapy cannot change this, it can help the parent do the monitoring in a manner that causes the least interactional friction and is the most effective for the child's learning. With most families, in fact, this aspect is a critical part of treatment. Otherwise, all the other agreements and arrangements are likely to come to naught.

Instructional Guidance

What is demanded from the parent is competence in *instructional guidance*. This is akin to, if not quite the same as, the making of prescriptive requests. As will be obvious in a moment, instructional guidance skills are important not only for homework but in many other contexts as well.

Like prescriptive requests, instructional guidance requires attention to both content and tone. Recall what was explained in Chapter 6 about prescriptive directives (e.g., "It is time now to put your toys away"). They need to be clear and concrete, age-appropriate, delivered one at a time, phrased as statements rather than questions, and made to target a small enough behavioral step. They should also be followed by a few seconds' delay, and, if the child complies, combined with brief praise.

Each of these same qualities is needed in instructional guidance. This is not surprising if one thinks about it. At the core of both making requests and giving guidance is a need that information be transmitted in a way that helps the child translate the information into practical action. What is said by the parent serves as a signpost for the child's action.

With children with hyperactive behavior two of these qualities take on even greater significance.

The first is the clarity of what is said. The ADHD (or ADD) child's cognitive window is less open, meaning that the request on guidance must be more clear than with other children. This must be emphasized to parents. The therapist should also look for opportunities, if the family does a dramatization, to give feedback (positive or negative) about this point.

Second is the matter of dividing more global messages into smaller units. This is key with most children with ADD or ADHD. The parent scales down the acts named to the right size.

For example, imagine that the child is working on mathematics homework. The parent may find that an instruction like "Add all the different sums together and get their total" is too global. Instead, the parent might say, "Copy this sum, here, over on this part, here, of the paper. Good. Now copy this sum just under it. Right. See, this is going to make a column. Now copy this sum under that one. Yes. And this one, at the bottom. Right. Now all four of these sums are in a good column, and you can add them together." The idea is to locate the level of specificity that works for the child. Otherwise the parent will aim too high, creating unending frustration for parent and child alike.

IMPROVING SELF-REGULATION

The ability to self-regulate is an important component of effective agency. Whenever one's frustration, anger, or anxiety intensifies, it is more difficult to act in the world. Children with hyperactive behavior tend to be particularly lacking in self-calming skills.[17]

This lack has negative effects on time management, doing homework, and any other kind of structured task. It also affects social relations. Who wants to play with a child who has trouble with anger, can't handle frustration, can't slow down to match everyone else's pace, and can't tolerate losing at a game?

Many children with hyperactive behavior also have sleep problems. This is an even more direct result of an inability to self-calm (Christophersen & Mortweet, 2001).

Self-calming can be learned, fortunately. Excellent cognitive-behavioral techniques exist for this. Some involve guided imagery. Others use muscle relaxation. Still others work with breathing. Many children can profit from such techniques, but for children with hyperactive behavior they are particularly valuable.

The usual format is individual therapy. A behavior therapist works alone with the child. My preference is to have the *parent* help the child learn the self-calming procedures. This is done as a part of the family sessions. The therapist guides the parent in guiding the child.

Why that arrangement? First, because of the transfer problem. It is not easy for children to learn these new habits and to use them at home. If the parent knows the procedures, she can guide the child through them at home. This can be done on a daily basis for one or several weeks. Even after that, it can be repeated, if needed, at some later point. Usually this will be in preparation for some event with unusual stress, like a school test.

Second, such an arrangement has, for many families, a useful systemic implication. The parents of children with hyperactive behavior often are overinvolved in attempting to "rescue" the child from out-of-control agitation. They jump in and solve a problem or make things better. The drawback, however, is that the parent then takes everything over. The child learns little about how to solve the problem, or about how to make things better for himself in such a moment. The value of having the parent do the self-calming "training" is that now the parent is helping the child *help himself*. It fashions one more template, for both of them, for a different type of interactional aid.

Third, the child and the parent are training themselves in this way, to enter into *shared* states of calm. They are quieting down and relaxing together. (As will be seen shortly, in order to guide the child, the parent must calm herself as well.) Implicitly, they are practicing a new form of joint behavior. They are learning a model for "relaxing downward" in unison, as opposed to rocketing each other "upward" in unison.

Fourth, this joint calming can be effectively coupled with other "family-calming" systemic work, also described shortly.

In order to intervene in this manner, the therapist must first demonstrate to the parent how to guide the child in certain self-calming procedures. I use three kinds.

Guided Imagery

Guided imagery is a highly effective self-calming strategy. Today it is widely used in many contexts, for both children and adults.[18] Most children with hyperactive behavior can benefit greatly from it. The child needs to be 5 years of age or older.[19]

In individual therapy, the classic way to show the strategy is simple. A subject is asked to close his eyes. He is told to imagine a happy, peaceful scene. It might be a pretend scene, a remembered one, or a mixture. Often children opt for a forest (frequently an "enchanted" forest), a sunny beach, or images of foods they love to eat.

The child is asked to describe the scene in full sensory detail. Naturally a calm, slow voice is used for these questions.

- What do you see?
- What can you hear?
- What smells are there?
- Are there any tastes with this?
- What does it feel like in your body?

One can ask about more specific details too:

- How does the ice cream feel on your tongue?
- Describe where you feel the sand on your skin.

- As you walk through the forest, what does the ground feel like as your feet touch it?

The whole procedure usually takes around 15 minutes—or less, usually, with a child of 5 or 6 years of age or with a child who soon gets restless. (You ask fewer questions of such a child.) Toward the end, you can inquire how the child is feeling now, doing this. Typical answers are: "okay," "happy," and "relaxed."

The aim is to have the child learn how to do this by himself, eventually. As a stepping stone, the parent learns how to take the child through these steps. How should this be shown to the parent?

One easy way is for the therapist first to do it once with the parent (or both parents) and the child together. In other words, the parent also closes her eyes and imagines a scene. This has advantages. Having gone through the procedure herself, the parent will have a better feeling for how to guide the child. Also, the parent may want to start using the strategy on occasion for herself.

After both of them have tried this with their eyes closed, the therapist can next propose that the parent now guide the child through the procedure again. The parent does so, with the therapist giving any relevant feedback. If the child does not want to repeat the experience so soon, the therapist and the parent can briefly discuss how it is executed from the guiding side.

Once in a while a parent prefers not to join in and try the procedure herself. In this case, the therapist can do it with the child while the parent watches. Then the therapist and parent simply discuss how the parent will do the same at home. Still another alternative is for the therapist first to describe how to do the procedure, without demonstrating it. Then the parent tries to do it, guiding the child. The therapist gives feedback.

A plan can be made for when and how often the parent and child do the exercise at home. I usually suggest that the procedure be practiced once each day. The time of day should also be decided upon.

The therapist explains that the eventual goal is to have the child learn to do it by himself, without the parent. After practicing with the parent for more or less a week, the child may feel he can do it by himself. He should then practice it alone, preferably at the same time of day, for at least an additional week.

Art techniques can be incorporated into this exercise as well. The child draws on paper one or more images from the imagined scene. He can take the drawing home, put it somewhere, and use it anytime as another support for self-calming. Most young children like this. The drawing feels to them like something very personal.

For children who seem poorly motivated to enter into the procedure, I suggest that the parents set up a regular small reward for the daily practice moment. This is arranged, too, during the session.

Progressive Relaxation

Progressive relaxation also works well for most children 5 years or older. Often I propose that a child with hyperactive behavior learns this once she is familiar and comfortable with self-quieting through guided imagery. For children who turn out not to like guided imagery, progressive relaxation can be a good alternative.

One starts with a short explanation. Children almost always need clarification about what a "tensed" muscle as opposed to a relaxed one is. A small spongy ball can be useful for conveying this. The therapist shows how the ball can be squeezed, then allowed again to expand. The child can take the ball and try this several times.

As with guided imagery, I teach the parent how to lead the child through the technique by having the parent join the child the first time we try it, if he is willing. The parent then guides the child through the exercise for several days until the child reaches the point where she feels she can do it alone.

Progressive relaxation is best done with the child lying on the floor, on a bed, or sitting in a comfortable chair. Distinct muscle groups then are successively named and worked with. Exactly which muscle groups are named and the order in which they are taken is totally open.[20] A good principle, however, is that the younger the child, the more short and simple the technique should be.[21] Children with hyperactive behavior can have an especially hard time lying still for more than a few minutes, so a rather abbreviated procedure usually works better.

The sequence I typically use is first the arms, then the stomach and buttocks, and then the legs.[22] One starts out:

Tighten your right hand into a fist. Squeeze it very tight. [This should be for about 5 seconds.] Now let it relax. [Pause for around 3 seconds.] Now tighten your forearm, the part of your arm between your hand and your elbow. . . .

Next come the right upper arm and shoulder; then the equivalent working up the left hand and arm; then stomach; then buttocks; then foot, calf, and thigh on each side in turn. For children who seem unusually tense in the face or who have facial tics, I might add parts of the head and neck or even just the lips. When a child has a great deal of difficulty staying still during the procedure, I reduce the number of body parts even more. For example, each fist in turn, stomach, and then each foot in turn. The child and parent can practice this much at home, for now. In a couple of subsequent sessions I introduce additional body parts.

Note the type of instruction: "Tighten your right hand into a *fist. Squeeze* it *very tight.*" This is not a particularly nuanced mode of progressive relaxation. In principle, instructions that are more delicate and gradual could be used. But this simpler form functions better for children with ADHD. Their access to body sensation is more limited.

One such sequence is all a child can manage in a single therapy session. For that reason, if the parent has also done the relaxation, I don't ask him to guide the child a second time through. The therapist can just go over a few points about how the parent will conduct it at home.[23]

Breathing Techniques

Breathing techniques are another means for children to self-calm. Personally I use them less often, for the simple reason that they lend themselves less to a systemic mode. But some children like them, and they have been reported to be effective (Kendall & Brasswell, 1985; Benson, 2000). They do have the advantage that they can be more quickly learned.

With these I simply show the child what to do. I have the parents try it too, just so they understand what the child is experiencing when he does it (and so that they can use it themselves, if they want to). I don't have a parent take over any further instruction, as normally this is not needed.

The idea is that the child deepens his breathing. One technique is to imagine blowing up a balloon. With each breath cycle, the child inhales deeply and then exhales into the imaginary balloon. She continues until the balloon is "filled up."

A similar technique is pretending to blow bubbles. The child holds an imaginary bubble-blowing wand and blows a series of 10 large bubbles. For each bubble, he takes a deep breath in and then lightly (remember, that is how you have to do it with bubbles!) blows out. At the end of this lengthened, gentle exhalation, he tries to let a small pause take place in his breathing before he inhales again.

Pretend bubble-blowing can also sometimes be used with a child as young as 4 years old. I have even done it with a child of 3 years. Compared to the imagery and muscle relaxation techniques, less patience is required and it is conceptually more simple as well.

Systemic Issues

Concerning self-calming, two related systemic issues may also need to be explored. One or both turn out to be significant for most ADHD families.

The first concerns overinvolved assistance, which often takes place when the child with hyperactive behavior encounters practical difficulties. The lid of the jam jar won't come off; he can't find the TV program he wants; a homework problem baffles him. Instantly his frustration goes through the roof. How do the parents or siblings react?

Unfortunately, in many families, the knee-jerk response is: *I had better solve this problem for him.* And the parent (or sibling) does so, immediately. This is unfortunate for a straightforward reason. More than most children, the child with ADHD needs to learn coping skills. He needs to learn about problem-solving and about how to maintain effort even when a patch of frustration comes along. Instead, he is being trained in the opposite. He is learning: Don't bother coping, don't solve the problem, forget about maintaining effort, because someone else will do it for you.[24]

The family needs to acquire more flexibility in these moments. Depending on the situation, the child with hyperactive behavior needs one of two things: scaffolding or a minimal echo. Scaffolding, in the Vygotsky and Cole (1978) sense, means that the parent helps the child to overcome the difficulty. The parent doesn't take it over but rather gives the child encouragement and whatever tips or support he requires to deal with the obstacle himself. A minimal echo response with empathy is more low-key still. The parent only acknowledges the difficulty, nothing more. For example, "I know those jars can be really tough to open." The child is left to struggle with it. This is more

appropriate for a smaller-scale problem where the child probably can manage well by himself.

Exploring with a parent what lies behind her overinvolved
assistance is usually important. The reasons most often have to
do with the parent's own past. The parent may have felt emotionally (or even literally) abandoned by one or both of her own
parents, for example. Now she has dedicated herself to doing
"everything possible" for her own child. Or, the sounds of crying
or of an angry outburst may trigger traumatic memories (for
example, of family violence) from her childhood.

Replacing overinvolved assistance with more functional
behavior is not always easy, emotionally speaking. By first
going to the parent's own past, the therapist both increases the
parent's motivation and gives her a more useful framework of
understanding.

> Mrs. Bridge, a single-parent mother, got terribly upset when-
> ever Alex, her 6-year-old son, became frustrated or angry. She
> was constantly "tuned in" to him, hypersensitive to his slight-
> est signal of distress.
>
> In the past, Alex had displayed hyperactive behavior, with
> poor impulse control and frequent bouts of rage. Being in
> public was especially hard for both of them. Alex wanted to
> run around, handle objects, and have things bought for him,
> and not getting what he wanted often led to tantrums. Typi-
> cally Mrs. Bridge would first try to calm him down but then
> would become so agitated herself that she ended up scream-
> ing. This would make her feel guilty, and she would give in to
> what he wanted.
>
> An exploration of Mrs. Bridge's own childhood around
> these specific themes proved beneficial. She cried as she
> remembered how her own mother seemed distant and cold.
> She recalled having consciously decided when she was preg-
> nant with Alex that she would be the opposite of her mother
> and listen carefully to every wish her child might have.

A second systemic issue with respect to self-calming concerns agitated states on the part of other family members. One of the first questions to ask in this case is: Independently of the child's behavior, how much nervousness, speediness, quick escalations of aggressive tone, and the like are present in the overall family atmosphere? If the child is bathed in an atmosphere with little calmness, it will be the harder for her to learn to self-calm.

IMPROVING SELF-MONITORING

A child with hyperactive behavior needs to learn not only how to self-calm, but also when. This means he must improve his *self-monitoring skills* as well. He must learn to register his states of agitation and mentally represent them to himself.

Plenty of emphasis on self-monitoring is already built into the overall method presented in this book. When I do family therapy, I often ask, "What are you feeling now?" or "What is going on in your body now?" Words are found for feeling states, pictures are drawn of them, metaphors are found for them.

All the same, at the start of therapy, children with ADHD or ADD tend to be especially poor at self-monitoring. Their sped-up inner rhythm leaves no time for it. So anything additional that can help them is worth the trouble.

Scaling is very useful for many of them, I find. The scale itself provides a representational language, and then a visual display can be used to represent the scale (Chapters 11 and 12). For example, the therapist can have the child draw a vertical line. The line can be used, thermometer-like, to stand for gradations of calmness vs. agitation. "1" can stand for "calm", or "cool" and "10" for "totally out of control". The child writes the numbers.

These analogic metaphorical representations are primarily for the child himself. But they also serve as communicational vehicles between the child and his parents, as well as between the child and the therapist.

The goal, naturally, is that the child eventually learns to register and represent his state to himself *in the moment* of mounting agitation. Then, if the situation warrants, he can use self-calming imagery, muscle relaxation, or breathing to regulate himself. He can try to work his state down from an "8" to a "7," for example.

Positive self-talk can also be helpfully combined with the same strategies, in some contexts. Say the child is about to take a school test. She is becoming agitated. Her thoughts start to run: "I am stupid. I will never get the math problems right." She changes this into: "I know I can do this kind of problem. I practiced it at home." Then she can use the self-calming strategies to lower her agitation level further.

The other question has to do with responses to the child's agitation states. Do one or more family members typically react with rising agitation on their side? Do the child and a family member mutually goad each other into symmetrical escalations? Obviously, this will make it harder for the child to learn to self-calm. Her own agitation states are being reinforced not only by negative attention, but also by imitative learning.

Overassistance and agitated states on the part of the family are not etiological causes of hyperactivity. But they contribute supplementary layers of both structuring and triggering causation.

One good means of thematizing such systemic factors is to couple them with the introduction of self-calming techniques for the child. The systemic issue can be confronted at the same time, or it can be done in a session soon after. One parent has already been made responsible for helping the child learn at home to self-calm. It is thus a natural step to motivate him or her, and everyone else, to also learn to self-calm. "Family calming" or "mutual self-calming" (mutual in the sense of both parent and child) can be talked about and labeled as an aid to the child. And because the others were present during the work with the child with imagery and muscle relaxation strategies, they already know something practical they can do for themselves.

> Mrs. Lawrence, a young single parent, worked full-time in a challenging job. Cody, age 6, and Dennis, age 3, were hungry and exhausted when Mrs. Lawrence picked them up late in the afternoons. So, for that matter, was Mrs. Lawrence herself. Cody had aggressive and hyperactive behavior. Every evening the family atmosphere quickly turned into one of general chaos and screaming.
>
> Cody learned self-calming imagery in a session. We planned for Mrs. Lawrence to help him practice this in the evenings, before he went to bed.
>
> In the following session, Cody reported liking the imagery practice and said that it helped him. He also told me proudly that a couple of days ago Mrs. Lawrence had begun to yell loudly at him and Dennis. Cody suggested to his mother that she go into her bedroom and try the imagery procedure. Mrs. Lawrence confirmed this and said that she did it and she actually was able to calm down.

RECONNECTING PARENT AND CHILD

I almost always use *play restoration* (see Chapter 7) when treating families with a child who is hyperactive. This is, in part, for the usual reasons. As already discussed, the restoration of play can emotionally reconnect a child and parent who have lost their emotional closeness. This is a very frequent problem between hyperactive children and their parents.

But play restoration has an added benefit for children with ADHD or ADD. These children lack perseverance when conducting an activity. They also have reduced social skills. Play can be a valuable medium for parental help with both of these.

In many respects, how the therapist works with play restoration, technically speaking, is the same as with other families. But a few things are different enough that they are worth mentioning here.

First, usually it is not just the child's aggression that has caused the parent to retreat from playing. The child is also often not particularly competent at playing. He can't wait his turn. He can't tolerate the frustration of losing a game. He is uncreative with pretend play. He is poor at cooperating in a joint project.

This means that the parent will have to have considerable patience. The therapist must warn the parent about that. At the same time, the therapist should make certain that the parent understands the developmental implications of what she will be doing. True, the child can be aggravating. But realistically, his interpersonal playing style can change, and to the extent it does, through the parent's help, she is giving a gift. Eventually the child will have a much better chance at building satisfying peer relationships. It can be highly motivating for a parent to keep this dimension in mind.

A second difference is that the parent will have to provide more structure than would be the case in playing with a child without attention difficulties or hyperactive behavior. I emphasized earlier how a parent should follow a child's lead. But with these children this must be somewhat modified. Initially the parent can wait and watch, letting the child determine a play direction. But once the child has done so, the parent can join in quickly, helping the child to structure the next logical steps of the play.

Otherwise, the child is likely to drift rapidly from one play initiative to another, developing none of them. The parent must quantitatively increase the amount of scaffolding she provides. The idea is to help the child better formulate a goal and then stay focused on trying to reach the goal.

> Mrs. Samir liked the prospect of engaging in play with Fadi, age 7, who was hyperactive and had a learning disability. They both agreed to try it in the session. Mrs. Samir suggested that Fadi pick a game or toy that he would like to play with. Fadi took a puzzle and started to do it. He got quickly frustrated when he couldn't fit one piece into its place. He threw the puzzle aside and went to another game.
>
> I encouraged Mrs. Samir to put words to Fadi's goal of finishing the puzzle and to try to help him continue. Mrs. Samir said, "You really want to do this puzzle, don't you? And that piece with the chicken's head is hard to fit in. Why don't you take that yellow and green piece? It looks like it would go right in the hole."
>
> Fadi followed the suggestion. Mrs. Samir praised him. Fadi successfully completed the puzzle after three more such interventions by Mrs. Samir. Mrs. Samir praised Fadi again. I gave positive feedback to both of them.

With other kinds of games and play, a parent also can help the child with hyperactivity learn about turn-taking and about cooperating to do a joint project. Play also offers plenty of opportunities for the parent to use emotion words or to solicit them from the child. "Do you think the bear feels more sad or angry now?" This is another area where many children with ADHD and ADD need to improve their abilities.

Finally, with some children, plenty of limit-setting will probably be required the first few times the parent and child play. If the child begins to become aggressive with the parent or refuses to follow directives (such as "don't hit the table with the block"), clear boundaries should be set by the parent. Time-out can also be used, if necessary.

In my opinion, a systemic approach is the treatment of choice for hyperactivity. It maximizes the child's potential for positive development, and it aids the rest of the family as well.

NOTES

1. For reasons of space I will not go into how the therapist can help a family plan and coordinate aspects of treatment separate from the family sessions. For competent work with ADHD and ADD families, a family therapist must be well informed about the full spectrum of such options. Barkley (1998), Power and colleagues (2001), and DuPaul and Stoner (2003) are recommended readings.

2. Two genes involving the production and removal of the neurotransmitter dopamine from the synapse seem to be implicated, although this is not yet certain (Cook, Stein, & Leventhal, 1997).

3. Exactly how much alcohol leads to risk is unclear. Indications are that it might be any quantity of alcohol at all. The first two trimesters seem to be the critical period.

4. See Pliszka and Colleagues (1999), Barkley (1998, 2000), Amen (2002), and Everett and Everett (1999) for how to do an evaluation of ADHD and ADD.

5. In 1994, with the American Psychiatric Association's publication of *DSM-IV*, three basic subtypes of ADHD were defined. The first and most common is attention-deficit/hyperactivity disorder, combined type. This diagnosis includes the following three symptoms: inattentiveness, hyperactivity, and impulsivity. The second subtype has symptoms of only inattention and distractibility. Following custom, I will refer to this as ADD. The third subtype includes symptoms of both hyperactivity and impulsivity, but not inattention. This subtype is known as attention-deficit/hyperactivity disorder, predominantly hyperactive-impulsive type.

6. The claims about oppositional-defiant disorder are the most disparate, ranging from estimates of 15% (Milich, Widiger, & Landau, 1987) to as high as 60% (Shapiro & Garfinkel, 1986).

7. The question of bipolar disorder is more controversial. For one thing, there are very few studies on the frequency of bipolar disorder

in prepuberty children. Also, it is not clear exactly what should be taken as differential criteria distinguishing ADHD and bipolar disorder. Clearly this is a matter requiring much study.

8. Research has shown stimulant medications to be effective in improving behavior, schoolwork, and social relationships in 50% to 95% of the children with ADHD (DuPaul, Barkley, & Connor, 1998).

9. For an excellent discussion of medications for ADHD see DuPaul and colleagues (1998). They estimated that 1% to 3% of children with ADHD cannot tolerate any dose of any stimulant medication. They also found that over one half of the children tested in their clinic have decreased appetite, insomnia, anxiousness, irritability, or proneness to crying as side effects of medication.

10. For example, Anastopoulos and colleagues (1996) used a format for the parents of 10 group meetings. Power, Karustis, and Habboushe (2001) used group meetings with ADHD children.

11. Another difference concerns system dynamics. Everett and Everett (1999) believed ADHD families mostly display certain typical dynamics. I see ADHD system dynamics as varying much more widely.

12. This has been brought out in the research of Zakay (1992). Similar results were found with ADD children as well.

13. See Power and colleagues (2001), Barkley (2000), and Christophersen and Mortweet (2001) for research on token and point programs for children with ADHD.

14. This excellent book discusses group therapy for helping ADHD children and parents with homework. Power's program includes separate groups for parents and children.

15. I leave aside the question of how the family might be helped to be brought into a collaborative relationship with the school, as this varies greatly from school to school. See Pfiffner and Barkley (1998).

16. Power and colleagues (2001) came up with this clever idea. They, however, suggested that the parent prepare the "kit" (as they called it) alone. I prefer to make the undertaking more systemic, with parent and child doing the preparation together. Additionally, I have found that often another child in the family, who has no problems with homework, soon wants her own "supplies sack" as well and also wants

to organize it with the parent. I of course support this. It helps moti-vate the ADHD child, and it is also good for the sibling relationship.

17. Children with ADD have fewer problems in this area.

18. For example, for PTSD, sleep disorders, and anxiety (Chris-tophersen & Mortweet, 2001).

19. It is not just a matter of patience. Children under 5 are much less capable with complex visualization tasks.

20. Various opinions exist on this. I am not aware of research, with children or adults, comparing the effectiveness of different ways to divide up muscle groupings.

21. Kendall (1991) suggested using a minimum of three muscle groups with children.

22. See Christophersen and Mortweet (2001) for a good script for doing muscle relaxation with children.

23. A recorded audio CD is an option if a parent does not want to take over the responsibility or if the child does not want him to. Good commercial CDs for progressive relaxation can be purchased, or the therapist can make her own.

24. Parents frequently tell me that they began responding in this mode way back when the child was an infant. Similar behavior can be seen with video-supported intervention techniques with families with infants or toddlers who have symptoms of excessive crying (see Papousek, 2004).

CHAPTER FOURTEEN

Sibling Relationships

• •

Sibling relationships are probably the single most neglected issue in family therapy, yet intuitively their importance seems obvious. Many children have as much or more contact with a sibling than they do with either parent (Bank & Kahn, 1982; Dunn & Plomin, 1990; Kahn & Lewis, 1988). Sibling relationships are a crucial arena for social learning. In this arena a child has formative experiences, over the course of many years, that may involve sharing, loyalty, humor, admiration, and trust—as well as jealousy, betrayal, exploitation, and violence. Our sibling relationships mark us forever.

From a systemic perspective, the sibling subgroup is also of tremendous significance. It has the power to complement—or undercut—parental influences. For that reason alone, one of the strongest moves a family therapist can make, systemically speaking, is to give attention to these relationships. This is true even when the problem that has brought the family to therapy lies in another area. Whatever other therapeutic work has been accomplished, improved sibling bonds and more open sibling communication will add an extra layer of support to the change process.[1]

Often the circular causal links are even tighter. Although the family is not aware of it, the problem preoccupying them may have plenty of hidden ties to difficulties in the sibling subset, as the vignettes in this chapter will show.

This turn to the sibling relationships should typically take place during the extension phase. Often the topic is mentioned earlier, often by one of the siblings themselves. Usually this work with sibling issues goes quickly and does not require a lot of time in the therapy.

The concept of *goal renegotiation* has already been discussed (Chapter 12). As explained, the idea is first to achieve elimination or a significant improvement with regard to the initial problem. With many cases this can be accomplished in the first three to five sessions. At that point, the family is offered goal renegotiation. They may opt to end the therapy, or they may opt to continue, pursuing modified goals. Usually new insights gained during the first sessions now allow them to formulate altered goals.

This is the moment, for many families, in which issues about sibling relationships come into focus. Frequently, along with other goals, the family decides to work toward change with respect to one or more sibling relationships and with some aspect of how the parents treat the siblings *qua* siblings.

The actual work with these sibling matters might occupy an entire separate session, or it might be done over several sessions, or during parts of them.

HOW ARE SIBLINGS ISSUES RAISED?

Interestingly, one of the most common ways that sibling issues are raised are by a sibling herself. At one time this was surprising to me. Years ago, when I began concentrating on letting children have more of a presence in family therapy, one unexpected result was a thematizing of sibling matters. The parents would come in for help with a child, but it was that child's sister or brother who would verbalize (or sometimes draw or paint) the sibling subset problem. This was what happened with the Schmidt family.

The Schmidts were a German family living in Paris. They had come in because of difficulties with Tilo, age 4. Tilo's 8-year-old brother, Max, was also present.

The parents told me about Tilo's frequent rages and oppositional behavior, which took place both at home and in kindergarten. Max was described as a good, obedient, intelligent boy.

During the first session I asked everybody the "magic wand" question (see Chapter 11): "If you had a magic wand, and with this wand you could wish to change anything in your family so that you would be happier, what would you wish for?" Max responded that his brother would disappear. Mrs. Schmidt immediately turned to me. She said she was sure Max did not mean that. Suddenly Max became even more intense. He insisted that his wish was for his brother to die.

I inquired about how he would be happier without Tilo. He replied that his parents would stop fighting about his brother and that his mother would have time to play with him again. This expression of resentment and pain captured his parents' immediate attention. They had never considered the consequences of Tilo's difficulties for Max. Until now, Max had never communicated his suffering.

Notice the parents' surprise in this example. This is typical. Parents tend to become so concerned by a difficult child's problems that they half forget about their "good" child. How, in such a moment, should the therapist respond? Remember, this was a first session.

My recommendation is, first, to make sure the parents have heard the sibling. Give them an opportunity to reply to the sibling who has spoken out. The therapist too can acknowledge what has been said.

Then, normally, one suggests to the family that they plan to return to this important matter some sessions from now. The therapist can explain that, usually, the most rapid means for the family to profit from the therapy is for everyone first to remain focused upon the difficulties of the child for whom they initially sought help. This way, things can begin to change for that child. Then, a few sessions later (in the extension phase), the family's attention can be better given in therapy to the sibling.

This does not mean that nothing is done about the new issue now. It may be that a small step, requiring little session time, can be taken at once by the family. But a more in-depth exploration will wait until later. In the case just described, for example, we took a few minutes on the spot to plan some structured play time for Max with each parent.

This is the most efficient procedure, I find, in the majority of instances when a sibling thematizes such a problem during the first two or three sessions. (I discuss exceptions to this guideline later in the chapter.)

Now consider a different scenario. A family much like the Schmidts comes for therapy. But nothing is said about sibling issues in any of the first few sessions. Let's say that by the time of the fourth session, the family has achieved their initial goal. Tilo (or his equivalent in this family) is now doing better at home and at kindergarten. The parents are doing better with respect to setting boundaries, confirming good behavior, having clear rules, and the like. What then?

My strong recommendation here is for the therapist to initiate a brief, minimal exploration of the overall state of sibling relationships. The reason is simple: It is not easy for children to speak about these matters, especially to the family as a whole. The fact that no child has spontaneously brought up sibling issues does not indicate that nothing needs to be expressed along those lines. The therapist therefore can briefly provide a framework that will make it safer for such things to be said.

With some families, the therapist is confronted with a still different situation. The family has come for reasons having nothing to do (in their minds at least) with sibling themes. Nor does anyone, child or parent, spontaneously bring such matters up. But the therapist himself notices something in this area that seems to demand immediate attention. He may then need to suggest this right away, instead of waiting until the resolution phase has ended.

For example, the therapist may think that something in the functioning of the sibling subset is having substantial, direct effects upon the problem for which the parents are seeking help. Such was the case with the Millers.

> Mr. and Mrs. Miller had two daughters, Lily, 17 years old, and Allison, 8 years old. Allison had been in individual therapy for depression for the past 6 months.
>
> Lily had been in a boarding school for a year. Allison's depression began exactly 2 months after Lily left the home. Lily and Allison had shared a room and had been very close. As both Mr. and Mrs. Miller worked full-time, Lily had parented Allison a lot.
>
> Since Lily had left for boarding school, she had not written to Allison or telephoned her. She did not want to come home for vacations or for weekends. The sudden onset of Allison's depression was clearly linked to her separation from Lily. Sessions were organized to include Lily so these themes could be addressed.

Another reason for immediate action is when abusive, destructive behavior is going on among the children and the therapist estimates that the degree of danger is too high to wait. For example, the therapist has heard about violent threats, or recent aggressive behavior that appears truly dangerous, or sexual exploitation that needs to be stopped at once.[2] The parents may have been unaware of what was happening. Or they have been minimizing it or outright denying it.

Mrs. Talbot was a single parent with a son, Jean, 12 years old, and a daughter, Marie, 8 years old. Jean had been hospitalized in a psychiatric clinic for evaluation. He came home on weekends. He had been setting fires, acting sadistically toward other children, and torturing animals. The clinic staff had urgently recommended family therapy.

When I asked Marie the "magic wand" question, she said that she wanted Jean not to come home anymore. I asked how it would be better for her if he stayed at the clinic all the time. She explained that often at night, when Mrs. Talbot was sleeping, Jean came into her room and did "dirty things" to her, things that "hurt."

Mrs. Talbot responded with irritation and assured me that Marie must be dreaming and imagining these things. Mrs. Talbot then added that in her opinion Marie watched too much television.

Sometimes such information may have come from another agency or from the child protective services.

INQUIRING ABOUT THE SIBLING RELATIONSHIP

If it is the therapist who introduces the topic of sibling relationships—or reintroduces it after a family member brought it up in a previous session—a short explanation is warranted.

- The relationship among sisters and brothers is very important. Now might be a good time to talk more about how it is going at home among the children.
- In an earlier session one of the children mentioned that she was not so happy about what happens between her and her

brother. Now seems like a good time to explore this relationship a bit more, as things are going better with the problems you came in with.

The exploration itself can continue with questions directed to both the parents and the children. For example, addressing a child:

- Can you tell me what you like about your sibling?
- What would you like to her change?
- What does your sister do that makes you angry?

Similar questions can be asked to each parent:

- What do you think about what the children just said, about what they would like to change about each other? Do you agree?
- What are you unhappy about concerning how your children get along with each other?
- What would you like to change about how they treat each other?
- What do they do to each other that results in your being angry?

Exploring family representations of what is unique and special about the various sibling relationships is useful too. Both the parents' and the children's perspectives should be heard.

- What about your children's relationship makes you proud as a parents?
- What do you appreciate that goes on between them?
- Which values as parents have you transmitted to your children about how siblings should treat each other?
- What is special about you and your brother?

278

- What do you especially like about your sister?
- What can your sister do especially well?

Afterwards, the therapist might ask about the history of the sibling relationships, again addressing both parents and children.

- How has the relationship between Christian and Patrick changed over the years?
- Have there been times when there were exceptions to how it is now?
- What do you think has caused the relationship between Christian and Patrick to change for the worse over the past few years?
- Since problems in your family began, what changes have you noticed in the relationship between your son and daughter?

The children can be asked similar questions:

- Was there a time when you got along with your sister better than now?
- When did you get along with your sister the best?
- Was there a time you got along worse with your sister?
- Why do you think you now fight all the time, but when you were younger you got along better?

Another information-rich area to explore is what happened when a younger child was born. Issues of sibling jealousy often have their origins here. How did the older child react?

- How did Jason react when you told him that you were pregnant and going to have another child?
- Was he present during the birth?

279

- What do you remember about how Jason reacted when the baby was brought home from the hospital?
- What changed for Jason once the new baby was in the home?

The children themselves should also be addressed. Many of the same questions can easily be translated into children's language:

- What was it like for you when your parents came home with your brother? What do you remember?
- What changed at home after the baby was there?
- Did your parents change? How?

Another group of questions, often relevant, involves significant events and crises in the family's life. How did these affect the sibling relationships? Examples include serious illnesses and hospitalizations, moves, separations, divorce, accidents, and deaths.

- What were important crises or turning points in your family's life?
- How have these affected Christian and Patrick's relationship?

Never overlook the troublesome area of competition and jealousy. Ask at least a little about this, and, depending upon the family, perhaps a lot.

- What can your brother do better than you?
- What would you like to do as well as, or even better than, your sister?
- When you feel jealous of your sister, what is it usually about?
- What do you think your brother is jealous of that you can do better than he can?

- What can your sister do that makes your mother or father proud that you cannot do as well?
- In what way do you think your mother or father would want you to be more like your sister?

The therapist should also be aware that parents often see sibling relationships as a kind of closed-off universe impervious to any influence coming from the parents' side. Indeed, parents frequently feel helpless in this regard. They may be taken aback to hear from the therapist that this is not so, and that considerable research shows quite the opposite. It is useful for them to learn that they have a lot of potential leverage in this domain, as you will see later in this chapter.

Therapists can also explain that in order to bring about change in a sibling relationship, the therapeutic work usually must take place on two levels. One level concerns how the siblings behave and communicate with one another. The second level concerns how the parents treat the siblings *qua* siblings. Both levels need to addressed.

TYPES OF SIBLING SUBSET PROBLEMS

Types of sibling subset issues range from sibling incest to sibling hatred. I will cover a few of the most common ones here.

Fighting and Aggression

Out-of-control fighting and aggression is one of the most common types of sibling subset issues. When confronted with this issue, the first step is to obtain more information. Questions like the following can be asked:

- What usually happens when your children fight?
- How would you three [the siblings] describe what happens?
- Where do the fights usually take place?

- Which time of day do most of the fights occur?
- In your perception, Tom, who usually starts the fights?
- Out of the last 10 fights, how many did each child start?
- How does a fight typically continue?
- What is each child's preferred fighting style?
- How do the fights typically end?
- In the last 10 fights, did someone seem to win? How many times did each child win?
- What normally has to happen before you [the parents] intervene?
- What do you [the children] have to do before your parents intervene?
- In the last 10 fights, how many times did you [the parents] have to intervene?
- If you [the parents] are both present, who typically intervenes?

Moving to the behavioral sequences at a certain point is essential. Always get everybody's version of the event. Each parent should also be asked.

- Tell me in detail about a recent example of a typical fight.
- Tell me just what happened, step by step.

You can also ask about the "worst" fight, as well as about any "positive exception" fights.

- Tell me about the worst fight you have had.
- Tell me in detail about a recent fight where in some way things went better than usual.

An art technique (see Chapter 4) is often useful for bringing out more aspects. You can ask if the children are willing to draw a picture of the fight being discussed. I also frequently use dramatization (see Chapter 2). A recent fight is selected. Each member plays her own role. This not only brings out more information, but also helps with the next therapeutic step, which is identifying underlying feelings I discuss later in the chapter.

Evaluating What is Said

As she listens, the first job of the therapist is to evaluate what she hears. She should especially be thinking about three questions: 1. How bad has the situation become? 2. What are the parents doing or not doing about it? 3. What contributing causes may be in play? Let's look at each of these separately.

1. How bad has the situation become? This is one of those knotty normative dilemmas. On the one hand, who is to say where to draw the line? Who decides what is acceptable or unacceptable sibling conflict? On the other hand, it seems undeniable that many families need help with this issue. I find it helpful to ask about the following areas.[3]

First, is the behavior age-appropriate or not? For example: I recently saw a family in which a 9-year-old, an 8-year-old, and a 6-year-old were biting each other during fights. I was shown a series of scars on arms and other body parts. A good rule of thumb is that biting past the age of 2 is not age-appropriate. Serious hitting and kicking past the age of 5 is not appropriate.

Second, how frequent is the fighting? Don't just rely upon what the parents say about this; get information from the children as well. If the parents describe the children's fighting as "poisoning their family life the whole day long," this may or may not be true. Some parents only pay attention when there is trouble; when the children play calmly, the parents no longer notice. Compare everyone's point of view here.

Third, how proportional is the intensity of the fighting to its typical triggering cause? Here is an example of disproportion: In a family I worked with, a 4-year-old boy recounted a situation in which he and his 6-year-old brother were watching television. The brother went to the bathroom. When he returned, he found that the 4-year-old had taken his chair. In retaliation the brother hit and kicked the 4-year-old, pushed him to the floor, and kicked him some more. What is relevant here is not just the degree of aggressiveness but also the low threshold for its emergence.[4]

Fourth, how abusive or dangerous are the individual behaviors? In a quarrel with siblings, what seems to be the intent of a child's fighting style? Is it just to stand up for himself? Or is it to hurt, injure, or humiliate a sibling? How mean or sadistic are the words spoken and the actions taken? Find out, too, whether any child's physical possessions are ever deliberately damaged.

Fifth, how much ganging up takes place? When one child becomes abusive with a sibling, does the third sibling regularly join in? Do playmates join in as well? Or even a parent? In one family I treated, a daughter had composed a quite humiliating song that belittled her brother. She was fond of singing it at dinner. Typically the rest of the family would then join in the singing.

Sixth, how much unexpressed emotional hurt are the conflicts causing for one or more of the children? Because children normally mask this, some good listening will probably be required. I go into that shortly.

Seventh, what background cultural norms are at play? Cultures vary with respect to how much intrafamilial violence is sanctioned. I am not saying that a therapist working with a family whose background culture is relatively violence-permissive should ignore what he considers to be destructive consequences. Nevertheless, the cultural aspect may, at a minimum, necessitate considerable diplomacy on the therapist's part in how he addresses the family about these sibling issues.

2. What are the parents doing or not doing about it? First, when conflicts occur, do the parents intervene too early? Or do they normally act too late, or even not at all? Some parents become overly involved the moment the children bicker. In one family I saw, the mother reacted to light, playful roughhousing with fear that the children might "kill each other." Others downplay starkly vicious events with a statement like, "That's just what kids do."

Second, if there are two parents (or more caretakers), who intervenes? Do they more or less share this task when both are present, or has one parent become the "enforcer"? What are the different styles with which they intervene?

Third, have the parents established clear rules concerning fighting? Clear consequences?

Fourth, when a parent must mediate a conflict, does she do this competently? Is each child's point of view listened to and taken seriously? Are possible compromise solutions solicited from the children themselves, at least some of the time? Does the parent bring in a calmer tone and an atmosphere of expectancy that solutions can be found?

3. *What contributing causes may be in play?* This concerns other forms of parental behavior that may be indirectly feeding the siblings' antagonism with one another.

A common example is favoritism. If a parent's words or actions frequently appear to reflect a marked preference for one child over another, the second child is likely to experience strong resentment. This will effectively operate as a structuring cause. A small triggering event between siblings may then elicit seemingly exaggerated reactions. Then other residual anger gets mixed in.

Comparisons can have similar effects. "How come your sister manages to do her homework before dinner and you never do?" "Why can't you just relax and enjoy the car trip the way Jonathan is doing?" A parent promotes competitiveness with such messages. In some families, comparative comments and labels are pervasive. One child is portrayed as an angel, the other as a devil. The parents' representations of the children have become polarized to an extreme degree.[5]

Another source of anger can be a lack of parental differentiation between siblings. Often this plays out as an older child and a younger one being treated the same way with respect to rules and privileges. A child who is 4 and a child who is 8 may have to go to bed at the same time, for example. The parents believe they are being "fair," but the 8-year-old perceives the situation as grossly unfair. The older child's resentment then gets acted out toward the younger sibling in very direct forms.

A contributing cause of a different order can be the manner with which the parents handle conflicts between themselves. Violence and abuse on the adult level are likely to be mirrored in the children's relations with one another. The siblings follow the model of what they see and hear. Likewise, a child who himself experiences regular physical violence at the hands of one or both parents will be more prone to behave the same way toward a sibling.

So the therapist asks, listens, reflects. He gathers together for himself an overall picture of what is really happening in the area of sibling conflict. But what next? How should he actually speak to the family about the evaluation he has made? Luckily, it is usually not necessary for the therapist simply to deliver his "opinion" without any support for such a viewpoint having first come from the family. There is another, better way. I turn now to that.

Identifying Underlying Feelings

A key to working with sibling fighting is to get at the underlying feelings of the siblings themselves. Normally these are quite hidden. You don't survive in a vicious atmosphere by showing a vulnerable face. But the feelings are almost always there. The worse the abuse, verbal or physical, the more at least one of the siblings will hate it. This suffering can be strong, despite being little shown. Even in a bully/victim sibling dyad, the bully may have his own suffering. Often this has to do with the systemic issues just described, such as perceived favoritism in how a parent treats the other child.

The job of the therapist is let these underlying currents of sadness, pain, and resentment find open expression in the family. Frequently this can be made a natural next step of the exploration. One means is just to pose further questions.

- What is it like for you when your brother kicks you in the knees and deliberately tries to hurt you?
- Do you feel your sister is being fair when she takes your toys and breaks them?
- What do you feel when your brother calls you "a piece of shit"?
- When you hear screaming insults from your sister, how does it make you feel?

Another particularly effective path to these covered-up affects is through a dramatization. As already mentioned, a dramatization will reveal typical behavioral sequences. But it can also bring out what is occurring on a deeper emotional level. The therapist simply stops the action from time to time and inquires about what is happening on this level.

> With the Fontaine family, a dramatization portrayed a recent fight between Sophie and Sadie. At one point Sadie, the younger sister, ran crying to her mother. She claimed that Sophie was "breaking her arm," even though Sophie's physical attempt to grab back a toy Sadie had seized was nothing of the kind. The mother then punished Sophie, who was not permitted to relate her version of the event. In response to my question about how she experienced this sequence, Sophie expressed feeling betrayed by both of them, and furious.

Eliciting such reactions and evaluations from the children is almost always the best way to nudge the family into a discourse about what they would like to change in this domain. The therapist can, of course, mention how matters appear from her standpoint. But the family will be more receptive, and her comments will have more weight, if she waits until the children's own discomfort has found expression.

Exploring Alternative Solutions

A last step is for the family to work out, and perhaps rehearse, some alternative solutions. One level of this exploration is with the siblings themselves. With the therapist providing guidance, they can think through some new ways to respond to conflict situations. Ideas coming from the children, and negotiated among themselves, have a much higher probability of being implemented at home. Additionally, the act of negotiating is a new behavior in itself.

> Corinne and Melissa, ages 4 and 7, were looking for a way to settle disputes without fighting. During a dramatization, the sisters played out a recent occurrence that had taken place at mealtime. The family had a set of glasses where each glass was a different color. Both Corinne and Melissa were fond of a particular blue glass. At this meal, Corinne had already taken the blue glass, but at a moment when she was not paying attention, Melissa silently switched the blue glass and another one. Squabbling and crying ensued. Their mother arrived, gave the blue glass back to Corinne, and punished Melissa. Melissa now complained that, even though she shouldn't have taken the glass, her mother was unfair in that she gave the blue glass to Corinne much more often than to Melissa. Corinne agreed with this. Corinne then suggested that they take turns having the blue glass. They decided to write out a schedule for the glass at home.

More often than not, the parents must be worked with as well. Usually I suggest that, at home, the children can first try to come up with their own solutions. Then the parent's role can clearly be defined as a kind of mediator. The parent will attempt, as far as possible, to create a framework where the two (or more) siblings will negotiate with each other.

> Mrs. Bernel, the mother of Corinne and Melissa, explored how she could help the girls settle such disputes. I recommended that she stay calm and first listen to both sides. Melissa broke in and said that this "listening to both sides" was important to her. A good format, I suggested, would be to give each girl 5 minutes to explain her version of the conflict. Next, instead of Mrs. Bernel solving the problem, she would ask each girl to suggest two possible solutions. The girls would then choose what seemed to them the fairest and most workable solution.

Needless to say, a future dramatization can also be useful. Either a new way to handle conflict can be hashed out first and then practiced in the future dramatization, or the very act of constructing the future dramatization can be used to determine how the new alternative might look.

With some families, however, the therapist will find herself faced with a dilemma at this point. When she proposes a future enactment of how a next fight might go, the parents object. What they want, they say, is for the fighting to stop entirely! Peace and harmony is the desire.

How should this be managed? You might simply confront the parents, gently, about how realistic they imagine such a goal would be. Or, if you are willing at times to be more explicit about child development, you can briefly go into the positive advantages of letting the children have their occasional fights. What they most need to learn is how to deal with peer conflicts in a constructive fashion.

Assessing the Severity of Sibling Fighting

The following two case examples illustrate severe and dangerous sibling violence.

The Clark family was in a crisis. Their 5-year-old, Peter, appeared to have tried to kill their 5-month-old daughter, Julie. According to Mr. and Mrs. Clark, Peter had been threatening to "get rid of Julie" since her birth. At times he had pinched Julie, shaken her, taken away her bottle, and destroyed several of her toys. After each event the parents had punished Peter and told him he was a very bad boy. But they hadn't really taken Peter's jealousy and rage seriously, until now.

Two days ago Peter had picked Julie up, carried her to the window, and was planning to throw her out of it. (Peter himself confirmed this.) Luckily his father came in the room just as Peter was struggling to open the window.

As I learned more about the family, it came out that Julie cried constantly, had feeding difficulties, and since birth had slept little at night. The parents were exhausted and constantly on edge, from both lost sleep and the daytime stress. Prior to Julie's birth, Peter had slept in the parents' bed. Julie had now replaced him. In response to questions from me, the parents also affirmed that this situation had left them with almost no energy or time for Peter.

In this initial session I used a systemic art technique. I asked each family member to draw the family now, and then to draw it before Julie was born. Peter drew dark clouds, with rain falling onto the house, for his "now" version. Inside the house he was alone, with a wall separating him from Julie and his parents. His second drawing, of before Julie was born, showed a large sun and the parents holding Peter's hand.

The wall and the rain clouds in Peter's first picture became the subject of an intense family discourse. I helped Peter articulate his loneliness and how much he missed his parent's attention.

290

The Gravier family was required by the judge to come to treatment. Quentin, 9 years old, had recently stabbed his 6-year-old-brother, Alain, in the hand with a knife during dinner. His explanation was that Alain had taken the last piece of bread. This was not the first act of violence between Quentin and Alain. Based on the seriousness of Alain's wound, together with the chaos in the family (the parents' substance abuse, unemployment, and frequent moves among homes), the judge had decided to temporarily remove Quentin and place him in an institution. A social worker has accompanied Quentin to the family therapy session.

For years both parents had considered the boys' fighting normal. The parents themselves were also frequently violent with both children. They saw this as good discipline, a means for the boys to "learn a lesson." The two adults also were regularly verbally and physically aggressive with each other. Were the court system not compelling them to do so, they admitted, they would never have sought to change anything in their family.

In many respects these families were very different. Yet both share a basic aspect: The danger signals were present from early on. The parents had mistakenly assumed that the siblings' mounting troubles were nothing deserving of concern. Potential risks and negative outcomes were underestimated. Both cases required an alternative evaluative perspective from the therapist.

Disabilities and Chronic Illness

A sibling theme of a very different nature can emerge when a family has one child who is disabled or chronically ill. In therapy, such families normally seek help for how they can better organize themselves, cope with the stress, mourn, and (all too often) save their couple relationship. But typically they overlook another critical issue: how things are for the other sibling or siblings.[6]

Frequently, this second "healthy" sibling finds herself caught in a terrible bind. The parents' attention, time, emotional concern, and perhaps financial resources are mostly directed toward the impaired sibling. As a result, the needs of the "healthy" child are largely ignored. Yet the last thing this child wants to do is add to her parents' burdens, so she stays quiet. The parents push her into the background, emotionally speaking, and she keeps herself there.

On top of that, she may be asked to assist, perhaps extensively. Instead of playing or being with friends, she ends up sharing responsibility for a sibling who, for example, has cerebral palsy, cystic fibrosis, Down syndrome, cancer, or is deaf or blind.[7] The nonimpaired child may thus feel isolated from her peers, isolated from her parents, resentful, and angry, while at the same time cut off from any chance of communicating her suffering to anyone. She may also have a lot of irrational fears about her own health, mental or physical.

Detailed therapeutic work with this child's relationship to the rest of the family will probably be undertaken in the extension phase. The issue may become thematized earlier, however.

A typical time it emerges, for example, is when exploring the nonimpared child's representations of the sibling's illness or disability. Inquiry can be made, for example, about what this child believes about the causes of the other's condition. Some of her ideas, of course, will be based on medical information circulating in the family. But if the therapist searches further, often a unique, private version will be uncovered. This version is often highly confused. Frequently it is based on magical thinking and reflects both intense survivor guilt and powerful fears. The child may hold the parents responsible for the sibling's disability or illness. Or she may fear that the parents, too, could die from the same illness or become disabled. Typically, she fears that she herself will become "infected" and come down with the same impairment. This was the case with Isaac and Timothy.

Isaac, age 8, had a brother, Timothy, age 10, who had a severe congenital heart disease. Timothy had to be very careful not to exert himself. He was not allowed to run or play sports. The parents had frequently warned both boys that Timothy could die if he ran. Isaac had been delegated the role of reporting to the parents whenever Timothy was disobedient by running or playing too hard.

Isaac believed that he had holes in his heart, too, but no one could see them. Whenever he played soccer, which he loved, he afterward became fearful that he would die. Furthermore, Isaac's father had recently had a minor heart attack. Isaac was also petrified now that his father would die.

To reassure Isaac that he had no holes in his heart, his parents took him to a cardiac specialist who tested Isaac's heart. The doctor showed Isaac the pictures from the magnetic imaging and reassured Isaac.

Isaac's father spoke to him as well about the different kinds of heart attacks people can have. He explained to Isaac everything that he had now undertaken to "heal his heart," such as engaging in sports, eating better, and stopping smoking. Both the trip to the doctor and the explanations from his father helped calm Isaac down.

Any feelings of shame should be allowed a voice as well. This may not be easy; the nonimpaired child may feel that her shame is even more out of bounds than her anger. Nevertheless, it is another common affective reaction. For the healthy child, the family is marked as different from others, and most children feel shame at being so different.

Whenever Barbara went out to play, she had to take Marion, her sister who had Down syndrome, with her. She felt both embarrassed and burdened. Her friends often made fun of Marion. But Barbara's parents told her she must protect and take care of Marion when that happened. Barbara was rarely allowed to play with anyone without including her sister. This had resulted in her being almost never invited to other children's homes.

Barbara felt very angry at her parents for all this. Yet she felt a lot of guilt about her anger, too. I supported Barbara to find words to express this anger to her parents. They were touched by Barbara's unhappiness and loneliness. They made a decision in the session that they would let Barbara go out often without her sister. Also, if Barbara had other children over to play, they would occupy Marion and keep her away from Barbara's friends.

Any other forms of resentment on the part of the nonimpaired child should be explored too. Frequently these include a sense of being left out, desire for parental attention and emotional care, and hunger for play with a parent.

Needless to say, however, in such an exchange the therapist must simultaneously be extremely supportive of the parents. Caring for a disabled or ill child is a hard road to travel. The point is not to criticize the parents. It is simply to alert them to the emotional and developmental needs of the "healthy" child who has been left too much in the shadows.

Some practical negotiation and further problem-solving will now ensue. The overriding question is: How can the nonimpaired sibling be permitted a childhood? Given the demands of the situation, compromise is unavoidable. Things can't match how they are in most other families. Yet solutions can be worked out. Partly these will have to do with how the parents can plan to give some attention, however limited, to this child's need for contact with them. Partly they will have to do with how the child at times can get out of the home and engage in activities with other children.

The last step to undertake here concerns the sibling relationship itself. (I suggest "last" as it is much easier to accomplish once these other points have been covered.) What needs to change? For example, in what ways might the two of them better relate to each other as peers? How can they play together and have open disputes and conflicts together? How can they share humor, trust, and mutual respect? Can some mutually satisfying activities or areas of interest be found?

> Olivier, age 8, had just returned home from a long stay at the hospital. He had leukemia and had become very weak from chemotherapy. Valerie, 6 years old, and Olivier decided that they wanted to have a pet that they could both play with and care for. The parents thought this was an excellent idea. They got a puppy. Olivier and Valerie fed, walked, and played with the puppy together, bringing much laughter and fun to their relationship.

Sometimes the parents must provide a still more detailed framework for such shared activity. This is a big topic deserving of a chapter in itself. I will just indicate a few possibilities to give the reader the general idea.[8]

It is best to suggest play activities that encourage interaction—for example, building blocks, Legos, Playmobil, dolls and dollhouse, puppets, or board games, to mention a few. Naturally the activity should not highlight the disabled child's deficits.

A specific time framework may need to be proposed. Developmentally delayed and sick children vary in their capabilities to sustain play. A time framework limited to 20 minutes may be right, for example. With preschool children, it may need to be even shorter, maybe 10 minutes.

The parent can also organize a play environment with minimum distractions. The television and the computer can be shut off, the Game Boy tucked away in the closet. This encourages more interactive playing. Perhaps other toys and things are also better put away. These steps will happen more easily if the parent takes them over.

Parental praise, judiciously dosed, should be used. "Eric, it's very nice of you to help your brother play with you." Or, "I like to watch you two play together. Good sharing."

Some rules and guidelines are also likely to be needed. Limits such as no throwing, no hitting, and no name-calling will have an extra importance. The parent may need to monitor the play from a distance. Remember, the rules must apply to both children.[9]

Depending upon the child's impairment, there may be constraints on what is feasible. But it is important that the siblings try to expand their relationship as far as can be reached. Both will benefit. The nonimpaired child will be able to act more freely and naturally, and in ways fitting her age, when she is with her sibling. For the impaired child, of course, the stakes are high too. These interactions with a sibling probably will be the impaired child's primary means of learning about how peers can share a world.[10]

The "Parental Void"

A still different sibling state of affairs is what I call living in a "parental void." The parents are absent either physically, mentally, or emotionally. One or both parents may be incarcerated, institutionalized, severely ill, hospitalized, or dead. Perhaps the parents are no longer the legal guardians, and the children live with other relatives. Or, the parents may live at home but for all practical purposes have abdicated the parental role due to drugs, alcohol, criminality, or mental illness. The children are at high risk for severe neglect, abuse, or abandonment.

In yet other situations, the children have been forcibly separated—placed in separate foster homes or in different institutions. Family therapy work, in collaboration with the relevant agencies or institutions, may be their one chance to stay connected as siblings.

Common to all "parental void" situations is the special need of forging sibling relationships with as much loyalty and mutual support as possible. I strongly believe this should be made a regular practice within the mental health system. It makes double sense in terms of both cost-effectiveness and the children's development. The help that siblings are capable of giving to one another in such adverse conditions can be stunning, but they have to be helped to help one another.

This is something the family therapist can undertake. A series of sessions can be dedicated to seeing some or all of the siblings without their parents. I at times call this "sibling family therapy."[11] Often it starts with a focus upon immediate crises, but its purpose is much deeper. It can provide the children with the feeling of belonging and with essential skills in giving and receiving emotional nourishment.

> The Duroc family had been referred by a social worker who was concerned about the children's welfare. Mr. and Mrs. Duroc had been alcoholics for many years. Their many attempts to stop drinking had been unsuccessful. Mr. Duroc was a truck driver. He was often on the road for a week at a time.
>
> Elise, 10 years old, had assumed a parental role and regularly cooked, cleaned the house, and watched after her 8-year-old brother, Hugo. She made sure Hugo was bathed, correctly dressed, and had enough to eat. She walked Hugo to and from school every day. Elise also took care of her mother when her father was away. Elise and Hugo's relationship was very aggressive and full of rivalry. Hugo and Elise's rage toward their parents had been displaced onto each other. Sibling sessions helped them understand this and then learn how to fight constructively with each other. Another goal that was achieved through sibling sessions was building loyalty and solidarity with each other. They were helped to enjoy each other, and to protect each other when their parents were abusive.

Family therapy can have a powerful transformative effect on sibling relationships. This is rich, satisfying work to do for the therapist—and much worth the doing. A better foundation can be laid, potentially for a lifetime. After all, we usually know our siblings longer than we know anyone else. They are unique and potentially deeply meaningful relationships.

NOTES

1. It is remarkable how little this point has been explored in the family therapy literature. Exceptions to recommend are Bank and Kahn (1982), Kahn and Lewis (1988), Angel (1996), Tilmans-Ostyn and Meynckens-Fourez (2002), and Cook-Darzens (2002).

2. Threats should not be underestimated. A recent study (Singer & Flannery, 2000) clearly showed that threats by children and adolescents against other children need to be taken seriously. Actual acts of violence, both at home and at school, proved with high frequency to have been preceded by open threats.

3. See also Wiehe's (1990) useful ideas.

4. There is also such a thing as too little aggressive reaction. In one family, an anxious 7-year-old did not react at all when his 3-year-old brother ran off with and destroyed his favorite toy.

5. Frances Schacter (1985) explored this process in some depth.

6. Refer to Meynckens-Fourez (2002) for a good chapter on this subject.

7. For elaborations of this point see Bank and Kahn (1982), Gath (1974), Stoneman, Brody, Davis, and Crapps (1988, 1989), and Powell (1982).

8. See Powell (1982) for a more lengthly discussion.

9. With due allowance, in the case of a developmentally delayed sibling. This child must also learn to play without initiating aggressive behavior. But to eliminate or reduce such behaviors may take time.

10. As Stoneman et al. (1988, 1989) pointed out.

11. After what Karen Lewis (1988) in an article on multiproblem families called "sibling therapy."

Epilogue

• •

Families are here to stay. And, most likely, so is family therapy. Our profession will continue to evolve, but who knows how? My strong expectation is that as family therapists start giving children a more prominent role in the therapy process, there will be no going back. The results one sees are too convincing, and stimulating.

What I have tried to spell out here is one way to go about bringing the child more fully into the therapy experience. As I hope has been evident, it is a way which devotes more space to each child, yet still keeps the therapy framework as systemic as possible. Rather than simply intervene more directly with a child, one stays consistently focused on family communication and relationships. The change occurs in terms of how the child is helped to find a place within these systemic exchanges.

Without question such a goal could be realized in other fashions. My hope is that the ideas presented in these pages will encourage others to not only try out some of the described techniques, but also to experiment and explore different directions. Children have such interesting perspectives on the world, and are so creative. This can have an influence on the therapist: to unlock their creativity can help unlock one's own.

Separate from technical innovations, we also must continue to refine our theoretical thinking in family therapy. I would have liked to have been able to devote more space to this thinking here, as child development research is currently flourishing. Its many and steadily accumulating empirical findings compel us to reevaluate numerous background assumptions.

It is exciting to me to have this book appear in English, my native language. It was first published in French in 2005 and then in German in 2007 (France, Germany, and Switzerland being the principal sites where I conduct professional training). Now it can be read as it was originally conceived and written. May this English version find its way to those who can make good use of it.

Bibliography

● ●

Aarts, M. (2000). *Marte meo. Basic manual.* Harderwijk, The Netherlands: Aarts Productions.

Abrams, K., & Heese, E. (2006). Examining the role of parental frightened/frightening subtypes in predicting disorganized attachment within a brief observational procedure. *Development and Psychopathology,* 18, 34–361.

Ackerman, N. W. (1958). *The psychodynamics of family life.* New York: Basic.

Ackerman, N. W. (1966). *Treating the troubled family.* New York: Basic.

Ackerman, N. W. (1970). *Family therapy in transition.* Boston: Little, Brown.

Ainsworth, M. D., Blehar, M. C., Waters, E., & Wall, S. (1978). *Patterns of attachment.* Hillsdale, New Jersey: Erlbaum.

Amen, D. (2002). *Healing ADD.* New York: Berkley Books.

Anastopoulos, A. D., Barkley, R. A., & Shelton, T. L. (1996). Family-based treatment: Psychosocial intervention for children and adolescents with attention deficit hyperactivity disorder. In E. D. Hibbs & P. S. Jensen (Eds.), *Psychosocial treatments for child and adolescent disorders: Empirically based strategies for clinical practice* (pp. 267–284). Washington, DC: American Psychological Association.

Angel, S. (1996). *Des frères et des sœurs.* Paris: Reponses, R. Laffont.

Bank, S., & Kahn, M. (1982). *The sibling bond.* New York: Basic.

Barkley, R. (1997). *ADHD and the nature of self-control.* New York: Guilford.

Barkley, R. (Ed.). (1998). *Attention-deficit hyperactivity disorder: A handbook for diagnosis and treatment.* New York: Guilford.

Barkley, R. (2000). *Taking charge of ADHD: The complete, authoritative guide for parents.* New York: Guilford Press.

Barkley, R., DuPaul, G., & McMurray, M. (1990). A comprehensive evaluation of attention deficit disorder with and without hyperactivity. *Journal of Consulting and Clinical Psychology, 58,* 775–789.

Bateson, G. (1972). *Steps to an ecology of mind.* New York: Ballantine.

Bateson, G., Jackson, D., Haley, J., & Weakland, J. (1956). Toward a theory of schizophrenia. *Behavioral Science, 1,* 251.

Beebe, B. (2003). Brief mother-infant treatment: Psychoanalytically informed video feedback. *Infant Mental Health Journal, 24*(1), 24–52.

Beebe, B., & Jaffe, J. (2008). Dyadic microanalysis of mother-infant communication informs clinical practice. In A. Fogel, B. King, & S. Shanker (Eds.), *Human development in the 21st century: Visionary ideas from systems scientists* (pp. 176–187). New York: Cambridge University Press.

Beebe, B., Knoblauch, S., Rustin, J., & Sorter, D. (2005). *Forms of intersubjectivity in infant research and adult treatment.* New York: Basic.

Benson, H. (2000). *The relaxation response.* New York: Avon.

Berg, I. K. (1994). *Family-based services: A solution-focused approach.* New York: Norton.

Biederman, J., Faraone, S., Keenen, K., Knee, D., & Tsuang, M. (1990). Family-genetic and psychosocial risk factors in DSM-III attention deficit disorder. *Journal of the American Academy of Child and Adolescent Psychiatry, 29,* 526–533.

Biederman, J., Faraone, S., Mick, E., Spencer, T., Wilens, T., Kiely, K., Guite, J., Ablon, J., Reed, E., & Warburton, R. (1995). High risk for attention deficit hyperactivity disorder among children of parents with childhood onset of the disorder: A pilot study. *American Journal of Psychiatry, 152,* 431–435.

Black, M. (1962). Metaphor. In M. Black (Ed.), *Models and metaphors* (pp. 25–47). Ithaca, NY: Cornell University Press.

Black, M. (1993). More about metaphor. In A. Ortony (Ed.), *Metaphor and thought (2nd* ed., pp. 19–41). Cambridge: Cambridge University Press.

Blatner, A. (1994). Psychodramatic methods in family therapy. In C. Schaefer & L. Carey (Eds.), *Family play therapy.* London: Jason Aronson.

Bodin, A. (1977). Videotape applications in training family therapists. In P. Watzlawick & J. Weakland (Eds.), *The interactional view: Studies at the Mental Research Institute Palo Alto, 1965–1974* (pp. 129–142). New York: Norton.

Boszormenyi-Nagy, I., & Krasner, B. R. (1986). *Between give and take: A clinical guide to contextual therapy.* New York: Brunner/Mazel.

Boszormenyi-Nagy, I., & Spark, G. (1973). *Invisible loyalties: Reciprocity in intergenerational family therapy.* New York: Harper & Row.

Boszormenyi-Nagy, I., & Ulrich, D. (1981). Contextual family therapy. In A. S. Gurman & D. P. Kniskern (Eds.), *Handbook of family therapy.* New York: Brunner/Mazel.

Bowen, M. (1976). Theory in the practice of psychotherapy. In

P. J. Guerin Jr. (Ed.), *Family therapy: Theory and practice.*
New York: Gardner.

Bowlby, J. (1969). *Attachment and loss : vol. 1. Attachment.* New
York: Basic.

Bowlby, J. (1980). *Attachment and loss : vol. 3. Loss, sadness and
depression.* New York: Basic.

Braswell, L., & Bloomquist, M. (1992). *Attention-deficits and
hyperactivity: A model for child, family, and school intervention.* New York: Guilford.

Bray, J. H. (2005). Family therapy with stepfamilies. In J. Lebow
(Ed.), *Handbook of clinical family therapy* (pp. 497–515).
Hoboken, NJ: Wiley.

Bray, J. H., & Kelly, J. (1998). *Stepfamilies: Love, marriage and
parenting in the first decade.* New York: Broadway Books.

Breslau, N., Brown, G., Deldotto, J., Kumar, S., Exhuthachan,
S., Andreski, P., & Hufnagle, K. (1996). Psychiatric sequelae
of low birth weight at 6 years of age. *Journal of Abnormal
Child Psychology, 24,* 385–400.

Bretherton, I., & Oppenheim, D. (2003). The MacArthur story
stem battery: Development, administration, reliability, valid-
ity, and reflections about meaning. In R. Emde, D. Wolf, &
D. Oppenheim (Eds.), *Revealing the inner worlds of young
children* (pp. 55–80). New York: Oxford University Press.

Brisch, K. H. (2004). *Treating attachment disorders.* New York:
Guilford.

Byng-Hall, J. (1995). *Rewriting family scripts.* New York:
Guilford.

Cabié, M. C., & Isebaert, L. (1997). *Pour une thérapie brève.*
Toulouse: Collection Relations, Érès.

Carr, A. (2000). *Family therapy: Concepts, process, and practice.*
New York: John Wiley & Sons.

Castellanos, F. (1997). Toward a pathophysiology of attention deficit/hyperactivity disorder. *Clinical Pediatrics, 36,*
381–393.

Cavell, T. (2000). *Working with parents of aggressive children: A practitioner's guide.* Washington, DC: American Psychological Association.

Christophersen, E. R., & Mortweet, S. L. (2001). *Treatments that work with children.* Washington, DC: American Psychological Association.

Christophersen, E. R., & Mortweet, S. L. (2003). *Parenting that works.* Washington, DC: American Psychological Association.

Cierpka, M. (Ed.). (1996). *Handbuch der familiendiagnostik.* Berlin: Springer.

Cierpka, M., & Cierpka, A. (2000). Beratung von familien mit zwei- bis dreijährigen kindern. *Praxis der Kinderpsychologie und Kinderpsychiatrie, 49,* 563–579.

Cook, E., Stein, M., & Leventhal, D. L. (1997). Family-base association of attention-deficit/hyperactivity disorder and the dopamine transporter. In K. Blum (Ed.), *Handbook of psychiatric genetics* (pp. 297–310). New York: CRC Press.

Cook-Darzens, S. (2002). *Thérapie familiale de l'adolescent anorexique. Approche systémique intégré.* Paris: Dunod.

Davis, J. (1988). Mazel Tov: The Bar Mitzvah as a multigenerational ritual of change and continuity. In E. Imber-Black, J. Roberts, & R. Whiting (Eds.), *Rituals in families and family therapy* (pp. 177–210). New York: Norton.

De Shazer, S. (1982). *Patterns of brief family therapy: An ecosystemic approach.* New York: Guilford.

De Shazer, S. (1985). *Keys to solution in brief therapy.* New York: Norton.

De Shazer, S. (1991). *Putting difference to work.* New York: Norton.

De Shazer, S. (1994). *Words were originally magic.* New York: Norton.

Dowing, E. and Vetere, A. (2005). Narrative concepts and therapeutic challenges. In E. Dowling and A. Vetere (Eds.), *Narrative therapies with children and their families. A practi-*

tioner's guide to concepts and approaches (pp. 7–24). London: Routledge.

Downing, G. (2003). Video-microanalyse-therapie: Einige grundlagen und prinzipien. In H. Scheuerer-English, G. Suess, & W. Pfeifer (Eds.), *Wege zur sicherheit: Bindungswissen in diagnostik und intervention*. Giessen, Germany: Psychosocial Verlag.

Downing, G. (2004). Emotion, body, and parent-infant interaction. In J. Nadel & D. Muir (Eds.), *Emotional development: Recent research advances* (pp. 429–449). Oxford: Oxford University Press.

Downing, G. (2008a). A different way to help. In S. Greenspan & S. Shanker (Eds.), *Human development in the 21st century: Visionary ideas from systems scientists* (pp. 200–05). Cambridge, UK : Cambridge University Press.

Downing, G., Bürgin, D., Reck, C., & Ziegenhain, U. (2008b, in press). Interfaces between intersubjectivity and attachment : Perspectives on a mother-infant in-patient case. *Infant Mental Health Journal*.

Downing, G. & Tronick, E. (2007). Manuscript in progress.

Dretske, F. (1981). *Knowledge and the flow of information*. Cambridge, MA: MIT Press.

Dretske, F. (1988). *Explaining behavior: Reasons in a world of causes*. Cambridge, MA: MIT Press.

Dretske, F. (1995). *Naturalizing the mind*. Cambridge, MA: MIT Press.

Dunn, J., & Plomin, R. (1990). *Why siblings are so different*. New York: Basic.

DuPaul, G., Barkley, R., & Connor, D. (1998). Stimulants. In R. A. Barkley (Ed.), *Attention-deficit hyperactivity disorder: A handbook for diagnosis and treatment* (pp. 510–551). New York: Guilford.

DuPaul, G., & Stoner, G., (2003). *ADHD in the schools: Assessment and intervention strategies*. New York: Guilford.

Erickson, M. H. (1980). *The collected papers of Milton H. Erickson on hypnosis.* Rossi, E. (Ed.). New York: Irvington Press.

Erickson, M., & Durz-Riemer, K. (2003). *Infants, toddlers, and families: A framework for support and intervention.* New York: Guilford.

Everett, C. A., & Everett, S. V. (1999). *Family therapy for ADHD: Treating children, adolescents, & adults.* New York: Guilford.

Eyberg, S. (1988). Parent-child interaction therapy: Integration of traditional and behavioral concern. *Child and Family Behavior Therapy, 10*, 33–45.

Eyberg, S., & Boggs, S. (1989). Parent training for oppositional defiant preschoolers. In C. E. Schaefer & J. M. Briesmeister (Eds.), *Handbook of parent training: Parents as co-therapists for children's behavior problems* (pp. 105–132). New York: Wiley.

Feldman, R. (2003). Infant-mother and infant-father synchrony: The coregulation of positive arousal. *Infant Mental Health Journal, 24* (1), 1–23.

Fisch, R., Weakland, J., & Segal, L. (1982). *The tactics of change: Doing therapy briefly.* San Francisco: Jossey-Bass.

Fivaz-Depeursinge, E., & Corboz-Warnery, A. (1999). *The primary triangle: A developmental systems view of mothers, fathers, and infants.* New York: Basic.

Fogel, A. (2008). Relationships that support human development. In A. Fogel, B. King, & S. Shanker (Eds.), *Human development in the 21st century: Visionary ideas from systems scientists.* Cambridge: Cambridge University Press.

Fonagy, P., Gergely, G., Jurist, E., & Target, M. (2002). *Affect regulation, mentalization, and the development of the self.* New York: Other Press.

Forehand, R., & McMahon, R. (1981). *Helping the noncompliant child: A clinician's guide to parent training.* New York: Guilford.

Forehand, R., & McMahon, R. (1984). Parent training for the noncompliant child: Treatment outcome, generalization, and adjunctive therapy procedures. In R. F. Dangel & A. Polster (Eds.), *Parent training: Foundations of research and practice* (pp. 298–328). New York: Guilford.

Freeman, J., Epston, D., & Lobovits, D. (1997). *Playful approaches to serious problems.* New York: Norton.

Frick, P., Kamphaus, R., Lahey, B., Loeber, R., Christ, M., Hart, E., & Tannenbaum, L. (1991). Academic underachievement and the disruptive behavior disorders. *Journal of Consulting and Clinical Psychology, 59,* 289–294.

Friedberg, R. D., & McClure, J. M., (2002). *Clinical practice of cognitive therapy with children and adolescents: The nuts and bolts.* New York: Guilford.

Gammer, C., & Cabié, M. C. (1992). *L'adolescence, crise familiale.* Toulouse: Collection Relations, Érès.

Gath, A. (1974). Sibling reactions to mental handicap: A comparison of the brothers and sisters of mongol children. *Journal of Child Psychology and Psychiatry, 28,* 715–730.

Gil, E. (1991). *The healing power of play.* London: Guilford.

Gil, E. (1994). *Play in family therapy.* London: Guilford.

Goldenberg, I., & Goldenberg, H. (2004). *Family therapy: An overview.* Pacific Grove, CA: Thomson.

Gorell Barnes, G. (2005). Narratives of attachment in post-divorce contact disputes: Developing an intersubjective understanding. In A. Vetere & E. Dowling (Eds.), *Narrative therapies with children and their families: A practitioner's guide to concepts and approaches* (pp. 189–204). London: Routledge.

Greenspan, S., & Shanker, S. (2004). *The first idea: How symbols, language, and intelligence evolved from our primate ancestors to modern humans.* Cambridge, MA: Da Capo Press.

Greenspan, S., & Wieder, S. (1998). *The child with special needs:*

Encouraging intellectual and emotional growth. Cambridge, MA: Perseus.

Guerney, B. G. (1964). Filial therapy: Description and rationale. *Journal of Consulting Psychology, 28,* 303–310.

Guerney, L. F. (1983). Introduction to filial therapy. In P. A. Keller & L. G. Ritt (Eds.), *Innovations in clinical practice* (Vol. 2, pp. 26–39). Sarasota, FL: Professional Resource Exchange.

Haley, J. (1963). *Strategies of psychotherapy*. New York: Grune & Stratton.

Haley, J. (1973). *Uncommon therapy: The psychiatric techniques of Milton Erickson, M. D.* New York: Norton.

Haley, J. (Ed.). (1985). *Conversations with Milton H. Erickson, M. D.* New York: Norton.

Hesse, E., & Main, M. (2006). Frightened, threatening, and dissociate parental behavior: Theory and associations with parental adult attachment interview status and infant disorganization. *Development and Psychopathology, 18,* 309–343.

Hetherington, E. M., & Kelly, J. (2002). *For better or for worse: Divorce reconsidered.* New York: Norton.

Imber-Black, E., Roberts, J., & Whiting, R. (1988). *Rituals in families and family therapy.* New York: Norton.

Issacs, M., Montalvo, B., & Abelsohn, D. (1986). *The difficult divorce: Therapy for children and families.* New York: Basic.

Kahn, M. & Lewis, K. (1988). *Siblings in therapy.* New York: Norton.

Karen, R. (1998). *Becoming attached: First relationships and how they shape our capacity to love.* New York: Oxford University Press.

Keith, D., & Whitaker, C. (1997). Play therapy: A paradigm for work with families. In C. Schaefer & L. Carey (Eds.), *Family play therapy* (pp. 185–202). London: Jason Aronson.

Kelly, J. B. (2007). Children's living arrangements following separation and divorce: Insights from empirical and clinical research. *Family Process, 46,* 35–52.

Kendall, P. C. (Ed.). (1991). *Child and adolescent therapy: Cognitive-behavioral procedures.* New York: Guilford.

Kendall, P. C., & Brasswell, L. (1985). *Cognitive-behavioral therapy for impulsive children.* New York: Guilford.

Kopp, R. (1995). *Metaphor therapy.* New York: Brunner/Mazel.

Lakoff, G., & Johnson, M. (1980). *Metaphors we live by.* Chicago, IL: University of Chicago Press.

Lakoff, G., & Johnson, M. (1999). *Philosophy in the flesh: The embodied mind and its challenge to western thought.* New York: Harper Collins.

Landgarten, H. (1987). *Family art psychotherapy: A clinical guide and casebook.* New York: Brunner/Mazel.

Landgarten, H. (1994). Family art psychotherapy. In C. Schaefer & L. Carey (Eds.), *Family play therapy.* London: Jason Aronson.

Lankton, S. R., & Lankton, C. H. (1983). *The answer within: A clinical framework of Ericksonian hypnotherapy.* New York: Brunner/Mazel.

Leveton, E. (1991) The use of doubling to counter resistance in family and individual treatment. *The Arts of Psychotherapy, 18,* 241–249.

Lewis, K. (1988). Young siblings in brief therapy. In M. Kahn & K. Lewis (Eds.), *Siblings in therapy* (pp. 93–114). New York: Norton.

Lycan, G. (1996). *Consciousness and experience.* Cambridge, MA: MIT Press.

Lycan, G. (1999). *Philosophy of language.* London: Routledge.

Lyons-Ruth, K., Melnick, S., Bronfman, E., Sherry, S., & Llanas, L. (2004). Hostile-helpless relational models and disorganized attachment patterns between parents and their young children: Review of research and implications for clinical work. In L. Atkinson & S. Goldberg (Eds.), *Attachment issues in psychopathology and intervention* (pp. 65–94). Mahwah, NJ: Lawrence Erlbaum.

Marvin, R., Hoffman, K., & Powell, B. (2003). The circle of security project: Attachment-based intervention with caregiver-preschool dyads. *Attachment and Human Development, 4*(1), 107–124.

McDonough, S. (2004). Interaction guidance: Promoting and nurturing the caregiving relationship. In A. Sameroff, S. McDonough, & K. Rosenblum (Eds.), *Treating parent-infant relationship problems: Strategies for intervention* (pp. 79–95). New York: Guilford.

McElreath, L. S., & Eisenstadt, T. H. (1997). Child-directed interaction. In C. Schaefer & L. Carey (Eds.), *Family play therapy* (pp. 271–292). London: Jason Aronson.

McGoldrick, M., & Gerson, R. (1985). *Genograms in family assessment*. New York: Norton.

McGoldrick, M., Gerson, R., & Shellenberger, S. (1999). *Genograms: Assessment and intervention*. New York: Norton.

Meins, E. (1997). *Security of attachment and the social development of cognition*. East Sussex: Psychology Press.

Meynkens-Fourez, M. (2002). Fratrie et handicap d'un collateral. In E. Tilmans-Ostyn & M. Meynckens-Fourez (Eds.), *Les resources de la fratrie* (pp. 183–198). Toulouse: Collection Relations, Érès.

Milich, R., Widiger, T., & Landau, S. (1987). Differential diagnosis of attention deficit and conduct disorders using conditional probabilities. *Journal of Consulting and Clinical Psychology, 55*, 762–767.

Minuchin, S., & Fishman, H. (1981). *Family therapy techniques*. London: Harvard University Press.

Mio, S., & Katz, A. (Eds.). (1996). Metaphor: *Implications and applications*. Mahwah NJ: Lawrence Erlbaum.

Nerin, W. (1986). *Family reconstruction: Long day's journey into light*. New York: Norton.

O'Connor, J., & Hoorwitz, A. (1988). Imitative and contagious magic in the therapeutic use of rituals with children. In E. Imber-Black, J. Roberts, & R. Whiting (Eds.), *Rituals in families and family therapy* (pp. 135–137). New York: Norton.

Papousek, M. (2000). Einsatz von video in der eltern-säuglings-beratung und psychotherapy. *Praxis der Kinderpsychologie und Kinderpsychiatrie, 49*, 611–627.

Papousek, M. (2004). Regulationsstörungen der frühen kindheit: Kliniscche evidenz fur ein neues diagnosisches konzept. In M. Papousek, M. Schieche, & H. Wurmser (Eds.), *Regulationsstörungen der frühen kindheit* (pp. 77–110). Bern: Hans Huber.

Papp, P. (1982). Staging reciprocal metaphors in a couples group, *Family Process, 2104*, 453–467.

Papp, P (1983). *The process of change*. London: Guilford.

Patterson, G., Dishion, T., & Chamberlain, P. (1993). Outcomes and methodological issues relating to treatment of anti-social children. In T. Giles (Ed.), *Handbook of effective psychotherapy* (pp.43–88). New York: Plenum.

Patterson, G., Reid, J., & Dishion, T. (1998). Antisocial boys. In J. Jenkins & K. Oatley (Eds.), *Human emotions: A reader* (pp. 330–336). Malden, MA: Blackwell.

Pfiffner, L., & Barkley, R. (1998). Treatment of ADHD in school settings. In R. Barkley (Ed.), *Attention-deficit hyperactivity disorder: A handbook for diagnosis and treatment* (pp. 458–490). New York: Guilford.

Pliszka, S. R., Carlson, C. L., & Swanson, J. M. (1999). *ADHD with comorbid disorders: Clinical assessment and management*. New York: Guilford.

Powell, T. (1982). Parents, siblings, and handicapped children: *A social interaction program*. Storrs, CT: University of Connecticut Press.

Power, T. J., Karustis, J. L., & Habboushe, D. F. (2001). *Homework success for children with ADHD*. New York: Guilford.

Reich, G., Massing, A., & Cierpka, M. (1996). Die mehrgenerationenperspektive und das genogramm. In M. Cierpka (Ed.), *Handbuch der familiendiagnostik*. Berlin: Springer.

Reinecke, M. A., Dattilio, F. M., & Freeman, A. (1996). *Cognitive therapy with children and adolescents. A casebook for clinical practice*. New York: Guilford.

Rochat, P. (2001). *The infant's world*. Cambridge, MA: Harvard University Press.

Rosenberg, J. B., & Lindblad, M. B. (1978). Behavior therapy in a family context: Treating elective mutism. *Family Process* 17 (1), 77–82.

Satir, V. (1964). *Conjoint family therapy*. Palo Alto, CA: Science & Behavior Books.

Satir, V. (1972). *Peoplemaking*. London: Souvenir.

Satir, V. & Baldwin, M. (1983). *Satir step by step: A guide to creating change in families*. Palo Alto, CA: Science and Behavior Books.

Satir, V., Banmen, J., Gerber, J., & Gomori, M. (1991). *The Satir model: Family therapy and beyond*. Palo Alto, CA: Science and Behavior Books.

Schacter, F. (1985). Sibling deidentification in the clinic: Devil vs. angel. *Family Process*, 24(3), 415–427.

Schaefer, C., & Carey, L. (Eds.). (1997). *Family play therapy*. London: Jason Aronson.

Schneewind, K. (1991). *Familienpsychologie*. Stuttgart: Kohlhammer.

Schützenberger, A. A. (1993). *Aïe, mes aïeux!* Paris: La Meridiennne.

Searle, J. (1979). *Expression and meaning: Studies in the theory of speech acts*. London: Cambridge University Press.

Searle, J. (1995). *The construction of social reality*. New York: Free Press.

Searle, J. (2001). *Rationality in action.* Cambridge, MA: MIT.

Selekman, M. (1997). *Solution-focused therapy with children.* London: Guilford.

Semrud-Clikeman, M., Biederman, J., Sprich-Buckminster, S., Lehman, B., Faraone, S., & Norman, D. (1992). Comorbidity between ADHD and learning disability: A review and report in clinically referred sample. *Journal of the American Academy of Child and Adolescent Psychiatry, 33,* 875–881.

Shapiro, S., & Garfinkel, B. (1986). The occurrence of behavior disorders in children: The interdependence of attention deficit disorder and conduct disorder. *Journal of the American Academy of Child Psychiatry, 25,* 809–819.

Singer, M., & Flannery, D. (2000). The relationships between children's threats of violence and violent behaviors. *Archives of Pediatric Adolescent Medicine, 154,* 785–790.

Steele, H., & Steele, M. (2005a). Understanding and resolving emotional conflict. In K. E. Grossmann, K. Grossmann, & E. Waters (Eds.), *Attachment from infancy to childhood* (pp. 137–164). New York: Guilford.

Steele, H., & Steele, M. (2005b). The construct of coherence as an indicator of attachment security in middle childhood: The friends and family interview. In K. A. Kerns & R. A. Richardson (Eds.), *Attachment in middle childhood* (pp.137–160). New York: Guilford.

Stern, D. (1995). *The motherhood constellation: A unified view of parent-infant psychotherapy.* New York: Basic.

Stern, D. (2004). *The present moment in psychotherapy and everyday life.* New York: Norton.

Stern, J. (2000). *Metaphor in context.* Cambridge, MA: MIT Press.

Stierlin, H. (1975). *Von der psychoanalyse zur familientherapie.* Stuttgart: Klett-Cotta.

Stierlin, H. (1978). Delegation und famili. Frankfurt/Main: Suhrkamp.

Stolorow, R., Atwood, G., & Orange, D. (2002). *Worlds of experience*. New York: Basic.

Stoneman, Z., Brody, G., Davis, C., & Crapps, J. (1988). Childcare responsibilities, peer relations, and sibling conflict: Older siblings of mentally retarded children. *American Journal of Mental Retardation, 93,* 174–183.

Stoneman, Z., Brody, G., Davis, C., & Crapps, J. (1989). Role relations between children who are mentally retarded and their older siblings: Observations in three in-home contexts. *Research in Developmental disabilities, 10,* 61–76.

Thiel-Bonney, C. (2002). Beratung von eltern mit säuglingen und kleinkindern: Videogestützte beobachtung und videomikroanalyse als interventionsmöglichkeit. *Psychotherapeut, 47,* 381–384.

Tilmans-Ostyn, E., & Meynckens-Fourez, M. (2002). *Les resources de la fratrie.* Toulouse: Collection Relations, Érès.

Tronick, E. (2007). *The neurobehavioral and social-emotional development of infants and children.* New York: Norton.

Van Fleet, R. (1994). *Filial therapy: Strengthening parent-child relationships through play.* Sarasota, FL: Professional Resource Press.

Van Fleet, R. (2000). Short-term play therapy for families with chronic illness. In H. Kaduson & C. Schaefer (Eds.), *Short-term play therapy for children* (pp. 175–193). New York: Guilford.

Vetere, A. & Cooper, J. (2005). Children who witness violence at home. In A. Vetere and E. Dowling, *Narrative therapies with children and their families. A practitioner's guide to concepts and approaches* (pp. 75–89). London: Routledge.

Vetere, A. & Dowling, E. (2005). *Narrative therapies with children and their families. A practitioner's guide to concepts and approaches.* London: Routledge.

Vygotsky, L. & Cole, M. (Eds.). (1978). *Mind in society: The development of higher psychological processes.* Cambridge, MA: Harvard University Press.

Wachtel, E. (1994). *Treating troubled children and their families.* London: Guilford.

Walsh, F. (1994). *Normal family processes.* London: Guilford.

Watzlawick, P., Bavelas, J., & Jackson, D. (1967). *Pragmatics of human communication.* New York: Norton.

Watzlawick, P., Weakland, J., & Fisch, R. (1974). *Change: Principles of problem formation and problem resolution.* New York: Norton.

Whitaker, A., Van Rossem, R., Feldman, J., Schonfeld, I., Pinto-Martin, J., Torre, C., Shaffer, D., & Paneth, N. (1997). Psychiatric outcomes in low-birth-weight children at age 6 years: Relation to neonatal cranial ultrasound abnormalities. *Archives of General Psychiatry, 54,* 847–856.

White, M., & Epston, D. (1990). *Narrative means to therapeutic ends.* New York: Norton.

Wiehe, V. (1990). *Sibling abuse.* New York: Lexington Books.

Woolgar, M. (1999). Projective doll play methodologies for preschool children. *Child Psychology and Psychiatry Review, 4,* 126–134.

Wortmann-Fleischer, S., Hornstein, C., & Downing, G. (2005). *Pospartale psychische störungen. ein interaktionszentrierter therapieleitfaden.* Stuttgart: Kohlhammer.

Zakay, D. (1992). The role of attention in children's time perception. *Journal of Experimental Child Psychology, 54,* 355–371.

Zeig, J. (1982). *Ericksonian approaches to hypnosis and psychotherapy.* New York: Brunner/Mazel.

Zilbach, J. (1986). *Young children in family therapy.* New York: Brunner/Mazel.

Index

● ●